SOUL WOUNDEDNESS

Soul Woundedness

SPIRITUALITY ON THE STREETS OF SEATTLE

Paul Houston Blankenship-Lai

FORDHAM UNIVERSITY PRESS   NEW YORK 2025

Copyright © 2025 Fordham University Press

All rights reserved. No part of this publication may be reproduced, stored in a retrieval system, or transmitted in any form or by any means—electronic, mechanical, photocopy, recording, or any other—except for brief quotations in printed reviews, without the prior permission of the publisher.

Fordham University Press has no responsibility for the persistence or accuracy of URLs for external or third-party Internet websites referred to in this publication and does not guarantee that any content on such websites is, or will remain, accurate or appropriate.

Fordham University Press also publishes its books in a variety of electronic formats. Some content that appears in print may not be available in electronic books.

Visit us online at www.fordhampress.com.

Library of Congress Cataloging-in-Publication Data available online at https://catalog.loc.gov.

Printed in the United States of America
27 26 25   5 4 3 2 1
First edition

*with the wild, liberatory love already present in all things
and my teachers, family, and friends
who walk slow with me.
with my editors, Richard and Nancy, and
the people living on the streets:
whose hospitality made this book
possible for us
to gather
into a question
about what is really going on and
how we can together create
a more loving love.*

and with Evelyn Ja, my beloved wife and dearest friend.

Contents

PROLOGUE   ix

NOTE ABOUT QUOTATIONS   xiii

Introduction   1

1 The Wound of Faith   15

2 The Wound of Rejection   35

3 The Wound of Human Being   59

4 The Wound of God   91

5 The Wound of Love   116

Conclusion: A More Loving Love   134

NOTES   159

BIBLIOGRAPHY   177

Prologue

This is a story about young adults who live on the streets of Seattle. It's about the social wounds that penetrate them soul deep. I will tell you a story about how certain "street kids," as they may like to be called from time to time, tend their soul wounds through creative spiritual practices to cultivate a life worth living in an almost unlivable local world.

These pages are heartbreak and agony. To be homeless, I found, is to live besieged by wounds like ravaging rejection, the mere presence of human beings, and a haunting, seemingly failed promise of God. When you are homeless you are violently uprooted from the complex conditions needed for a livable life. Your soul is intimately afflicted and the liberative mysteries of who you are get tangled in the seductive web of destructive ignorance.

I spent more than five years with people who live on the streets of Seattle. I wanted to learn about what their everyday life is like, the real differences spirituality makes, and what spirituality on the streets can teach us about how to love. The extensive research and writing I practiced—which anthropologists crafted as "ethnography"—was scathing. In the face of the affliction I witnessed, it became hard for me to go on being human. I wanted instead to be a yellow daffodil, unnoticed and growing silent into a symphony of natural beauty. A hope that this book might gather us as friends into a more loving love with people experiencing homelessness held me tenderly in this flesh, especially when I experienced a traumatizing period of homelessness.

This is not just a heartbreaking, agonizing story about suffering on the streets. It is also a story about the unyielding beauty of the human person and how the fire of divine love is too wild, strong to be tamed and overcome. This book is an invitation to notice the radical beauty and divine love that pulses through people on the streets; even when they do things you think you'd never do in alleys you'd never walk down; yes, still, when they die in fumes of social hatred and abandonment, holding and being held still by their unrealized dreams. Poverty will continue to afflict the world until we allow ourselves to be harnessed into and transformed by the concealed dreams of people experiencing homelessness.

As I write this prologue, the number of people experiencing homelessness is shattering records. In *City of Grants Pass, Oregon v. Johnson*, the United States Supreme Court is deliberating whether it is cruel and unusual to punish people for sleeping outside. In his campaign to become president of the United States, Donald J. Trump is describing people experiencing street homelessness as violent insurrectionists. To make cities more beautiful and livable, Trump is promising to arrest people sleeping on the streets and rehabilitate them in mass encampments on inexpensive parcels of land. Last month, in February 2024, the National Governors Association met in Washington, D.C., to learn how to respond effectively to what has become a crisis of affordable housing. More and more people find that a safe, reliable physical dwelling, which is intrinsic to personal and social wellbeing, is out of reach. Fentanyl, an intensely addictive opioid, is further devastating people on the streets and causing unprecedented death by overdose. In the unlikely happening that someone living homeless on the streets finds permanent supportive housing, they are nevertheless likely to experience social homelessness and remain homeless within themselves. We move through the wounds of a world in the hands of a loneliness epidemic. At an hour in world history in which we most need each other, our hearts are often breaking alone and weakened by rampant divisiveness. The brutal realities of our world have conspired against the youth and made suicide a leading cause of death. For some, the hope of being at home in this world has been eclipsed. And many of us are "compassion fatigued." We are tired of seeing people homeless and exhausted when politicians talk about the next plan to end homelessness. Understandably, we are routinely frustrated, angry, and uncertain about what precisely will heal political divisiveness and solve an unnecessary global calamity that international war and global warming threaten to worsen.

At a recent service at a nondenominational church, a pastor claimed our physical space a "refuge for the homeless" as the doors of the church were locked to prevent unhoused people from causing a disruption inside and wounding the wounds of the housed.

This book is an open door and a space to dwell in a question with people who are homeless. I sincerely hope this question wounds you, nonviolently: How can we love with people experiencing homelessness more lovingly?

I propose that a more loving love with people experiencing homelessness can become real through *a spirituality of loving social power for the violently uprooted*. A spirituality of loving social power invites creative spiritual practices that manifest an Economic Bill of Rights through nonviolent direct action and authentic ways of befriending ourselves and each other on the streets. I write to transform how we experience the streets in our everyday lives so that they become places to consciously practice our diverse spiritualities. I also call upon the global Christian church to help facilitate interdenominational, interfaith monthly meetings in candlelit darkness where we temporarily suspend our theological and other differences and try, for just one slow hour, to be simply, compassionately present with each other. Listeningly.

The book is a story, finally, that is mostly unwritten. It is a story by someone who has become more curious about how to understand and love with people experiencing homelessness, not less. Peace, friends, peace. Our subtle, shadow cruelties and hatreds with each other are themselves practices that make us homeless.

This is a happily weak book by itself, friend, because it wants you and needs you and wonders what good work you are called to do. Here is an unfinished story, then, that we can go on writing together for the world with the sentences and open spaces that create our lives.

Multifaith Prayer Room
Seattle University
March 2024

Note about Quotations

Nearly exact quotations are put in double quotation marks. They are derived from semistructured interviews recorded on a small electronic device. Single quotation marks are used when a scene is reconstructed from fieldnotes and memory. The need(s) for anonymity and recognition tussle with each other. An electronic device, like the ethnographer, isn't neutral. I have labored to render the human and nonhuman creatures that appear in this book honestly and compassionately. My hope is that these words become seeds of understanding that fall on the ground of ethical reflection and bloom into a more loving love with people experiencing homelessness. But alas. The ethnographer is a finite creature seduced by the invisible bars of their own cage. Like the creatures in this book, and you, perhaps, I open my heart to the possibility that I might need your forgiveness and mercy. Again, and again.

We should be willing to act as a balm for all wounds.
—ETTY HILLESUM

Introduction

'my soul hurts.'

Our backs are against the wall. A bulky advertisement is plastered on the 7-Eleven window above our heads: '$10 Large Pizza and 5 Classic Wings.'

'Got any cheddar for this broke cracker?' 'Spare a few and it will come back to you.'

Hitch is calling to "yuppies" on "the Ave" in Seattle's University District. I say the hook shyly. 'Paul,' Hitch says, 'you're my yuppie friend.'

Hitch is teaching me how to "spange." For Hitch, spanging is a street practice that differs from "panhandling." Panhandling is desperate begging. It is the flesh of a despair that Hitch is on the run from, and that renders the kind of homelessness he thinks he is not experiencing. Spanging, though, is real work. It can be dignifying and creative; it potentially is lucrative and liberative. Spanging is a materialized wish for something good: a smoke, a smile, an opportunity to "practice good karma," enough money to "get well" and ward off the horror of withdrawal.

For Hitch, spanging is also a spiritual practice that connects him consciously to an empowering force in "The Universe," a name street kids frequently use for spiritual forces they believe are alive in the world and working for one's good.[1]

'Sometimes,' Hitch says, smirking, 'I tell someone that Jesus is watching them.'

I am surprised. Hitch is hostile to Christianity; Christian jargon is a mostly unfriendly force in this "None-Zone."[2] Through the cacophony of street sound—with a tired rage tangled with shame and hope—Hitch says to a woman approaching: 'You cannot run from Jesus.'

'Fuck her anyway.'

Hitch and I are white and gender queer. I am a Christian; Hitch is emphatically not. As we sit on the streets today, I am securely housed in a downtown Seattle apartment. The streets are home to Hitch; for me they are a place of aliveness to learn with the world how to love. Later, as these pages will tell, the streets will become a place of terror for me when I experience a brief period of homelessness.

'Look at this, Paul. I found this bracelet right here last night.' The discovery, Hitch tells me, as he brings it to my eyes, is 'a gift from The Universe.'

I read the inscription on Hitch's bracelet aloud and ponder the difference it makes in his everyday life on the streets: "It is better to give than receive."

His pockets are full of rocks. He has a necklace of the Buddha on. Like the Buddha, Hitch says, the rocks keep him grounded.

There is a pool hall across the street. 'Let's play pool,' I say. 'I'll get a pitcher of beer so we can be inside for a while.' 'I need to be drunk before going indoors. Don't you listen, Paul? Fuck.'

We get up and walk and talk and then sit down at a post office. We smell dog piss, rain-soaked cigarette butts, and freshly baked bread. It is evening. The sun is warm on my shoulders. Soon, after we eat dinner at the "feed" down the alley, Hitch will retire to his tent, which is one among many along Interstate 5. Alone he will carefully count the money from his spange, laid out with care on his sleeping bag. I will continue walking the streets, listeningly. We are in this moment, however, held together in street silence: car horns and anonymous chatter fill the soundscape, and we don't speak.

'Paul,' Hitch tells me, breaking the street silence, 'my soul hurts.'

'Every day I hold it in. Look,' he says, 'chills: up and down my arms. Does the energy in your soul ever feel like it's going to break out of your body? Sometimes,' Hitch says, 'I feel like it's going to snap me into a million pieces.'

Listening to them speak, part of me is afraid their energy will crack open my skull and break all of me into a million scattered pieces.

Hitch says he felt like this, for the first time, when he got jumped. He got 'swarmed with blows' one day after school. 'It is like that now,' he says, 'except life itself is throwing the punches. And they are coming from everywhere, all the time.'

Hitch asks if I know how Buddhist monks control their soul energy. 'If I can learn to control my soul energy,' he says, 'maybe this suffering won't go soul deep.'

what really matters: a more loving love

This book is about the relationship between homelessness, spirituality, and culture. It is about social wounds that go soul deep in people who are homeless and how those wounds are tended through spiritual practices to cultivate a life worth living in an almost unlivable local world. The story I tell is derived from more than five years of intimate time with the people who live on the streets, which I describe below. What's at stake is a trustworthy perspective about everyday life on the streets of Seattle, the differences spirituality makes there, and what street spirituality can teach us about the world. Though we've learned a lot about homelessness, we know relatively little about the intersection between homelessness, spirituality, and culture. What *really* matters about this book, however, is a more loving love for people experiencing homelessness, which I propose is the realization of a world in which everyone has a safe and empowering home, always—and really feels at home in this world through a spirit of friendship. Though many find it difficult to study love, love can be experienced as a constructive space of collaborative interdisciplinary engagement across culture, rigorous inquiry and experimentation, and, potentially, holistic transformation.[3] Love is always simultaneously a perennial answer to the human condition and an endless, open question. Love is also a daring adventure and a place of hospitality that gathers us with our real differences to work for a more beautiful world. The varieties and consequences of love represent one of the least studied and most promising dimensions of life to learn about, reflect upon, and actualize.[4]

Before I arrived in Seattle in the summer of 2016 to spend time with street kids like Hitch, I was doing fieldwork on the streets of Berkeley, Oakland, and San Francisco. During this time, I am grateful to have learned from anthropologists Lawrence Cohen at UC Berkeley and Tanya Marie Luhrmann at Stanford. They taught this novice theologian about the craft of ethnography, which is the method anthropologists use to study culture or local worlds. Cohen and Luhrmann encouraged me to spend a lot of time on the streets, take extensive fieldnotes, ask questions respectfully, and listen deeply. The theologians at the Graduate Theological Union in Berkeley I studied with—Elizabeth Liebert, Wendy Farley, and Arthur Holder—encouraged this slow, open, compassionate beginning as well. Upon listening to my teachers, it seemed to me that a more loving love for people experiencing homelessness could become possible only after a "long, loving look at the real" and by humbly living the questions that came to matter on the streets.[5] Through experimentation and frequent embarrassment, I lived five questions on the streets. These questions companioned me in Seattle and animate the spirit of this book.

The first question I lived is what spirituality is like for people who live on the streets of Seattle. I asked, that is, how people understand spirituality and put it into practice. The second question I lived is what difference spirituality makes in everyday life on the streets. If people pray, I am curious what difference, if any, their praying makes. What difference does it make when someone gets a bracelet from The Universe, like Hitch claimed to? Does spirituality ease suffering, generate life-giving connections, and help people get off the streets? Does it further alienate people from themselves, one another, and the chance of getting off the streets? Does it help people feel at home in the world even though they are homeless?

The third question that animates this book is about what difference a book about street spirituality might make. A book with our blood, sweat, and tears on the pages is what's at stake. A book that brings us lovingly to the streets and the polls together is at stake. An unhelpful, unread book that only makes me an author would produce in me spiritual decay. I wrote this book to make a real, positive difference in the lives of other creatures. Since little ethnographic research has been done on the spiritual lives of people experiencing homelessness, I hope this book will place a new light on our evolving understanding of homelessness and contemporary spirituality. Since understanding for the sake of understanding alone is not good enough, however, I also hope that this book will shepherd everyday conversations, public policy, and faith-based action to reduce the suffering that people who are homeless experience and help everyone have a home and feel at home in the world, always.

During my time on the streets, faith-based organizations often asked me about my research. They wanted to know what I was learning and how that learning might help their work. I was invited to have coffee conversations, serve on panels, speak at religious services, and consult with program developers. I was asked to participate with an international research team of theologians and social scientists working to respond to homelessness, which resulted in a book.[6] In the process of learning about the relationship between faith-based organizations and people experiencing homelessness, I decided to do fieldwork at a faith-based organization and turn one of my research questions around. Based on fieldwork I did with Christian "street ministers" in Seattle, I asked what difference people who are homeless make in their own spiritual lives. The fourth question that guides this book is therefore about how and why people who are homeless transform some securely housed Christians' spirituality and what that transformation can teach us about Christianity and culture.

The final question I live in this book is about God. This is a question about how people experience and name the divine on the streets, to be sure, but it is also about the reality of a living God and how and where I think God is after scathing but nevertheless encouraging research. Writing like God is real will be a scandal (or a good laugh) to most social scientists who put their faith truth in methodological agnosticism. What may be more shocking is that it will be scandalous to write like God might be real for many theologians as well. Unavoidably, we bring our embodied, authentic selves into the worlds we inhabit and the research we do. Even when I tried to drown God in Lake Washington, which I describe in the first chapter, I could not stop asking about God's real presence in the world.

The Austrian poet Rainer Maria Rilke can be companion for our experience of this book. Lest we close our eyes to the kindness of uncertainty and look for a shelter made by hasty, inadequate answers, I invite us to consider his wisdom in *Letters to a Young Poet*: "I ask you . . . to have patience with all that is unresolved in your heart and try to love the questions themselves like closed rooms, like books written in a foreign language."[7] I hope this book clarifies your understanding of homelessness and spirituality on the streets of Seattle, dear reader—but only if that clarity births new, surprising questions that nurture your love with people (and their nonhuman companions) experiencing homelessness. Love is itself a question that must remain somehow unanswered.

It is important that you, the reader, understand who I am, even though an author, in their becoming, must, I think, always remain in creative friendship with the reader as a question written in a foreign language for a more loving love. I grew up living and working with people experiencing homelessness in San Diego because my mother ran a Christian organization dedicated to helping people in poverty. Some of my fondest memories as a child are sharing life and sometimes my bedroom with someone who was unhoused or at risk for being unhoused—and learning about their world, sharing our worlds. I also grew up in an apocalyptic charismatic Christian world birthed by Lonnie Frisbee and the Jesus People Movement of the late 1960s and 1970s. From childhood, I could not help but ask about spirituality and homelessness. Today I am a Quaker-Buddhist who appreciates learning about and sometimes practicing with other religious and spiritual traditions. I am a white human who is learning how to be an effective antiracist ally and how to companion the more-than-humanness of our world amid the urgent realities of climate change. I am gender queer, heterosexual, and married. After finishing the first draft of this book, I became homeless. I lost full-time employment at Seattle University when its School for Theology and Ministry began to close due to low enrollment and an unsustainable financial outlook. During this time, I wandered for several months in Hawaii, California, Oregon, and then back to Seattle. The small room where I finally secured housing in Seattle turned out to have a mold problem and no ventilation, which made me ill and rendered me temporarily homeless again. While homelessness initially felt like a spiritual adventure, as it did for some of the street kids you will meet in this book, it soon became a nightmare that haunts me to this day, even though I am now securely housed and far more privileged than most people in this book. It is not possible, finally, for me to describe who I am without also writing about the mental health challenges I experience, which stem from a history of multifarious abuse and the ongoing impact of post-traumatic stress. Like you, perhaps, I come to the pages of this book hoping to learn how to be a wounded healer.

ethnographic fieldwork (deep hanging out)

The ethnographic fieldwork this book is grounded in began in the summer of 2016 and continued through summer of 2023. The most intensive period of fieldwork transpired between 2016 and 2019. During these years, I'd spend up to ten hours a day on the streets, six days a week. After 2019, my fieldwork became much more limited. Between 2019 and 2020, I lived a few hundred miles from Seattle—in Spokane, Washington—where I wrote a draft of this book and remained in touch with people on the streets through Facebook, Instagram, and text messaging. In 2020, in the middle of the COVID-19 plague and the development of CHAZ (Capitol Hill Autonomous Zone), born from George Floyd's murder by a police officer in the daylight, I moved back to Seattle and spent more time on the streets.

When, in 2016, I first moved to Seattle, I imagined that spending time with a diffuse homeless population in many different neighborhoods would help me understand and render a complete picture of homelessness. After a few months, however, rendering a complete picture of homelessness seemed impossible. And undesirable. Different neighborhoods in Seattle hold different but related worlds of homelessness, I found; in this difference there are stories worth paying close attention to. I decided to focus my attention on one population in two neighborhoods that lived in a local world where spirituality really mattered. It was "street kids"—roughly between the ages of eighteen and thirty-five, living on the hip streets of Capitol Hill and the University District, claiming to be liberated by the streets and with a "fuck you" orientation to the world—that drew my heart and curiosity. Their "fuck you" to the world became, for me, a love query.

To understand street life, I did a lot of what street kids do: hang out, walk around, spange, strum guitar strings. I wore the same clothes to "pass" as someone homeless. I learned to fall asleep while sitting against a wall in the daytime. I begged for spare change and leftovers. I ate food out of the trash. I stood in long lines at the food bank for "hobo BBQs." I regularly dined at "feeds" (soup kitchens). I went "dumpster diving." I'd urinate on a tree, in a library restroom, in a putrid port-a-potty. I felt the weight of human judgment penetrate me and grow like deadly cancer, strangle my heart.

I shared beer and cheap vodka when it was cold out and pretended not to be disgusted; I shot pool in local bars when it rained. I held my breath when someone blew "blues" (fentanyl) near my face and heroin smoke moved into my nostrils. I watched street kids heat and shoot heroin in parking lots, alleyways, and tents. I came to feel the power of heroin to ease a ravaged mind. I hung out in tent encampments and needle exchanges and alleyways and squat houses. I feared getting arrested or, as street kids often said, "stuck on the streets" and "fucked." I drank coffee in coffee shops. I stared out the window and at my phone, scrolling Instagram. I listened to music with headphones. I sat on the streets for hours—reading, playing games, and being bored because being bored is a school of street life.[8] I walked. I walked so much that I broke a bone in my foot, which put me in an orthopedic boot many street kids signed with delight. I noticed beauty. The streets of Seattle are dazzling. As I describe in "The Wound of Human Looking," I often practiced a spiritual practice on the streets called "manifestation," which is a sincere, strategic, and open wish to render a material good from "The Universe." Since I met many "Luciferians" on the streets, I read the Satanic Bible and took a dive into this fascinating world even though it made me feel deeply unwell—and afraid, as I was as a child, that I'd become possessed by Lucifer and banished to an eternal lake of fire where I could hear only weeping and gnashing teeth.

Being homeless is not just a sad story. It can be fun. So, I had fun. I'd lie in the sun in a hammock and just talk and laugh. I'd paint and draw. I'd remember goodness with others.

I accompanied street kids to hospitals, court appointments, and day centers. Street kids followed me to my apartment, I was told, in case I turned out to be "a narc." I couldn't tell if that was a lie dressed as a warning or a kind telling of the truth. Sifting through "bullshit" for something like the truth is a common street practice, so I tried my best to do that too. Though a steady undercurrent of fear permeated my fieldwork, I felt deeply unsafe only a handful of times, like when an older Indigenous person living homeless ran toward me with a knife. When a street kid stood up to defend me, I knew that, for some, at least, I became more than an anthropologist. When I understood why the event took place without taking it personally, given the genocidal history of Seattle, which I describe in the first two chapters, I felt just like an anthropologist. Try as I did to understand, I knew I was not a street kid and that I was likely just passing through this world, not at home in it. My distance with street kids was most acute when I'd go home and sleep in a warm bed and then greet them the next morning, rested and showered.

It must be noted that some street kids didn't want me around, researching and asking about their lives. I felt invasive. For others, I was a harmless but amusing trick: cheap entertainment. After an interview at a popular burger joint on the Ave, a street kid told me that she didn't trust me "for shit." She seemed to relish flaunting her weapons at me, which she carried around "for the revolution."

Over the years I spent on the streets as a participant observer, I took extensive fieldnotes: over a thousand pages. I wrote fieldnotes at the end of the day: in a bar, a coffee shop, or on the bus. I meticulously coded my fieldnotes by individual and the categories that emerged from them.[9] I discussed the themes with street kids to see what they made of my seeing and get their feedback.

I was reluctant to ask for a semistructured interview before I got acquainted with someone so there'd be at least a glimmer of trust between us. In exchange for an interview, I'd offer gift cards, cigarettes, and cash (depending on what I had available). Like Philippe Bourgois and Jeffrey Schonberg in *The Righteous Dopefiend*, I found it helpful, caring, and dignifying to pay to participate in a local world of homelessness.[10] I also recorded and transcribed over a hundred semi-structured interviews and coded them meticulously. I took hundreds of photographs with my iPhone. Through it all, I tried to be a sincere friend first and learn what it would take to help create a more loving love with and for people experiencing homelessness.

spirituality on the streets

This book demonstrates that spirituality on the streets is a response to "soul woundedness." Soul woundedness is a concept I use to understand, explain, and render what becomes at stake for a spiritual person whose life is being ravaged by a confluence of social wounds. It is an experience of being uprooted from oneself through violent social force and becoming existentially and then materially homelessness. To be existentially homeless is to feel nearly severed from an experiential power that makes life worth living.

Spirituality on the streets is a last finger on the ledge of life. It is the pursuit of a presence that can help make life worth living. Spirituality on the streets is a complex, evolving set of beliefs and practices formed in the local world of the streets through one's own intimate history and dream for the future. Spirituality helps someone hold on to life in the present and have faith that a more

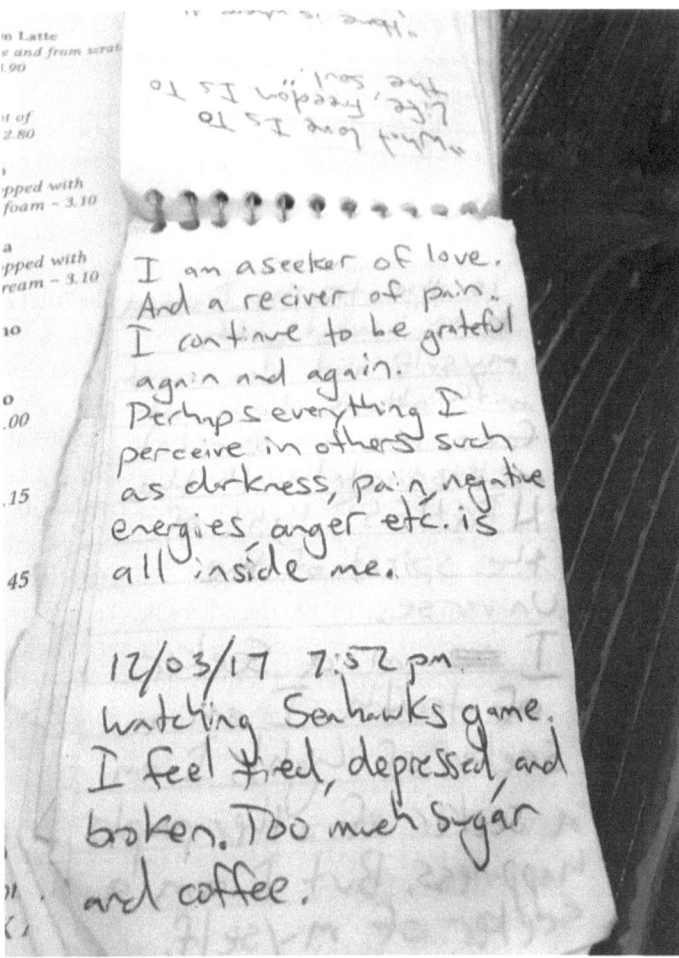

livable future might be possible. It gives one the energy to throw a middle finger with one's dangling hand, laugh at the seemingly meaningless chaos below, and find real joy. It creates beauty where others see only cruelty and deviance. On the streets, spirituality is a struggle for what I call *the spiritual conditions of being* through an empowering connection with spiritual presences.[11] As chapter 3 describes, however, spirituality on the streets is fraught. It may further "fuck" someone who lives a life that feels almost always "fucked." It may loosen one's finger finally from the ledge. Despite its failures, however, spirituality on the streets persists as a practical desire and question about how to feel at home in the world through everyday street practices that ease the excruciating pain of soul woundedness and render the spiritual conditions of being. Even when the word "spirituality" becomes meaningless or "too yuppie," as it sometimes does, the dynamic response to soul woundedness does not. To be human is to be something like what we call spiritual, in pursuit of a powerful presence within that is also beyond.

Each chapter in this book is about a social wound that constitutes soul woundedness. It discloses a social wound street kids experience and demonstrates how that wound is tended through spiritual practice. The final chapter is a response to the question about how to respond and tend these wounds for a more loving love with people experiencing homelessness. It is also about how I experience the presence of the living God.

Chapter 1 is methodological. It is about my ethnographic practice and how I learned to become present with people living on the streets. It explores ethnographic research as a wound of faith for love of the Other. Historically, many anthropologists have been suspicious about whether a religiously committed ethnographer can adequately understand and render a different local world because of their religious commitments. On the other side of academe, many theologians have been suspicious of social scientists for developing epistemologies that disorient religious commitments. I respond to the debate between theologians and anthropologists about how a religiously committed ethnographer can become present to real otherness and render a different local world. I propose that presence to real difference can emerge through apophatic spiritual practice that frees the Other from one's always limited conceptualizations. Chapter 1—and, indeed, this book—operates at the historically contested intersection of theology and anthropology and, in J. Derrick Lemons's term, is a "theologically engaged anthropology."[12]

Chapter 2 wonders about how street kids in Seattle became homeless. It shows that most street kids experienced their world before becoming homeless as uninhabitable because of an intimate, pervasive wound of rejection. Though intimate, pervasive rejection is not the only reason street kids became homeless in Seattle, it is a salient one. The street kids I spent time with were not at home in themselves before they became unhoused. Existential homelessness preceded their material homelessness. Chapter 2 also shows that street kids experience freedom, and a temporal but significant existential homecoming, through various forms of rejection. On the streets, rejection is an attempt to create the spiritual conditions of being. This chapter demonstrates that religious rejection is a spiritual practice that helps street kids distance themselves from the destructive conditions of street life, cultivate the spiritual conditions of being, and experience a presence that helps make life worth living in an almost unlivable local world. I propose that religious rejection is a form of "attuned care" because it can help create the conditions where street kids might become free, open, and let-be.[13] Religious rejection is also a spiritual practice because it tries to clear the numinous realm from spiritual entities that are oppressive, closed, and unwilling to let someone be. Religious rejection constitutes what I call *protest spirituality*. On the streets, strikingly, moreover, Lucifer is a salvific figure whose religious protest promises a life worth living; he offers a cure for the wound of rejection.

Though being on the streets affords unique opportunities to practice freedom, which is a necessary condition of being, freedom on the streets, I found, is always eclipsed by the cruel reality of street life. Chapter 3 describes how the streets form a unique "holding environment" that can keep life in place. Overwhelmingly, however, everyday life on the streets is characterized by the experience of feeling "fucked," "stuck," and "trapped." Chapter 3 queries the experience of stuckness on the streets through attention to what anthropologist Kathleen Stewart calls "ordinary affects."[14] It demonstrates that the ordinary affects of street life constitute an "affective atmosphere" imbued with the weight of degradation from the look of human persons.[15] The social wound that this chapter discloses, and opens, is the wound of human looking and human being. Like racism, homophobia, sexism, and classism, human looking is described by street kids as a weighty social power that keeps people stuck in homelessness. It is a wound picked apart by glances and the mere presence of another human formed by the media, political figures, and everyday conversations about people who are homeless. By examining how some street kids use spanging, dumpster diving, and manifesting as spiritual practices, I demonstrate that spirituality on the streets is about rendering a presence that tends the wound of human looking and human being. At stake is the transformation of the affective atmosphere on the street, The Universe itself, and the real looking faces of human persons. Spirituality on the streets is a struggle for the warm weight of compassion on one's skin, which might manifest a simple smile.

Chapter 4 queries how street kids think about God and what difference thinking about God makes. I show that perceptions of God are diverse, ambivalent, and contested. I also show that there are nevertheless coherent and meaningful patterns to people's God concepts and that these patterns of thought matter. God concepts help sustain purpose against ultimate meaninglessness and empower people to pursue a livable life in the grip of soul woundedness. This chapter also queries why the Christian conception of God usually fails to help. It reveals a wound of God in the experience of being human, which is a question about divine love's painful affective absence in the midst of senseless affliction and the presence of offensive material abundance that one does not have access to. I also show that the Christian conception of God fails because of its discriminatory connotations, the epistemological changes that have placed us in what Charles Taylor calls "the immanent frame," and because the unloving social conditions people live within make the "problem of presence" Christians face across space and time profoundly difficult to resolve.[16]

In chapter 5, I describe how some faith-based organizations experience people who are homeless and describe the difference homeless persons make in the spiritual lives of Christians who are securely housed. Though I spent a considerable amount of time learning about the ways many faith-based organizations across the United States experience and respond to people who are homeless, I focus on ethnographic research that I conducted with "street ministers" at a Christian organization, Operation Nightwatch, in Seattle. Here, I tell the local history of street ministry, describe the nature of the practice, and demonstrate the spiritual differences it makes for the securely housed Christian. I propose that homeless individuals are experienced as "wounds of love" that help make the project of Christian love possible. I also show that street ministry helps God become real to some housed Christians in a secular age, which gives their lives meaning in a world where ultimate meaning is impoverished and divine love feels painfully absent. I conclude this chapter by showing that the love street ministers offer people who are homeless helps some individuals but hurts others.

The concluding chapter opens a question about how we can render a more loving love with and for people experiencing homelessness through spiritual practice. Sincere personal and social transformation is what's at stake with a more loving love: a love that becomes real in the Homeless Other through the materialization of compassionate, sustained togetherness and permanent, supportive housing, not merely a love that lives only in the Housed Christian as they try to love the Homeless Other. Beginning with a narrative about a street kid I met on a bridge who was planning to kill herself, I develop what I call *a spirituality of loving social power for the violently uprooted*. This spirituality is a call for two adaptable spiritual practices that begins by suggesting that a social infrastructure of love is needed to support a street kid's own soulful desires for a life worth living and that this infrastructure can be cocreated through spiritual practice. The first spiritual practice I propose is intended to engender solidarity with street kids and broader homeless communities through direct political action. I challenge faith-based organizations to develop spiritual practices that touch, evoke, and transform what I call *the social soul* of the human person through nonviolent civil disobedience. The social soul of the human person refers to the powers within the social world that influence (but do not determine) the personal soul of human persons. I challenge faith-based organizations to imagine and engage the streets as a site of social transformation where spiritual practices can help engender the social conditions for a life worth living. I provide a historical example of the Poor People's Campaign led by Martin Luther King Jr., which has been revived by William Barber II. Like the street kids in this book, who dream what feels like an impossible dream to stay alive, I also dream for what sometimes feels impossible: a solution to homelessness that comes by way of temporary, collective homelessness.

In *Across That Bridge: A Vision for Change and the Future of America*, the late civil rights leader and legislator John Lewis writes that "to truly revolutionize our society, we must first revolutionize ourselves."[17] Lewis renders an astute, seasoned observation about the spiritual climate in the United States and the possibility of real social change. To be sure, we need to develop a social infrastructure of love. This kind of development is needed because the social conditions for a livable life are absent for poor people and a more loving love needs a social infrastructure. To not be homeless, people need affordable housing, health care, fair-paying jobs, and a supportive community. A social infrastructure of love is also needed because most people in the United States are existentially homeless themselves. Most of us are wandering away from ourselves. We are internally uprooted. Still, as Blaise Pascal noticed in *Pensées* in 1670, we struggle to be alone with ourselves in a room. Unless we become more at home in ourselves and each other, I propose, we will fail to develop a social infrastructure of love. We will not become temporarily homeless with each other for a more loving love until we come home to ourselves. We need to be more loving toward our own woundedness to love people experiencing homelessness more lovingly. Loving oneself more lovingly is therefore a direct response to homelessness. It is a real step toward compassionate, sustained togetherness and permanent, supportive housing. Self-love is a nonviolent power that empowers our capacity for liberatory love with others. This book calls on faith-based organizations to develop creative, locally meaningful spiritual practices that help people love and come home to themselves and free their soulscape from the internal colonization of heartless capitalism, militarism, and the ubiquitous position of hatred. I suggest, as medicine, now and on the pages that follow, the historic practice of spiritual friendship.[18] Spiritual friendship—with oneself and the world—is an overlooked practice of revolution.

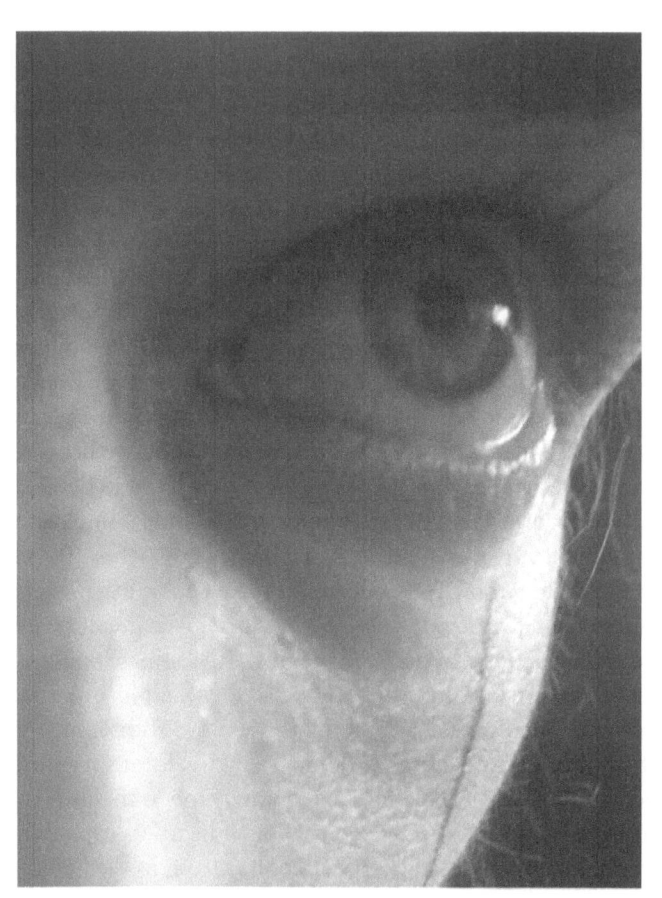

1
The Wound of Faith

'do you feel me?'

'I am little,' he says, 'but I become a monster when somebody fucks with me. That's why people on the streets call me Little Monster.' His blue sneakers scrape the ground. Abruptly, he stops the bike he pushes up and down, up and down the sidewalk. Standing still, we splinter and slow the anonymous train of street walking. Little Monster penetrates me with a long look and gathers me into him.

'Do you feel me?'

'I feel you,' I say. 'I feel you.'

In truth, I didn't feel him. Truer still: I was afraid to. I hurried past the uncomfortable emotion Little Monster's question evoked and focused on what I knew. I helped him step firmly into a street name and identity. I was fine with that. Howard Thurman put the need to be rooted in a name well: "To be known, to be called by one's name, is to find one's place and hold it against all the hordes of hell."[1]

Little Monster ran away from home. It wasn't a home to him anyway. He said none of his foster homes have been. He said abuse and arbitrary rules don't make a home, so he left. He ended up on the streets because he had no place else to go. On the streets he imagined there'd at least be people like him, going through what he is going through.

One of my teachers, Tanya Marie Luhrmann, told me that ethnography is like learning to swim. You can't learn ethnography, she said, by reading a book about it. You learn ethnography by going into the field, asking questions, and learning what it means to be a member of the local world you're trying to understand.

Little Monster's question became alive in me. I heard it on the streets when he wasn't around. I fell asleep listening to it play like a record in my mind. His question helped walk me into what I didn't know: who to spend time with, what questions to ask, where to look. On that day, before Little Monster's question about whether I could feel him, if that really was his question, I lost the water. I lost a certain knowledge about how to swim.

Ethnography insists on an epistemological stance Max Weber, a founding figure of sociology, referred to as *verstehen*: a temporary bracketing of one's judgments about the world to make room for a different perspective to emerge. Ethnography is the study of a local world "from the inside out," Luhrmann writes.[2] Getting inside a different local world, though, is hard. What is harder still, she told me, is to have a sense not only for how you see people but how the people you're seeing see themselves and make sense of their world: and, there, experience you experiencing them.

Christianity seeded, grew, and formed my interior landscape. A peculiar Christian invitation to love brought me to the streets to learn how to make love real. For most of the street kids I spent time with, however, Christianity is an intrusive foulness. It is a reality to be banished, not embraced. Spirituality on the streets is, in the first place, as the next chapter will demonstrate, an impassioned rejection of (what is perceived to be) Christianity. An ethnography on the streets of Seattle seemed to ask that I open, risk, and transform my Christian way of experiencing the world. The practice of an ethnography for a more loving love wounded me with practices of faithlessness.

The Pastoral Clinic is an ethnography by Stanford anthropologist Angela Garcia. It explores the relationship between placelessness and addiction in New Mexico's Española Valley, which has one of the highest rates of heroin addiction and fatal overdose in the United States. Garcia proposes that heroin addiction in the Española Valley is a symptom of historic and ongoing oppression; that it is a mistake to view addiction outside the fraught cultural context it is experienced in. During her research, Garcia became intimately acquainted with heroin addicts. She used the term "moments of incomprehensibility" to describe how much of the suffering she witnessed escaped her comprehension and remained unknowable to her.[3] Rather than abandoning the incomprehensible, however, Garcia attended to it. It became a place she inhabited to discern how to understand the local world she became a part of to render a presence that is good and caring for the people she got to know. Looking back, the street moment when Little Monster asked if I could feel him appears as a moment of incomprehensibility. I am still learning how to inhabit it, unknowingly.

This chapter is about how I began to learn how to swim. It is about how I started drowning in a water I no longer knew. It is about how I became present to a local world that I was a stranger in. This chapter proposes that apophatic spiritual practice, also known as the *via negativa*, is a useful spiritual tradition and technique one can draw from to understand different local worlds without uprooting oneself from one's own religious world. I propose here that love requires practices of unknowing: that a more loving love asks that we skillfully unknow what we (think we) know. This chapter encourages ethnographers, be they religious or secular, to develop *practices of unknowing* for a more loving love.

Engaging ethnography as a spiritual practice is not novel. In *The Weight of the World*, Pierre Bourdieu, in a way he knew would scandalize "the rigorous methodologist and the inspired hermeneutic scholar," described ethnography as a spiritual exercise. For Bourdieu, the spiritual exercise of learning about the Other through empirical research involved a "forgetting of the self" and, subsequently, "a conversion."[4] In *Death without Weeping*, Nancy Scheper-Hughes builds a bridge between ethnography and theology. "If theology entails a 'leap of faith' of oneself toward an invisible, unknowable Divine Other," she writes, "anthropology implies an 'outside-of-myself' leap toward an equally unknown and opaque other-than-myself, and a similar sort of reverential awe before the unknown is called for."[5] Eileen Campbell-Reed and Christian Scharen, among other theologians working in tandem with social science, have also framed ethnography as a spiritual practice.[6]

contested epistemologies

Ethnography is a site of epistemological contestation. Anthropologists gave the world the method of ethnography; the diverse academic world has since transformed it. Not all anthropologists are pleased. The diverse uses of ethnography—among scholars in fields such as political science, psychology, theology, and religious studies—raise questions about methodological adequacy. One site of epistemological contestation over ethnography is the place between social science, anthropology, and theology.

Ethnography is a question about how to discover real otherness in the world.[7] If real otherness is found (and it not always is), ethnography is also a question about how to keep otherness other as it is explained and rendered. To keep otherness other in ethnography is to protect and nurture the intimate differences of another life and distinct local world. An ethnographer must not reduce the living mysteries they are trying to understand to their own always limited understandings. Historically, many ethnographers have been suspicious about the degree to which a religiously committed person can do ethnography well. Their claim is that religious commitments may obscure the possibility of discovering real otherness.[8] A seasoned anthropologist at an ethnography training at UC Berkeley put the matter to me crudely. "Your theology doesn't belong in ethnography," he said. "It should have nothing to do with it." His sentiment of discontent became present at an American Academy of Religion conference. Over a breakfast at a Mexican restaurant in San Diego, an anthropology colleague told me that his tenure might be jeopardized if he continued writing about how anthropology might companion theology in the quest for a better, more nuanced understanding of the world. The word "theology" in relation to anthropology, he said, is anathema to his tenure reviewers.

In 2006, the anthropologist Joel Robbins wrote an article entitled "Anthropology and Theology: An Awkward Relationship?"[9] In the article, Robbins reflects on the epistemological questions the burgeoning field "the anthropology of Christianity" raises for the discipline of anthropology. One question Robbins explores concerns anthropology's "awkward" relationship to theology. Historically, Robbins recognizes, anthropologists have engaged theology with suspicion. For some anthropologists, Christianity is what Mary Douglas called a "purity danger."[10] In relation to anthropology, that is, theology is out of place; it is like pollution in a liberated, secular landscape. Because of the enriching possibilities he believes theology holds for anthropology today, however, Robbins encourages anthropologists to develop a more generous and hospitable hermeneutic. To that end, Robbins charts three routes by which anthropologists might engage theology today.

The first route explores how theological ideas shaped anthropology. Robbins considers Talal Asad, who excavated the Christian roots of the concepts of religion and culture, as a pioneer on this path.[11] The second way to engage theology, Robbins suggests, is by examining the difference theology makes in local Christian worlds. Susan Harding's *The Book of Jerry Falwell*, which demonstrates how the theology of church leaders shaped the fundamentalist world she studied, is cited as a pioneering study here.[12] Robbins's third map into theology is, still, the most uncharted. In response to how he perceives John Milbank's *Theology and Social Science* to "mock" anthropology for its unwitting entanglement in ontological violence, Robbins proposes that anthropologists find inspiration in theology to realize social ontologies in the field that might engender hope and flourishing.[13]

Robbins's article is deeply influential among anthropologists and theologians. It animated a lively and robust conversation about the difference theology makes to anthropology.[14] Today, the conversation engages theology for more than a revelation about anthropology's epistemological roots, data that might inform ethnographic projects, and ontological inspiration. In *Theologically Engaged Anthropology*, for example, theology matters for anthropological theorizing itself and potential collaboration on shared problems related to human flourishing. Don Seeman, for example, an anthropologist, suggests that theology can help an anthropologist break out of their "cultural and ideological straitjackets" to better understand, explain, and render what is experienced on the "shoreline of lived experience."[15]

A tension that remains in the discussion is about what a religiously committed person should do with their religious commitments in the field. In *On Knowing Humanity: Insights from Theology for Anthropology*, a volume of contributions from Christian anthropologists and theologians, the authors argue that anthropology's ontological commitments to secularism and liberalism undermine its capacity to adequately understand, explain, and render religiously based perspectives. What is at stake for these authors is the recognition that Christianity is not reducible to culture and the possibility that it can contribute to the analytic core of anthropology.[16] Central to the volume is the notion that people are created in the image of a loving God to be in loving relationships with the human and nonhuman world. This is a defining feature of their version of Christian ontology and the religious commitment by which they propose Christian anthropology should adjudicate the social. Divine love, they say, is both our tool and our *telos*.[17]

An adjacent conversation in academe is transpiring among progressive, mainstream Christian theologians and ethicists. In *Ethnography as Christian Theology and Ethics*, Christian Scharen and Aana Marie Vigen wrote an impressive manifesto for theologians who want to incorporate ethnography into their work, responsibly and with sophistication. The essays in *Ethnography as Christian Theology and Ethics* share the root theological commitment of *On Knowing Humanity*: that people are made in the image of a loving God to love God and the world.[18] What is at stake in Scharen's later book, *Fieldwork in Theology*, is "waking up to the world God loves."[19] The figure of the divine lover remains the most operative force in the ethnographer's social world and the principal reality the ethnographer is attuning themself to. The purpose of these conversations about a Christian ethnography is a question about how ethnographic data can be used by Christian institutions for seemingly Christian purposes.

When I devised this project and entered the field, I was firmly committed to the notion that people are made in the image of a personally loving God to love the human and nonhuman world. At the heart of the cosmos, I thought, stood a divine figure akin to Aslan in C. S. Lewis's *The Chronicles of Narnia*. He is not a safe lion, but he is good. Tender and fierce, he lives in passionate and loving pursuit of the world for their flourishing. When I began my fieldwork in Seattle, however, I wondered if it was violence and ethnographic blunder to impose this Christian theologizing onto the world. I did not want to see the streets, as I was on the streets, at least, and to the extent possible, through the eyes of a loving lion. It seemed clear to me that Christian anthropology and ethnographic theology had not sufficiently demonstrated what Eloise Meneses suggests is needed to learn something true about other people: namely "a willingness to allow our preconceptions to be altered by the strange realities of their existence."[20] While Scharen and Vigen also discuss the importance of "de-center[ing] our own assumptions and evaluations," theological ethnographers hadn't pushed Christian ethnographers far enough in challenging our Christian preconceptions of the world either.[21]

Still, it did not seem necessary to unchristian myself in order to do ethnography. The challenge I faced was how to allow myself to be altered by the world I sought to understand—and love—without needlessly unbinding my religious commitments. In time, through challenges from people like Little Monster, I developed practices, informed by the apophatic tradition of Christianity, that opened my religious commitments in the field to make room for the real otherness to emerge. I sought to develop spiritual practices of unknowing to help decenter my core theological assumptions in the field and learn how to see the world from the perspective of the people I spent time with.

To make room for real otherness to emerge, the Christian ethnographer can conceive of the field as a landscape of apophatic prayer. I propose that a Christian ethnographer enter the field as though they are walking in "a cloud of unknowing" and experiencing John of the Cross's "dark night." Through apophatic spiritual practices, by which one generates epistemological humility through the recognition of the inherent limitations of theology, and prays one's image of God away, one learns how to become open to real otherness in the world; one learns, perhaps, how to give the breath of life and love in ethnography. The persistent faith of apophatic spirituality is that, though wounded by unknowing and an eclipse of meaning through practices of faithlessness, one will remain guided by a real love for a more loving love.

spiritual practice and the *via negativa* in ethnography

In this chapter, which explores how I engaged ethnography as a spiritual practice, I have invoked terms that require definition. Those terms are *spiritual practice, apophatic prayer,* "the cloud of unknowing," and "the dark night." *Ethnography* also requires a more concise definition.

Elizabeth Liebert's definition in *The Soul of Discernment* is a helpful place to begin. Liebert defines spiritual practice as "something we do repeatedly that helps us move closer and closer to God."[22] I propose that ethnography can be framed as a spiritual practice that can help one become closer to God. Closeness to God through ethnographic research can happen when an ethnographer distances themself from how they experience God in the present. The field is a place to imagine forgetting God. God may be found (or lost) in the letting go of God and the painful eclipse where God becomes absent. In the field, the ethnographer must free the God that lives in their clenched fist. In an ethnography that struggles, in fear and trembling, for a more loving love, this loosening is divine because it is for love which, though presently and necessarily unknown, is trusted as the fundamental energy of the divine in the world.

In a 2017 essay titled "Academic Life and Scholarship as Spiritual Practice," Liebert further illuminates her definition of spiritual practice. In that essay, Liebert defines spiritual practices as regular, repeated, intentional, embodied actions that are shared with and evaluated by a community of shared practice according to agreed-upon standards of excellence that enhance the good, true, and beautiful that one seeks and is sought by.[23] Liebert's definition of spiritual practice is akin to the sociologist Robert Wuthnow's. In "Spirituality and Spiritual Practice," Wuthnow defines spiritual practice as "those activities in which individuals engage in order to become more aware of their spirituality or to enrich and grow in their spiritual lives. Whereas spirituality indicates a transcendent state of being or an ineffable aspect of reality," Wuthnow continues, "spiritual practice is a more active or intentional form of behavior."[24] Wuthnow further explicates spiritual practices as being intentional, "oriented toward the attainment of intrinsic or internal goods, . . . embedded in social institutions," implying moral obligations, requiring self-reflection, historic, and related to other social practices.[25]

I now turn to a brief discussion of apophatic spirituality. The point here is not to be completely adequate to the complexity of apophatic spirituality. That would require a library, let alone a book. The point of this discussion, rather, is to define apophatic spirituality so that the reader can understand how I am using it. Apophatic spirituality is a particular way of relating to God. Most fundamentally, apophatic spirituality is based on the notion that God is fundamentally unknowable. In Kierkegaard's language, there is an "infinite qualitative difference" between humanity and God.[26] To speak of God apophatically is to recognize that God lives beyond language. Thinking that God can be confined in a thought, a practice, or theological proposition, apophatic spirituality reminds us, is idolatry. Elizabeth A. Johnson puts it well: "The living

God literally cannot be compared with anything in the world. To do so is to reduce divine reality to an idol. This divine magnitude means that no matter how much we know, the human mind can never capture the whole of the living God in a net of concepts, images, or definitions, or preside over the reality of God in even the most exalted doctrines."[27]

God's unknowability, however, does not mean that God cannot be known or spoken about at all. Apophatic spirituality dares to speak about God, but it does so through creative negation at the limits of language. It is for this reason that apophatic prayer is also referred to as *via negativa*. God is experienced through negation and in the liminal space negating creates. From one perspective, the point of apophatic spirituality is to empty the mind of what I call *the divine imaginary*. At stake in engendering divine emptiness is to recognize that we do not have the cognitive or emotional equipment to completely understand God. From another perspective, however, apophatic spirituality is not about lack but abundance. The divine reality overflows and exceeds the categories of human comprehension. For Denys Turner, the apophatic is an exercise in *exhausting* the power of language to speak about God that culminates in a brilliant, impregnated darkness.[28] To practice apophatic spirituality is like trying to stand under the weight of Niagara Falls. It is impossible for a human to feel the beautiful weight of its presence and remain alive. Therefore, apophatic spirituality is both divine emptying and a divine filling. Negation itself is not what is at stake in apophatic spirituality. At stake is experiencing a presence living in *excess* that, as Stephan Quarles writes, might become an experience of "sweeping praise."[29]

In Christian spirituality, apophatic spirituality contrasts with kataphatic spirituality. They are not opposites. Both spiritualities represent different paths to a conscious experience of the divine presence and relate in dialectic fashion.[30] Whereas apophatic spirituality operates at the *limits* of language, however, kataphatic spirituality operates at the *embrace* of language. Kataphatic spirituality worries less about losing God in language or making an idol of an image. It is more concerned with accepting that image and being lovingly alive with it. *The Spiritual Exercises* of Ignatius of Loyola exemplify kataphatic prayer. In *The Spiritual Exercises*, Ignatius encourages people to use their imaginations to experience and embrace God. Ignatius considered the imagination a reliable site of divine encounter, paint for a spiritual masterpiece that can be one's own life.

In the Christian tradition, apophatic spirituality is first and most robustly demonstrated in the work of Pseudo-Dionysius. Though Pseudo-Dionysius lived in the late fifth and early sixth century, he wrote as though he were a first-century convert of Paul of Tarsus named Dionysius the Areopagite.

Speaking of God, Pseudo-Dionysius writes, requires an "unknowing of what is beyond being as something above and beyond speech, mind, or being itself."[31] Pseudo-Dionysius finds resources for the unknowability of God in the Hebrew Scriptures where, for example, Moses is moved into unknowing upon asking God for God's name (Exodus 3:14). Pseudo-Dionysius was a student of the Neoplatonist philosopher Proclus. His apophatic spirituality, therefore, is also rooted in Neoplatonism. Indeed, early Christian spirituality is itself a juxtaposition of Jewish and Platonic matrixes.[32]

Throughout the history of Christianity, apophatic spirituality has used different metaphors. There is no one apophatic way. Earlier, I invoked "the cloud of unknowing" and "the dark night." Briefly, I will discuss them to demonstrate how I use them analogously on the streets of Seattle. *The Cloud of Unknowing* was written in the fourteenth century. Though its author is anonymous, many scholars presume that *The Cloud* was written by a Carthusian priest, likely a recluse living in the East Midlands of England. *The Cloud* is written as a letter from a spiritual father to a spiritual son. The spiritual father's intent is to help his son learn the art of contemplation, which is meant to result in the experience of divine love. To this end, the author of *The Cloud* suggests putting a "cloud of forgetting" between himself and God. All thoughts, even supposedly holy ones, are to be put into this cloud of unknowing. The reason, the author claims, is that knowing cannot reach God: knowing, in fact, can be an impediment to the experience of God. What can reach God, however, the author claims, is the impulse of love. As the author writes, "it is love alone that can reach God in this life, not knowing."[33]

"The dark night" may be the most popular metaphor in the Christian tradition of apophatic spirituality. "The Dark Night" is an eight-stanza poem written between 1578 and 1579 by a Spanish Carmelite named John of the Cross. Approximately two years later, John wrote two commentaries on the poem. The first is titled *The Ascent to Mt. Carmel* and the second is titled *The Dark Night*. Like Pseudo-Dionysius of *The Divine Names* and the anonymous author of *The Cloud*, John wrote *The Dark Night* to counsel people in his spiritual care. Fundamentally, the treatise is meant to be an adaptable map for a spiritual pilgrim through darkness and disillusion on their quest for the presence of God.[34]

The Ascent to Mt. Carmel and *The Dark Night* tell a sequential story of the human pilgrimage to spiritual union with God. Mt. Carmel is a metaphor John uses for the climactic, embodied, and ecstatic state of loving union with God. On the ascent to Mt. Carmel, the spiritual pilgrim must traverse through a series of purifications—or, as John calls them, "nights." The nights are both active and passive; they are experienced in one's "senses" and "spirit." The nights are active in terms of human effort. Principally, human effort involves a struggle of the human will to detach from things that prevent a closer attachment to God and evokes its own disorienting darkness. The passive nights, conversely, refer to the effort of the divine. In the passive nights, God labors to free a person from unhelpful attachments. The night is dark because the soul feels as though it has been abandoned by God. The light that lit and nurtured its world is eclipsed. In the night, the soul is beside itself.

The result of the purification is not meant to induce a solitary bliss. For John of the Cross, a person is loved into and through darkness to grow in faith, hope, and love. The new love, born from disorientation, is for the world. The love born in the dark is for the wounds of the world and meant to be seen in the crystalline light of day. In "The *New Self* of John of the Cross," spirituality scholar David B. Perrin argues that John's corpus is a striking, divine invitation to convert from a self preoccupied by vain attachments that inhibit love to a self that burns with divine love.[35] The invitation to a love born of darkness, Perrin suggests, is nothing less than a humanization of the divine and a witness to the ongoingness of the Incarnation of Christ.[36]

Wendy Farley's work illuminates why apophatic spirituality really matters to the tradition of Christian spirituality and what the various metaphors try, forever imperfectly, to convey. As with Pseudo-Dionysius, the author of *The Cloud*, and John of the Cross, Farley advocates apophatic spirituality as a school of divine love.[37] What makes apophatic spirituality a practice of love, according to Farley, is that it can liberate one from inadequate conceptualizations of the divine and other people. One's image of the divine holds other people. It can fix one's gaze upon the world. Apophatic spirituality is a cure for an idolatry that inhibits love. It loosens one's grip on the illusion that people and God can ultimately fit into boxes we construct for them and helps us understand that our "natural way of seeing" may be quite unnatural. When we cling to our images about other people and the divine, we may wound them. Love, though, is liberatory. It is courageous. Going the negative way, Farley writes, is an act of great faith. Apophatic spirituality does not preclude naming, but it recognizes that love is the mystery behind every name and that even speaking the numinous as love is itself a wise mistake. To walk the *via negativa*, Farley writes, is to take a lover's walk into a space of unknowing.[38]

I just proposed that ethnography can be a spiritual practice in the apophatic tradition of Christian spirituality. The extended discussion about apophatic spirituality above has been an attempt to describe how apophatic spiritual practice is compatible with secular ethnography. Now, I will demonstrate that secular anthropologists have treated ethnography as a presence-making enterprise that attempts to render a presence that is good. I propose that apophatic spirituality is useful ethnographically because it can help one become present to real difference, which is the *raison d'être* of ethnography. I also suggest that without the kind of presence ethnographers artfully and rigorously seek, and which I suggest Christian ethnographers can seek through apophatic spiritual practice, we are derelict in our capacity to love. We cannot love what we do not adequately know and what hasn't become sufficiently present to us through practices of unknowing. Love is a possibility that emerges through practices of unknowing.

presence

Ethnography, as Clifford Geertz put it, is about "being there."[39] For Geertz, "being there" is a multifaceted process. First, being there means becoming sufficiently present to the local world being studied to establish rapport with the people in it. In my case, that meant spending time on the streets and getting to know the people who live there. It is here where Renato Rosaldo's reference to ethnography as "deep hanging out" makes sense.[40]

Being there, however, is not merely about establishing a physical presence and getting to know people. To really be there, one must learn what it *means* to be a member of the social world being studied. It is about learning the subtle differences, as Geertz puts it, between twitches and winks.[41] Veena Das's description of ethnography as a "dwelling science" is helpful: what matters in becoming present to a local world is an attentive dwelling-with whereby one becomes attuned to what is at stake in the ordinariness of daily life.[42] This kind of dwelling might allow the meaning of the Other to be born in the ethnographer.

So, "being there" is about more than becoming physically present to a local world. It is about more than developing meaningful relationships with the people present. It is also about more than *learning* what really matters in a local world. Inevitably, an ethnographer returns home from the field—if one has a home—and, inevitably, feels confused. I had thousands of pictures and fieldnotes and interview transcriptions to sort through. My "deep hanging out" needed to become deep understanding about real difference. "Being there," Geertz teaches, must give way to "being here."[43] Ultimately, the ethnographer becomes present to a local world to render it present to others through a mediation of different frames of meaning.[44] Presence—not merely having "been there" but having been there so deeply that one can eventually bring others there—is what makes ethnography methodologically distinctive. Ethnographers render worlds present through their presence.

Again, though: a presence merely rendered is not the point. Why do others come to your page? How do you want others to dwell on your pages and what might you want this dwelling to do? To merely stand back, removed, and gaze at different lives in affliction? Ethnography is not tantamount to typing out a list of facts and quotes and then putting them down on a page. It is about more than letting other people become the objects of attention. That's voyeurism. The presence upon presence one seeks in the field can be explained. The puzzlement and strangeness about otherness can be reduced. People go to the page to learn about the vastness of the human experience. Geertz writes: "The claim to attention of an ethnographic account does not rest on its author's ability to capture primitive facts in faraway places and carry them home like a mask or a carving, but on the degree to which he is able to clarify what goes on in such places, to reduce the puzzlement—what manner of men are these?"[45] He continues: "It is not against a body of uninterpreted data, radically thinned descriptions, that we must measure the cogency of our explications, but against the power of the scientific imagination to bring us into touch with the lives of strangers. It is not worth it, as Thoreau said, to go round the world to count the cats in Zanzibar."[46]

If Geertz is right—and I think he is—that ethnography inevitably makes real connections between different worlds, then it is necessary to question one's ethical obligations to these new connections: how one lands and what one does on this shore of new human experience. For this reason, Paul Rabinow is right to characterize ethnography as an ethical quest.[47] One, then, does not become present to a local world to merely hang out and pass the time. One does more than learn about what is at stake in a different world to reduce its puzzlement and make strange connections familiar. For many ethnographers, the presence one seeks to render is also a question about how to do something good in the world. I sought to render an ethnographic presence of street life—mindful of but not paralyzed by my inadequacies, imperfections, and inextricable connection to power—that might, in however small a way, engender social healing.[48] I sought an ethnography that would break your heart and move you to compassion: a presence that can help create a world that can sustain and nourish life in the midst of complex and overwhelming social woundedness.[49]

making space for the Other to be Other

Ethnography, then, is about presence. More precisely, it is a question about how to become present to a local world to render a presence that might be good for that local world in a larger, more-than-human world. Based on a narrative from my early days on the streets of Seattle, I make one central proposal about how a religiously committed ethnographer can become present to a different local world. The proposal, I must say, is limited in scope; it is meant to evoke a dialogue rather than suggest a final, authoritative answer.

I propose that presence emerges from a distance that is cultivated and revered through apophatic spiritual practice. Let me explain. On the one hand, presence is about being close. Being close involves respectful listening and careful attention. If the smell of the streets has permanently stained your skin and you struggle to wash it from your mind, it is possible that you have become present to people living on the streets.[50] Much of my ethnographic work involved learning how to become sufficiently present to street life in order to understand what it was like to live there, what spirituality was like, and what difference it made in everyday life.

On the other hand, however, presence is about being distant. Being distant involves recognizing that the Other is not reducible to the way you think and feel. If you have cultivated a field between yourself and the Other so that the Other can emerge to you in their freedom, it is possible that you have become distant. That is love. "To love purely is to consent to distance," Simone Weil wrote. "It is to adore the distance between ourselves and that which we love."[51]

Like Farley, the anonymous author of *The Cloud*, and John of the Cross, Weil is writing in the tradition of apophatic spirituality. She, too, proposes that epistemological distancing is a requisite for understanding and rendering loving action in the world. In what remains of this chapter, I demonstrate the specific apophatic practices I developed in the field to distance myself from how I conceived God, the people I spent time with, and the streets. A different ethnographer, however, will develop their own authentic practices of unknowing.

The Stranger

Little Monster is pinching the filter of a cigarette between his right thumb and index finger. "Come on," he says, "follow me." He pushes his bike back down the street, hoping I'll tag along.

"Sorry," I say.

My day started in a small urban park located in Pioneer Square, Seattle's most historic neighborhood. It took me half an hour to walk there from my downtown apartment. When I got there, a tour guide had just finished discussing the historical significance of the park. I stared at the totem pole he and the tourists were huddled around. In *Native Seattle*, Coll Thrush argues that totem poles help write Seattle's "place-story." Place-stories build the identity of a city and its people; they shape the stories we tell about the world and our place within it.⁵² On the surface, totems seem to evoke respect for Indigenous history. We might pause, looking at them, and imagine what it would have been like to live such a long time ago. On a deeper level, however, Thrush argues, totems can write Indigenous people out of the historical present. The erasure occurs because Indigenous symbols are employed not just to remember but to forget. Totems announce Seattle's separateness from its past; they mark the present as a new frontier. In effect, people may come to believe that Indigenous people used to populate Seattle; that now they're history and that the brutality of colonization is swept away and vindicated by technological progress. We might also overlook the fact that Indigenous people are still living in the city without adequate recognition and care.

While tourists and business professionals do frequent the park, it is occupied mostly by people who are homeless. I went to speak with Sam and Eddie, two older homeless women who hang out there during the day. They weren't there. I sat down on a park bench and waited for them to show up. There was a strange peace to the steady movement of cars driving and honking behind me. I let this strange peace move through me. I felt the sun rest gentle on my forehead. When I let the sounds and sights of the streets move through me, I felt like I was praying.

Moments later, I hear distant yelling. It gets louder, closer. A man enters the park holding a large stack of newspapers. He has brown skin. He is speaking in a language other than English. He seems homeless. He offers a newspaper to everyone he encounters. Some people accept a newspaper; others do not. If people do not accept one, he throws it at their feet. A white homeless individual, who is sitting on a bench across from me, stands up and yells back at him: "Nothing shall separate you from the love of God, mother fucker!"

Newspapers line the ground.

The newspaper is called *The Stranger*. It's a free, weekly paper held in dispensers throughout the city. On the front page is a large, solid-black circle. Light comes out from behind it. Beneath the rim of the light is this caption: "Total Eclipse of the Trump: astrologers predict doom for the president. P. 6." On page six there are seven yellow moons. In each moon, there is a sliver of then-President Donald Trump's face. "If we're lucky," the article reads, wryly, "whatever shift Trump undergoes will be an improvement and not the start of a nuclear holocaust. Or a race war."⁵³

The cover story is about the first total solar eclipse that will be visible from the United States in forty years—and the first to cross the entire country in a century. Since Seattle is close to the point of totality, the view is expected to be spectacular. The story is also about the relationship between astrology and presidential politics in the United States. A "Virgo astrologer," Margo Orr, points out that John F. Kennedy's assassination, the attempted assassination of Ronald Reagan, and the impeachment of Bill Clinton all occurred on or near eclipses. The popular Susan Miller from Astrology Zone cautions that nothing is stronger than an eclipse. She predicts that it will bring a scandal in the Trump orbit to light. In a column entitled "Free Will Astrology," *The Stranger's* own astrologer is more reticent. He believes the eclipse will kill egos, not persons. "In a normal person," he writes, "that could be a good thing, because it would relieve that person of illusions and delusions that he has about himself. In Trump's case," however, he concludes, "there could be a shattering."[54]

The yelling washes over me again, on the park bench I am sitting on. He—the man whose name I do not know—has come back to the park. I close the paper. A family from England is taking a picture by the totem pole. Evidently, he desires a conversation. He first tries to speak with the father. When the father ignores him, he moves toward the children. The mother steps in front of her children. In a shielding haste, the father tucks his camera under his coat. The mother throws out her hands in the air, covering her children. In panic, the family frets aloud about what to do. "You're British, are you?" He detects their accent. "Do you know the queen?"

He puts his hand on the father's shoulder. "Please, leave us alone," the father pleads. "We just want to enjoy the park." The father comes up to me and asks what to do. I want to say "play it cool . . . you'll be alright . . . just walk away . . . " but I haven't the courage to speak.

"Crackers! Crackers! Fuck the queen!" They are penetrated by abusive racial expletives as they hurry out of the park. I remain seated on the park bench, staring nervously at the newspapers moved by the wind.

a tour of the streets

"Well . . . are you coming?" Little Monster wants to give me a tour of the streets. He imagines that will help my research and, I believe, render a material good for him. Like cigarettes or cash. Or, perhaps, I muse, a friend. Given the experience I had in the park earlier in the day, I am hesitant but ultimately decide to go.

Our first stop is an alley behind a homeless shelter. There, Little Monster introduces me to Jed. "Don't talk to him unless you want smokes or weed," he says. "Got it." Our second stop is behind Chief Seattle Club, an organization that provides care to Native Americans. Little Monster asks a volunteer on a cigarette break if he can have a smoke. "You're too young, kid." "All right," Little Monster tells me, "let's go. There's someone I want you to meet."

Little Monster pushes his bike out of the alley. Following closely behind him, I step in a large puddle. My right foot is soaking wet. I begin to think his tour is a ruse. A white male comes up to him and demands his private attention. "Can't," Little Monster says. "It's an emergency," the white male protests. "Later," Little Monster retorts.

Little Monster grabs two flattened cardboard boxes lying on the ground. He places the cardboard boxes next to a group of men standing in front of a dumpster. "Sit down," he tells me. He calls out to one of the men—whom he calls "Knife"—and asks him to come over. "This is Paul," he says. "He's writing a book about spirituality on the streets."

Knife is intrigued. "What do you mean you're writing a book about spirituality?" I give the speech I've rehearsed time and again in front of academic audiences: "I want to know what people pray about and how they think about God and what that has to do with life on the streets. Would you like to do an interview sometime?"

"I don't mean any offense," Knife responds curtly, "but you don't know what you're talking about."

Knife brings me away from the group. He puts his hand on my shoulder. "Look, you're not one of those people who's going to tell me to read a Bible verse, are you? I don't talk to those people." I assure him I am not.

"This is interesting then." Knife pauses. "You see, I've been asking God to send me someone to talk about this with. Usually, God sends me an attractive woman, though. You look good but you're not a woman. I don't think you're the one I am supposed to talk to."

Knife looks me up and down. He stares into my eyes. I think he is searching for a place inside of me that will tell him who I really am. He becomes upset. Our conversation woke rage in him. "God is nice and all," he tells me, almost yelling, "but he doesn't fuck around. Do you understand? He will take your life if you hurt one of his kids. That's in the Bible."

I tell Knife that perhaps I am not the person he is supposed to speak with. Feeling uncomfortable, afraid, and out of place, I gather myself to go. "Look," Knife responds, "what do you need to know?" I want to leave and no longer know what I need to know. "I talk to God and I talk to Satan, too. Okay? That is what you need to know. Jesus and Satan are not enemies—they're friends."

I thank Knife and Little Monster for their willingness to speak with me. Before I can leave, however, Knife gathers my attention again. "Before you come back," he said, "you need to answer this question: Why is it that I can see God and Satan even though I am not dead?"

I leave the alley in haste and ride a streetcar to what locals describe as "the Other Seattle." Homelessness is less visible in this Seattle; it is eclipsed by tower cranes, luxurious condominiums, and hipster coffee shops. I order coffee at one of these coffee shops, ease into a comfortable chair, and begin to write.

journaling

An ethnographer takes copious notes. The world they construct comes to life from the words in their journal.[55] Sipping a black coffee, I wrote down what had just happened: the trouble I had relating to Little Monster, the tour he gave me, and especially what Knife said about Satan. Several images came to mind. Anton LaVey, the founder of the Church of Satan, who was also known as "The Black Pope," came to mind first. Like Anton, I imagined that Knife was drawn to the figure of Satan out of rebellion over Christian hypocrisy.[56] I judged Knife for glorifying rebellion and being satisfied with a cheap moral compass. The image of the hapless victim of social circumstance came to mind next. I imagined Knife suffering from a serious mental illness caused by a life of inequitable pain. I judged there to be nothing real about his conversations with Satan; that he is listening to the impersonal, internalized force of injustice when he thinks Satan speaks to him.

In addition to writing about the images that came to mind during my encounter with Knife, I wrote about the emotions I felt. In *Emotions and Fieldwork*, Sheryl Kleinman and Martha Copp suggest that ethnographers often avoid exploring the emotions they experience in their research out of concern about being considered unscientific and solipsistic. In their view, however, emotions can be helpful companions on the journey toward robust and clear-eyed cultural understanding.[57] Elizabeth Liebert makes a similar point about the relationship between emotion and prayer in *The Way of Discernment*. With careful discernment, she suggests, our emotions can help lead us closer to God.[58]

Fear was more salient than the various images that came to mind when I wrote about Knife. Certainly, the fear was related to the obvious fact that I was in a dangerous neighborhood and that I had witnessed traumatizing racial violence. The center didn't seem to hold in Pioneer Square. The fear ran deeper than the immediate present, however. It was connected to the religious socialization I experienced as a child and the God that I came to know. In the religious world I grew up in, Satan roamed the world like a wrathful lion, preying on the souls of sinners. He was not a good lion. God would let him swallow you into a lake of eternal fire if you got to close to his mouth. We children were taught to be very afraid of Satan. Most of us still are.

Paradoxically, I discovered myself by journaling about my encounter with Knife. I did not in fact know whether Knife had a serious mental illness or if he befriends Satan because of Christian hypocrisy. I had not gently held and slowly wondered about him with him. My emotional experience of Knife, like the thoughts I had about him, were drawn mostly from my own story, not his. He did not yet freely emerge to me; I did not experience his name. He never told me, and I never asked. In reaching this place of unknowing—of seeing my world rather than the world of those on the streets—a presence beneath the surface became possible. I had questions rather than answers and, most importantly, an open heart.

swimming

Religion, the French philosopher Simone Weil wrote, is nothing else but a looking. It is the sacred way human persons learn to fix their soulful gaze upon the world.[59] Prayer, for Weil, consists principally in cultivating attention to what is present. This kind of attentiveness means "suspending our thought, leaving it detached, empty, and ready to be penetrated by the object."[60] Love, the rendering of a life-giving presence to the Other, which is also Christianity's faith about the fundamental energy of the universe, also requires a peculiar looking. Weil writes: "This way of looking is first of all attentive. The soul empties itself of all its own contents in order to receive into itself the being it is looking at, just as he is, in all his truth."[61] Love, in Weil's analysis, means learning to free the Other from ourselves and simply ask: "What are you going through?"[62]

Summers in Seattle are warm. The nights are long. Whenever I could, after a long day on the streets, I'd swim in Lake Washington. When I dunked my head under water, I'd imagine the people I got to know. Eyes closed and submerged, I held them gently in my mind. Breathing out in the water, I tried to release them from the grip of my emotion and understanding.

I would do the same with God. I would call Aslan to mind. In the water, as I pushed my breath out of my mouth and let my heart beat out of my own chest, I prayed that Aslan would run free from me. I imagined pushing Aslan out of my mind through my breath and seeing him sink to the bottom of the lake. I prayed that I would experience what the world was like without him, what it was like to experience the different spiritualities that I would encounter on the streets.

When I got out of the lake, and threw my towel around my body, I looked out at the water. I imagined that I left my thoughts and emotions—and my faith—in the lake. This practice of faithlessness, which wounded me, did not work like magic. I still feel fear when I think about what Knife told me about Satan. Anton LaVey and the hapless victim of social circumstance run through my mind still. Despite the obvious limitations of the practice, however, the thoughts and feelings I had about others and God became less salient. They had less grip on me. The practices helped me become open to real otherness in a different local world.

I never emptied my soul into Lake Washington. It's an absurd proposition. Nonetheless, I found a way—my own way—of consenting to the distance between me and the people I began spending time with on the streets. As a result, I found it easier to look away from myself and ask the person in front of me: What are you going through?

The practices of journaling and swimming helped me expand the distance between me and the people that I came to know. They helped me understand that presence can emerge through spiritual practices that prevent the Other from being reduced to the way I think and feel. I propose that becoming present ethnographically—to people and to social problems—requires challenging our fundamental existential commitments and actual practices that dip us regularly into the waters of unknowing, walk us into the disorientation of spiritual darkness, and invite us into the presence of the Other.

Ethnography is a question about learning how to become sufficiently present to a different local world. I have proposed that Christian theologians and anthropologists develop what I call *practices of unknowing for a more loving love*. I imagine that such practices might help other ethnographers, whether religious or secular. How, practically, and through what techniques, do secular ethnographers cultivate distance from the people and places they think they know? *How*, that is—not just *what*—might they need to unlearn to learn?

Reality is not fixed; our capacity to grasp social problems is finite. Before the infinite presence of the incomprehensible, every ethnographer must find personal ways to embody epistemological humility. I found ethnographic practices of unknowing in conversation with people who are homeless, on a pad of paper, and in a lake; another might find them in the sky, or by licking the sap of a tree.

the eclipse

The eclipse came a few days after Little Monster's tour. I went back to the park and noticed that there weren't any newspapers on the ground. There were, however, a lot of tourists and business professionals standing on it. They were looking up at the sky with sunglasses on; they were taking pictures of the shadows on the ground. My grandmother always said staring at the sun will cause blindness. I stared at the sun until my vision got blurry and I became paranoid that there'd be irreparable damage to my eyes.

I saw Sam and Eddie, the homeless women I came looking for before Little Monster's tour, sitting on a park bench. I asked what they made of the eclipse. They weren't looking up at the sky. They were drinking beer from a can and sharing a conversation. "Oh, is that today?"

2
The Wound of Rejection

lucifer

Lucifer's hands shake as he rolls another cigarette. Some tobacco, which rests gentle on his palm, falls from the rolling paper and lands on the church steps we are sitting on. His street wife, Lilith—renamed after the supposed "first Eve" who refused to live bound by religious patriarchy—is spanging up the street to pay for their next bottle of alcohol.

Lucifer is telling me a story about how he became homeless. In the summer of 2011, his father locked him out of their apartment in Queens for breaking curfew. A shrewd drug dealer took pity—and advantage. He offered Lucifer a free room in exchange for dealing drugs. It wasn't until after he moved in that Lucifer realized he was living in a "bordello." He liked the space at first—for the thrill, the cash, and the freedom—but found himself strung out. 'If I didn't leave,' he said, 'I'd either die or go crazy.'

When a friend brought him to Occupy Wall Street, he experienced a kind of social healing. The protest signified solidarity, meaning, and hope—and tended the wounds of rejection, betrayal, and isolation ravaging his life. Lucifer hurried back to his room in the bordello, pulled his backpack down from the closet, stuffed it full of clothes, and left for New York's financial district.

At Occupy Wall Street, Lucifer met a woman. She had a car and they both had a dream to travel west, so they hit the road. Their relationship broke down where her old Volvo did, however: on the California 101. They helped each other get to Seattle, where she had family, but split apart. Without a place to stay or money in the bank, and with a criminal record he reasoned would prevent him from getting a job, Lucifer slept on the streets.

He grew up Roman Catholic. Lucifer prayed to Jesus when bad thoughts came to mind. Praying, though, he said, made him "just fuckin' lose it." As a teenager, the reviled figure of Lucifer intrigued him. He came to believe that Lucifer never wanted to wage evil warfare. "That's Christian hogwash," he said. Instead, he learned online, Lucifer refused to submit to a meaningless power that undermined his capacity to be free. God gave Lucifer a choice, he said: either serve in heaven or find freedom in another place.

He lights the cigarette. He tells someone eavesdropping on our conversation, who asked us for a Bible, to "get lost." One day, he goes on, he gave his life to Lucifer in a meditation. There were no candles or chants: "If you'll have me," he told Lucifer coolly, "I will be one of your moral personas on earth." Today, Lucifer thinks that street kids in Seattle claiming to be Luciferians got that from him.

lilith

Lilith grew up on a lake in a small midwestern town. She enjoyed the world outside: the squirrels, the oak trees, the sun's glitter on the lake. Inside, life was hard. Her mother was addicted to prescription drugs, neglectful, and "kinda crazy." Lilith's father, a fisherman, was often gone. 'When I think about it,' Lilith told me, 'Nature raised me.'

In college, Lilith discovered a different social world. When she returned after her senior year, her hometown felt different. 'The whole place,' she told me, 'felt like a closed-in cardboard box.'

Lilith lifted the lid with a lover. They drove to California for a road trip and an adventure. Within a few months, however, the desert heat got too hot. And they were arguing all the time. When a friend offered her his couch in Seattle for a few hundred dollars a month, she took the opportunity to live in a city that seemed open, accepting, and free.

Within a year, Lilith felt stuck in an abusive relationship. She was a barista at a coffee shop on the Ave in the University District. Lucifer knocked on the glass door one night just after closing. Nervously, he asked for a glass of water. Hesitantly, she said she couldn't get him a glass of water, since they were closed, but that she could buy them a six pack of beer at the gas station down the street. They could share it, she said. Romantic love emerged as they drank beer into the night. Late in the summer they'd marry at the gas station by jumping over a broom in the company of friends. 'It was like an Irish ceremony,' she said.

Lilith started hanging out on the streets. She would sing and play music with the street kids on the Ave, who seemed like a big family. 'There was just something charismatic about the Ave,' Lilith recalled. After sleeping on the streets 'to try it out first,' Lilith quit her job at Red Couch Café. She bought a hammock with her last paycheck and moved into the local park. She said that, unlike a lot of street kids, she chose to be homeless.

In a few months' time, however, Lilith's alcohol use will reach a dangerous pitch. She will develop grave wounds on her back. Her wounds will compel her back into the cardboard box. She will tell me, before she and Lucifer hit the road: 'Remember when I said I wanted to be homeless and that it was my choice? Well, that's not true anymore.'

But today it is summer. It is not winter; the snow has not blanketed the ground. Today, homelessness feels like a choice and today the streets are liberative. The charismatic community is still on her side. Today, the police aren't threatening to arrest her if they see her sitting down on the Ave one more time. Today, people are smiling. They are sharing and she is sharing. Today, there are people playing music, having "hobo barbeques," and enjoying themselves.

rejection

Homelessness is concrete evidence of social failure. It is visceral proof that some things fall apart. In the face of this failure, the human person is confronted with questions of meaning. Making and being made by meaning is part of what it means to be human. How we make meaning out of social failure differs; these interpretive differences really matter: they shape our relationships to ourselves, each other, and the world. This chapter is about how street kids create meaning and power with their experiences of homelessness through spiritual and other practices of rejection. It is also about how rejecting one's perception of religion can be experienced as a spiritual practice that tends one's soul wounds to survive an almost unlivable local world.

When I began my research on the streets of Seattle, I was walking around collecting letters to God on a yellow pad of paper for cheap cigarettes. In front of an empty storefront—formerly an American Apparel—a few street kids told me that they weren't interested in writing a letter to God, not even for cigarettes. I put the yellow notepad away and wondered why they rejected my invitation to connect with God. And myself. Lilith told me, on a summer evening on the sidewalk, that the only way to understand street life was to sit down and hang out.

After sitting down for a while, it was clear that rejection was a constitutive feature of everyday life on the streets. Street kids rejected the police, the yuppies walking by, the homeless advocates trying to help them, researchers like myself trying to learn about the world with them, and the everyday people they wanted money from. They seemed to reject the world and their very selves.

It is a mistake to lose a person who is homeless in a general category of homelessness. There is no one becoming homeless story. Every person who becomes homeless is a complex individual with a unique story. In my research, it was clear that the "routes" by which street kids became houseless varied considerably.[1] Still, patterns emerged in the irreducible narrative pluralities. In the stories I heard, like Lucifer and Lilith's, the theme of persistent, pervasive, and intimate rejection came up. It was the first social wound I noticed people articulate. And the first spiritual practice that surfaced within me on the streets was religious rejection, though it did not initially strike me as a spiritual practice.

The social wound of rejection is multifaceted. Superficially, it may begin when one stands facing a locked door. Lucifer's homelessness began when his father locked him out of their apartment in Queens for breaking curfew. The closure of his girlfriend's car door in Seattle announced another chapter in his experiences of homelessness. Lilith became homeless in Seattle when her apartment became overwhelmed by domestic violence: she lost a door into a safe dwelling. The wound of rejection is therefore a story deeper than an immediate physical closure. For the street kids I spent time with, the wound of rejection emerged in childhood. External forces—like one's parents, school, and religious world—uprooted them from themselves. Street kids were existentially homeless before they became physically homeless, I found. Most street kids were not at home in themselves when they were living in a house or apartment.

It was not striking to me that street kids felt interiorly uprooted. The role religion played in a person's existential and physical homelessness was, however, I hadn't foreseen that religion might uproot people from themselves in a way that would push them toward physical homelessness. Religion—and one's experience of Christianity in particular—had not struck me as a contributing factor in the experience of homelessness. Heartbreakingly, it sometimes is.

the reality about reality and home in a person's homeworld

In 1965, at a time of cultural ferment, Peter Berger and Thomas Luckmann published *The Social Construction of Reality*. In the book, which Berger and Luckmann locate within the "sociology of knowledge," they ask how reality becomes real to people: how the world takes on an independent aliveness from one's own volition, how people come to know that the independent world is real, and how it appears natural to them.[2] The book, which found an audience among academics and social revolutionaries, was impressive because of what *kind* of reality Berger and Luckmann tried to explain. In *The Social Construction of Reality*, Berger and Luckmann are not interested in timeless, metaphysical reality. They are not theologians wondering about how God might be real. They are also not primarily concerned with a question of how social theorists define reality. Instead, what concerns Berger and Luckmann is how ordinary people—"the man on the street," as they say—come to live in a world that is real and meaningful to them.[3]

Berger and Luckmann propose that reality is a social construction.[4] They do not deny that the human person has a natural inwardness. For Berger and Luckmann, however, a person's natural inwardness consists of nebulous "drives" that are chaotic without the social world to guide them into an orderly place. In their view, a person's natural inwardness only becomes meaningful in the context of a social world. Without a social world, in other words, human life would not be possible; it would be meaningless chaos. The social, then, represents a shepherding of the human person's innate drives. One implication of this social shepherding is that human people are deeply malleable: by nature, Berger and Luckmann claim, people are marked by a sense of "world-openness."[5]

What is ultimately at stake for Berger and Luckmann is an analysis of precisely *how* reality is constructed, not merely an argument *that* reality is socially constructed. In their view, reality is constructed and maintained through a dialectic of externalization, objectivation, and internalization.[6] Externalization refers to how human persons externalize themselves to create a stable world that will make life possible.[7] In the process of externalization, the world that people create is apprehended as objectively real. Objectivation, then, refers to how people come to believe that the process of externalization, which is always already fragile and ongoing, created the world as it appears natural.[8] That, for Berger and Luckmann, is the great trick up social reality's sleeve: it appears natural and inevitable when it is in fact constructed and contingent. Internalization is the process whereby the social world that has been created through externalization and which appears objective is made real in human consciousness.[9] Internalization is the place where a socially constructed reality makes a home in a person: and one would, say, give one's life for their country or place a flag on a car to signify what really matters about the nature of the world itself. Berger and Luckmann describe the process in three sentences: "Society is a human product. Society is an objective reality. Man is a social product."[10]

For Berger and Luckmann, internalization is a result of socialization. Socialization is defined as "the comprehensive and consistent induction of an individual into the objective world of a society."[11] There are two forms of socialization: primary socialization and secondary socialization.[12] For Berger and Luckmann, primary socialization is the most important form of socialization.[13] It forms the skeleton of one's inner world. Though one may "leave it behind," it remains active in the present and the future. As Heidegger proposes in *Being and Time*, the human is "thrown" into a world.[14] The world they are thrown into is the world their significant other shaped; they did not create the ordered chaos. In primary socialization, the world matters primarily because of how it matters for others. The child is given a gender, a class, a school. For the most part, one does not choose one's own name, the command one will learn to respond to, even when, really, it's the sound of wind blowing in the trees. They may refuse to abide by the rules of the world, but they have no real option to live in another external world. The world they are thrown into is the true world, the inevitable world, the world they cannot run from. This world is *the* world. Schooling one to be in the world that one is thrown into is the intent of primary socialization, even if that is not the conscious will of one's primary socializers; ostensibly, this process is meant to create a human who can function reasonably well in the world that they have been forced to comply with. That has made a home in them without their consent.

Primary socialization is also a highly charged emotional process. The world one is thrown into is a world of pulsating affect and emotion. If one does not develop healthy emotional relationships in primary socialization, Berger and Luckmann contend, it will fail.[15]

According to Berger and Luckmann, it is in secondary socialization that an individual may see that their world is one world among many worlds. Heidegger again: one realizes that the world one is thrown into can be thrown off. Here *the* world becomes an amalgam of *multiple* worlds. Despite the discovery of the seemingly arbitrary quality of the world and the possibility of living in a new one, Berger and Luckmann argue that people never really leave the world that became real to them in primary socialization. "It remains," they write, "the home world, however far one may travel from it later in life into regions where one does not feel at home at all."[16]

In a later book, *The Homeless Mind: Modernization and Consciousness*, Berger and his colleagues broaden their work on the relationship between homelessness and inward experience. Here, "home world" refers more generally to the everyday "life world." Gone, they write, in *The Homeless Mind*, is a world in which there was one world. As a result of the technological prowess of modernization and secularization, which once held together an existential world with theological stitching under a "sacred canopy," Berger and his colleagues posit that the modern person lives homeless.[17] And to live socially and existentially homeless in a plurality of worlds that renders the possibility of one totalizing world less certain and more precarious, is to live less at ease. "Because of the religious crisis in modern society," Berger and his colleagues write, "social 'homelessness' has become metaphysical—that is, it has become homelessness in the cosmos. This is a very difficult to bear."[18]

The *Oxford English Dictionary* defines homelessness as "the state of having no home." Many of the street kids I spent time with would contest that definition. They did not consider themselves homeless; their lives protested false, impersonal conceptualization of "the homeless." Home, as I have shown, is often experienced on the streets.[19] A street kid named Strawberry told me that they felt home for the first time when they became homeless on the streets of Seattle. Costa Mesa, a traveler who came through Seattle a few times a year, told me home is his big backpack. 'It's really cheesy,' Hitch once told me, 'but it's true: home is where the heart is.'

a national and local discourse on homelessness

Homelessness is a complex social problem and a contested category. There are disputes about how to define homelessness, how many people experiencing homelessness there are, and why people become homeless in the first place. In the history of the United States, homelessness has become known through the experience of different human faces. The human faces of homelessness—and the "routes" by which these faces emerge into public perception—have changed over time.[20]

Recently, homelessness has been fashioned in terms of social failure. In the collapse of the welfare state, and in response to earlier research studies that put blame for homelessness on individuals, the homeless face is often seen through a film of social injustice.[21] This homeless face is a traumatized face that people with power have failed. Today's homeless face is a strikingly different face than appeared, for example, in England during the Tudor Poor Laws. During that time, the homeless face was seen through a film of individual deviance, sin, and laziness. It was a face that seemed to deserve rejection and punishment, not acceptance and public housing. The social world socialized people into a home world that felt naturally threatened by and accusatory of the homeless face.

Today, many people in Seattle understand homelessness through what I call *rituals of social failure*. Rituals of social failure socialize people to experience the homeless person as a victim of social injustice. When I told people in Seattle that many street kids felt at home on the streets, and experience a kind of freedom there, they usually thought me naïve and hermeneutically tuned into a national deliriousness (such as Fox News). Rituals of social failure are political baptisms that care nothing for your consent. They baptize people into political action to help make sense of homelessness and compel people in power to become more responsible for the problem of homelessness.

Alas, there have always been homeless people in North America. In *Down and Out, on the Road*, Kenneth Kusmer demonstrates that most homeless individuals in the colonies were homeless because of war trauma, rising inequality, immigration, and slavery.[22] It wasn't until the years following the Civil War, Todd Depastino proposes in *Citizen Hobo*, that the United States first grappled with homelessness.[23] According to Depastino, the collapse of Wall Street caused massive unemployment that produced a "tramp army" and culture of "hobohemia." Tramps and Hobos were men riding the rails in search of seasonal work. Usually, they found lodging in downtown districts. During this time, homelessness was perceived as a problem among white males. Hobos and Tramps were experienced as lone wolves howling through cultural and economic alienation. With the pen of writers like Walt Whitman and Jack London, "hobohemia" became a romantic tale in American folklore.[24]

The Great Depression caused a significant rise in homelessness. Estimates range from 200,000 to 1.5 million. While there were homeless women and families during this time, the public face of homelessness remained the unhinged white male. The numbers related to homelessness declined sharply during World War II, however, when most homeless persons became involved in the war industry. After the war, homelessness rose again sharply and was evident mostly in skid rows. Skid rows comprised of inexpensive motels, cheap restaurants, bars, and religious missions. Here again the public face of homelessness was white and male, although the face tended to be a *drunk* white male. No longer a tramp in search of work and adventure, the homeless male was an addict in search of a bottle and a bench. This lonely drunk face had comparably little sympathy.

Until the 1970s, the dominant face of homelessness was the Hobo or the Tramp. This man lived on skid rows. He was white and older. He was drunk with alcohol or wanderlust—or both. Certainly, he was not your average, everyday face. In the 1970s, however, a "new homeless" emerged.[25] Urbanization brought a wrecking ball to the cheap hotels or SROs (single-room occupancy units) people found refuge in. During this time, the public presence of homelessness increased. People experiencing homelessness were on the streets and in parks, not just in shelters or desperately impoverished parts of town one could easily avoid. The new face of the homeless was in your face.

In the 1980s, it became more common for women and children to be homeless. The rise of the new homeless coincided with the loss of affordable housing and draconian reductions in government spending. The homeless were not just children with their mothers. They were also unaccompanied youth, who were often thought to be fleeing abusive homes or transitioning out of the foster care system. The face of the homeless was a face of adolescence gone terribly wrong; an innocent face that had been failed. Deinstitutionalization is another important component in the uptick of homelessness and the emergence of the new homeless. Deinstitutionalization is a term for what happened when mental institutions closed because they were thought to be inhumane and because local communities promised more humane care. Tragically, that never happened. In response to this social failure, streets and shelters began to "house" and "care" for our mentally unwell.[26] At this time, the "crazy" face of homelessness emerged in the public experience.

Today, people of color are disproportionately homeless. African Americans are 13 percent of the US population, for example, but roughly 40 percent of the homeless population. In 2023, the United States Department of Housing and Urban Development found that Hispanic and Latino people experienced a 28 percent increase in homelessness from 2022, and that people who identify as Asian or Asian American experienced a 40 percent increase.[27] Today's homelessness has moved off the streets. People experiencing homelessness today live in abandoned buildings and vehicles—and perhaps on your own couch. Many are also, strikingly, working full-time jobs. The anthropologist Brian Goldstone demonstrates that the term "the working homeless" is ripe for our lexicon.[28] Gone are the days when there was one face of homelessness and one route by which people became homeless. Today's homeless are not "tramps." They are not just down and out on skid row. There is a multiplicity of homeless faces.

the faces of homelessness in seattle

Almost everyone experiencing homelessness in Seattle wants safe and affordable housing. In 2018, Seattle's "Point-in-Time Count" reported that 98 percent of homeless persons would take a good housing opportunity if it were offered.[29] The diverse faces of homelessness in Seattle were not thriving faces, not laughing faces; they were faces wrinkled and traumatized, faces that wanted desperately to get into permanent housing. Sculpting the faces wounded by social failure really mattered in public discourse. Melinda Giovengo, once president and CEO of YouthCare, a prominent organization in Seattle working to end youth homelessness, didn't mince words in an article she wrote for the *Seattle Times* in 2018: "Let me set the record straight: Homeless youth are not sleeping outside by choice."[30] Giovengo, and others who create and defend the rituals of social failure, work hard to dispel myths that profane their rituals. One myth is that people are homeless by choice. Another myth is that people come to Seattle to be homeless. During my time in Seattle, social workers and local activists showed that the faces of homelessness in Seattle are faces from the neighborhood.[31] They protest the "The Freeattle Myth," which suggests that people come to Seattle to be homeless because they want free stuff from Seattle's social services.[32] The dominant discourse on homelessness, which seemed to be changing due to the public's "compassion fatigue" and Seattle's failure to solve homelessness, said homeless people aren't looking for a free handout but for a helpful, neighborly hand up. They are faces that are not to blame;

rather, politically powerful faces and obstructionist conservatives are the faces to blame.

I was drawn to street kids because they did not seem to fit how people created and defended the category of homelessness in Seattle. Many had smiling and laughing and happy faces much of the time. Like their rejection of God and prayer, their street happiness puzzled me. Many of them, too, weren't from Seattle. These were traveling, skateboarding, artistic, beer-drinking faces. The street kids I spent time with often refused shelter and other forms of institutional care; they told me that the streets liberated them and helped them feel at home in the world. They spoke of apartments and jobs like prisons and poisons of the soul. They spoke of people who weren't homeless as fools who'd been duped by capitalist overlords. I could sense, talking to them, new chains around my ankles.

the nature of freedom on the streets

Early one summer afternoon, I ask Filth, who is a Latin American street kid I had gotten to know, if he's seen Plato. Plato asked me to help him find a used stroller for his dog's new puppies, so I'd been looking for him. Filth says he hasn't seen Plato. He also says he needs a chaperone. Filth says he got Felony Assault 2 and that he must deal with it in court today or there will be a warrant for his arrest.

I tell Filth I will be his chaperone.

Filth tells me he got Felony Assault 2 because he got in a fight with a Marine. He says he lost the fight but that he got a few good hits in. Filth tells me to look at his hands, his fingers. He smiles, telling me there's a Marine's blood on his hands.

Filth and I walk across the street. We catch the 11 bus from Capitol Hill to downtown. On the ride, Filth looks out the window. 'It's so different now.' He tells me these used to be *his* streets, that he and his friends ran them. If he got in trouble, all he would do is whistle. Then, he said, his "homies" would come running. They would have his back. 'It's so different now,' Filth repeats. 'Now there's nothing but tourists, tower cranes, and yuppies.'

Filth and I get off the bus and walk to the courthouse. Almost there, Filth tells me he can't go in yet. Filth says he has "delusions" when he gets near a courthouse. He needs to feel normal with alcohol first, he says. Filth points to his fingers: 'See,' he says. I see: they are shaking.

He leads me down the block, through bushes. We sit down on a patch of grass, hidden from the public. Filth pulls a bottle of vodka from his backpack and asks me to take a swig. I put my lips on the vodka bottle, though I feel disgust, and shake and swig because it's rude to refuse a street kid's liquor. I pass the vodka back to Filth and grieve the blood on his fingers. He drinks. He drinks and tells me about his daughter, tells me about how he learned to play guitar to help her fall asleep. He drinks and tells me about his mother, tells me about how she would go on a "drug binge" and leave him alone for days.

His hands stop shaking.

Filth tells me his mother had abusive partners, tells me that one of her partners told him to eat disgusting food. He said no, that he would not eat the disgusting food, and then his mother's partner grabbed him by the hair and slammed his face on the kitchen table.

'Out here,' Filth says—like he is answering a question the world forced upon him—'I am free. That's why I am here.' Filth begins to yell. He yells loud, with passion. 'Out here I am fucking free!'

Filth throws the vodka bottle into a bush. We walk to the courthouse. After waiting for more than an hour, Filth sees the judge. I watch Filth stand before the judge from behind a glass wall. He is not shaking. The judge lets him off. I am surprised that there is no clapping, no relief. How banal this ritual is.

Outside the courthouse, Filth thanks me for being his chaperone. He hugs me. Filth wants to celebrate the good news with his friends in the park.

On the train ride, Filth tells me to go on YouTube. He says he is on a video that will help my research.

The video, seen over ten thousand times, begins with an elderly white woman staring into the camera. She has strawberry blond hair and gold jewelry. Her eyes are green. 'I believe there are too many homeless people,' she says. She says she believes our country 'is not doing what it should to prevent that.' The woman says we should stop spending so much money on people in other countries and focus instead on the people who need help in our country.

Filth appears.

"Hey," Filth says, "what's up? Fuck Trump. Travel," he says, "live free, have fun." Filth tells the camera that America is going down the shithole and that people should enjoy life while they can. "Do the best you can before it's all gone," Filth says.

The camera pans to a cardboard sign on the concrete. The sign reads: "homeless and in love, traveling mystics." It advertises tarot readings, spells and charms, and custom jewelry. It asks for "anything" to help with travel.

A street kid named Rider appears on the video, telling the camera that he is a "dislocated, freight train youth." He comes from Chicago. Rider takes a drag off his cigarette and says he feels like the camera is "scanning his soul." He tells the camera that he can't imagine any other way to live. He says he tried having a job once as a telemarketer and that it felt like prostitution to phone old ladies on a fixed income for money. Rider says he only takes what he needs and that he has everything he needs. He says that he has a lovely, beautiful girl traveling with him. He says he is happy. He says he can say with the utmost conviction that he is happy.

The camera pans to his partner. She is beautiful. My name, she says, is Laugh. Laugh has dreadlocks and freckles and piercings on her nose and chin. She, too, is from Chicago. Laugh says she is traveling and selling her art. She suggests to the camera, to everyone who will watch this video about being homeless as fuck: "Stop whatever you are doing and do what I am doing because it is ten times more fun." Laugh smiles wide and adds that it's "worth it" and that that's "all I know to say."

On the streets, the word "freedom" is carved on park benches. It is tattooed on bodies, even faces. One street kid named her car, which she later ditched because of how many tickets she got for outdated plates, and who, a year later, overdosed in a tent on fentanyl, "My Freedom." Hitch, whose story I began this book with, wrote "freedom" in blue above the door of his tent, which he called "my Zen." Before he left each morning, Hitch passed underneath words like they sprinkled him with holy water: "Always be free." Freedom showed up in most of the stories people told me about how they became homeless.

The stories of how people became homeless in Seattle are rejection stories. They are also freedom stories. On the streets, I propose, rejection makes an experience of freedom possible.

We worry for good reason about the great unraveling of our social worlds. Researchers from our world's most credible institutions warn that individualism is a pervasive threat to our way of life. In *Habits of the Heart*, for example, Robert Bellah and his colleagues argue that people in the United States have been seduced by a cancerous discourse of unfettered individualism that is weakening our commitment(s) to the common good. The title of their book stems from the French social philosopher Alexis de Tocqueville's poetic study of life in early America. Tocqueville also worried about individualism. Bellah and his colleagues read Tocqueville as a figure simultaneously inspired and troubled by this social power. Tocqueville fretted that their individualistic "habits of heart" would make them free *from* one another, not free *for* one another.[33] Perhaps they are right. Now we bowl not in leagues but alone.[34] We scroll these days on our phones for each other but away from each other.[35] In a world that has never had more access to others, loneliness is a public health crisis.[36]

freedom on the streets

It is true that street kids seek freedom from other people and social commitments many people take for granted, but it is not true that street kids are unfettered individualists. That is not what is at stake in the desire for freedom that is constitutive of street life. The stories I heard about how street kids became homeless were not stories about the pursuit of unregulated freedom. Everyday life on the streets is mostly not an exercise of immature, youthful rebellion. Street kids in Seattle yearn for a connection to something and someone good as they yearn for freedom. The freedom they sought was a communal freedom, in fact, a freedom made possible by the conditions of street life. On the Greyhound bus they took to Seattle, a street kid named herself Guerrero de la Libertad for herself and others. "Freedom Warrior."

In Seattle, the perceived absence of social judgment renders a particular and compelling space of freedom present. The local culture in Seattle is an invitation to freedom for certain groups. It creates an opening where some people feel they can become themselves. Lucifer said he likes Seattle because of how diverse it is. He said you can be almost anything in Seattle—gay, bi, lesbian, an alcoholic, a heroin addict—as long as you're not hurting other people. 'Fuckin' a,' he said, 'you can even be a Christian in Seattle.'

Lilith was drawn to Seattle because it is considered diverse and open as well. Seattle was for her the opposite of the "cardboard box" she grew up in. Seattle cares by opening a hospitable world for people experiencing the wound of rejection. Lilith is proud to live in Seattle because of how it has been a sanctuary for people in the LGBTQ+ community, she said; she is proud to live in Seattle because of how the grunge scene flipped conservative America upside down. 'The thing about Seattle,' she said, 'is that most people will accept you no matter what.' 'You can be anything you want in Seattle,' a street kid named Samantha told me at a crosswalk. 'Even the dude whose pants are down around his ankles with his ass out. Seattle has always felt like home.'

A *War on People* is a stunning ethnography by anthropologist Jarrett Zigon. It is based on extensive fieldwork Zigon conducted with active and former drug users who are political actors in the anti–drug war movement. A *War on People* is a question about how people become ethical subjects in their everyday lives, build communities of care, and imagine alternative ways of being amid widely diffused biopolitical warfare. A *War on People* is also an intriguing exercise in what Zigon refers to as "an anthropology of potentiality." An anthropology of potentiality investigates and imagines worlds of being ethically and politically otherwise. It attends to what is emerging in a local world. It attempts to dwell in a question about how local worlds struggle to imagine and liberate their potential from a world stuck in irrelevant modes of thinking, injurious social imaginaries, and anachronistic forms of being.[37] It also treats fieldwork as an invitation of hospitality into the concrete particularities of everyday life within a local world and at the thresholds of possibility that become manifest therein.[38] An anthropology of potentiality treats the ethnographer as a potential political actor that can dwell in local thresholds, help bring emerging worlds into being, and provide fresh models of political visions to broader publics.

Zigon found that at the heart of the anti–drug war movement is a commitment to freedom: a freedom, that is, to live in a world in which people can use drugs if they want to.[39] To many, this is a jarring, disruptive, and negative freedom. Initially, Zigon wondered if the freedom that the anti–drug war activists sought was the variety that troubled Tocqueville. He wondered if he saw a careless freedom from external constraints, an irresponsible freedom from civic responsibility, and a violent freedom for social control: like vengeance masquerading as justice. After listening more carefully to what was at stake in the anti–drug war activist's commitment to freedom, however, Zigon found a different freedom. He found a freedom to help others live unburdened by violent imposition, a freedom to be open and become with others, and a freedom nurtured and made real by caring relationships. Zigon found a yearning for a freedom where other people were open and let-be. He found a disclosive freedom, which is a freedom where others can disclose themselves through the openings created in communal places.[40] He saw the anti–drug war activists struggling to become free and build a world where people would be let-be through local practices of "attuned care" rooted in a philosophy of nonjudgment and grounded in the materiality of what Zigon calls *sites of potentiality*.[41] Zigon refers to attuned care as a care that doesn't attempt to change the person to be as they are not, but rather cares for them as they are. It creates space to let someone be. For Zigon, disclosive freedom, which, following Martin Heidegger and Hannah Arendt, he considers a condition of being human itself, emerges when people come together to set an affective mood.

In Zigon's framework, Seattle is a site of potentiality. Many street kids experience the streets of Seattle as a place where they might become more free, open, and let-be. It holds the liberating potential for their becoming. As I said, Zigon demonstrates that sites of potentiality come into being through acts of attuned care. Current and former drug users create space for people to become free, open, and let-be. Attuned care is rendered at sites of potentiality through political events, community meetings, meal preparation, and hugging.

Attuned care on the streets of Seattle also helps people experience freedom, openness, and letting-be. Though it may surprise the unfamiliar observer, the streets of Seattle are a remarkably caring place. Innumerable are the acts of attuned care on the streets. I want to conclude this chapter by describing an act of attuned care on the streets in detail and then reflect on its social significance: religious rejection.

Rejection and protest are underappreciated acts of care, spiritual practice, and moral formation. Understandably, rejection and protest are experienced as challenging acts that thwart the status quo. They may seem immoral. They are sometimes angry and violent. They cause trouble, destabilization, and are hardly ever pretty. People often yell, not whisper. They bang their firsts, not hug. Still, I came to understand rejection and protest as acts of attuned care, spiritual practice, and moral formation on the streets because they help create the conditions where street kids might become free, open, and let-be.

The freedom street kids sought was enacted and experienced through religious rejection. Religious rejection and protest demonstrate another *habitus* that is a means of survival, a political world-building, and a spiritual practice. Religious rejection and protest are spiritual practices because they liberate and tend the human spirit and, as I describe more fully in the next chapter, clear the numinous realm from oppressive, superempirical power. Strikingly, if we slow down long enough, religious rejection can also disclose the innate beauty of the human person.

religious rejection on the streets of seattle

Religious (and, more to the point, Christian) rejection is pervasive on and off the streets of Seattle. There is a "fuck you" for the world in the air, for their perception of the Christian God. During interviews, I'd ask people to describe their spirituality. Descriptions would often be framed in terms that immediately differentiated one's spirituality from Christianity. Native, for example, who grew up in a Catholic foster home, told me that his spirituality 'is not like Christianity at all.' For Native, and most of the street kids I spent time with, Christianity is experienced as an oppressive force and an engine of their social woundedness. It helped birth their suffering and multifaceted homelessness, they claim. Christianity takes life and devalues it; it does not give life and dignify it. 'Christianity is all about damnation and shit,' Native said. 'Like I am going to go to hell for doing drugs and sleeping around. Fuck that,' Native told me. 'I get the importance of being a moral person,' he went on, 'but my spirituality is about valuing life. It's about everything having value, from the bench we're sitting on to the breath we're breathing.'

One of the most glaring examples of Christian rejection came from street kids who identified as "Luciferians." Four street kids I spent time with had "Luciferian" street names and roughly ten considered themselves "Luciferians."

Lucifer was a prevalent figure on the streets. Another street kid I got to know was named Zarathustra. He took his street name from Friedrich Nietzsche's figure who declared the murder of God, the murder he hoped would become more and more true and eventually kill the God of our social imaginaries to further free free spirits.[42]

The figure of Lucifer emerged in everyday interactions. One day I was spending time on the Ave in the University District with Cleopatra. Cleopatra had been stealing items from secondhand clothing stores: wigs, dresses, and jewelry. On this day, she was dressed in a long white dress and a green wig. She had a plastic snake around her neck. She said her outfit made her feel "fucking fierce." As we walked across the street, Cleopatra made a loud and long, deep, and rather strange noise. Once we got to the sidewalk, she told me that a woman had looked at her like a "piece of shit." That, Cleopatra said, is why she gave the woman her "Lucifer growl." Later that afternoon—as I drank gin and tonics with a professor in the faculty lounge at the University of Washington to discuss a public event on homelessness and Christian ministry we were putting on—Cleopatra was arrested for stealing secondhand clothes she had on—after resisting, running away from, and then assaulting the officer who accosted her.

Lucifer emerged in songs street kids listened to, the clothing they wore, the spiritual objects they purchased. For the most part, street kids did not worship a dark supernatural entity, though a few told me they did (some seemed sincere, and others clearly didn't. I didn't take Reaper seriously when, for example, he said he used to sacrifice small animals to Lucifer). Most street kids said that they ascribed to Luciferianism because it is an empowering spirituality. River said Luciferianism is 'all about self-empowerment. Like fuck you,' she said, 'I can take care of myself. Here are the horns of the devil—fuck you.' Star, who grew up with an abrasive and 'very, very conservative Christian mother' considers himself a "non-theistic Luciferian." 'For me,' Star said, 'Luciferianism is about self-empowerment and self-realization. Like when I say "hail Satan,"' he said, 'I am really hailing myself.' Indeed, Luciferianism was not always a conscious rejection of a specific Christian doctrine. For the most part, being a Luciferian had to do with evoking and then embodying a strong feeling. One day, for example, I went into a new age boutique on the Ave with Ghost. Ghost purchased an item with a Luciferian symbol on it. When I sought the meaning behind the symbol, he told me he didn't know. Holding it gently in his palm, he said he is drawn to "the power" behind it. I could feel the power on him and the affective difference holding the symbol made.

The figure of Lucifer appeared regularly on social media. Interestingly, Facebook and Instagram constituted a site of everyday Christian rejection for people who live on the streets. In a post from two street kids who traveled to Seattle, a meme showed a picture of an animal in a car with a satanic symbol on its head. It read: "Get in bitch, we're hailing Satan." Some street kids identify as Satanists or Luciferians on their social media pages. On Facebook, for example, a street kid named December identified as a "Satanic Queer." Many of her Facebook posts poke fun at Christianity. In one post, a Bible is burning up in flames. In another post, she says that "the book of homo, chapter 6 verse 66" says that "thee must be gay." In another, she writes that "prayers to Satan would be much appreciated" for getting into community college. Strawberry's Instagram name, which she uses for sex work, has the numbers 666 in it twice and, in her profile picture, she is dressed as a demon.

survival strategies on the streets

Social suffering pushes and pulls people to the streets. It also pushes and pulls ethnographers there.[43] Many ethnographers who study homelessness focus on the social suffering that people experiencing homelessness experience. The focus on social suffering is evident on the first page of many important ethnographic texts on homelessness. James Spradley, for example, is recognized as one of the first anthropologists to study homelessness in the United States. His ethnographic work took place on the streets of Seattle. His book *You Owe Yourself a Drunk* begins this way: "The American city is convulsed in pain. It is in the streets and alleys, fills the air, crowds into our living rooms."[44] Elliot Liebow is another early ethnographer who studied homelessness. His book *Tell Them Who I Am* begins: "On the street or in a shelter, homelessness is hard living. At first sight, one wonders why more homeless people do not kill themselves."[45]

While ethnographies on homelessness are considerably diverse, anthropologists have been studying homelessness as a site of social suffering for more than one hundred years. In this suffering, ethnographers query how people survive the streets and retain a sense of their humanity. In their comprehensive review of the scholarly literature on homelessness, Irene Glasser and Rae Bridgman suggest that the theme of how people survive the streets has received the most attention in anthropological literature on homelessness.[46]

In *Down on Their Luck*, David A. Snow and Leon Anderson provide an extensive review of how homeless persons in Austin developed strategies to survive the streets. They refer to these strategies as attempts to "salvage the self." At stake in salvaging the self, they write, is a meaningful identity; an existential shelter that can weather the traumatic storms of homelessness. Without a meaningful identity, people will collapse into the destructive conditions of street life and drown in their suffering, they claim. Snow and Anderson observed that homeless individuals often salvage their selves by "distancing" themselves from street life. Distancing might be by space from homeless peers, from the label of "homeless" itself, and from institutions providing care.[47]

Snow and Anderson also found that some street people would embrace identities to salvage their self. They called this "ideological embracement." Snow and Anderson note how a person named Banjo embraced the identity of Christianity, for example. On his banjo case, he painted "Wealth Means Nothing Without God." Banjo was often found preaching about "the power and grace of Jesus" on the streets of Austin and how Christianity helps him transcend his suffering on the streets.[48]

Indeed, many ethnographers of homelessness have found that "the embracement" of religion, and of Christianity in particular, helps people cope with their suffering. Nels Anderson's 1923 book, *The Hobo*, which may be the very first ethnographic study of homelessness in the United States, found that, among the "broken old tramps," who, unlike the youth, had lost hope for revolution and decided to adapt themselves to "things as they are," Christianity helped satiate the aspiration for life in a more complete sense. Christ was indeed living water. In Anderson's mind, the Christian mission had done better than any other organization could perhaps do to transform the inner lives of people on the streets.[49] In *Tell Them Who I Am*, Elliot Liebow found that nearly all the women he spent time with believed in God. In God, he wrote, they found not a fatalism or retreatism, but a profound comfort and source of power that got them through their real, everyday lives. "For homeless women," Liebow wrote, "religion was more than an opiate, more than a cry of the oppressed. For them, there really was A Balm in Gilead."[50]

spiritual but not religious

The United States is a people of historic religious discontent. As Nathan Hatch demonstrates in *The Democratization of American Christianity*, the United States was shaped by "religious outsiders" at war with ecclesial hierarchies, professional theologians, and orthodoxy.[51] Over the past several decades, however, religious discontent has escalated. In 1952, 75 percent of the country said religion was very important to them. In 1970, that number dropped to 70 percent. By the end of the 1970s, it was down to just 52 percent.

In the last decade, there has been a steady increase in the number of people who are more than religiously discontent; they are over it. In 2012, for example, the Pew Research Center found that one in five Americans reported no religious affiliation. Since 2015, that number has hovered around 23 percent.[52] It is highest among adults under thirty—close to 35 percent report that they have no religious affiliation.[53] Yet, though many do not affiliate with religion, they do consider themselves "spiritual." It is here, in the steady, remarkable, and relatively recent decline of religiosity in the United States, that the designation "spiritual but not religious" has emerged in the public discourse.

The sharp decline in religious affiliation and commitment to spirituality has been a lively academic question. Some see the statistical dip in religiosity and begin to praise a version of the secularization thesis. The classic view of the secularization thesis holds that, as the world modernizes, reason will triumph over magical thinking and people will discard religion like an old sweater: good while it lasted, but no longer useful. August Comte imagined sociologists as the priests of society. Freud fancied psychoanalysts as the truly enlightened ministers of the mind. Marx conceptualized religion as the flower on the chain of human suffering ready to be plucked so the material work of revolution could continue. In the disappearance of religion, the secularization thesis proposed, the Enlightenment fantasy would become a reality: humans would be free to realize their potential. As Nietzsche's "mad-man," Zarathustra, proclaimed through the woods, we will have killed God and, in the process, liberated humanity from the heavy, arbitrary, and self-imposed *God-weight*.[54]

Mark Chaves and Christian Smith dispute this notion of religious decline as unreliable, simplistic, and taken on bad faith. There is no invisible current in the cultural waters destined to wash religion away. It is as though God is not dead but asleep; it is up to a culture to wake or keep God in bed. Religion is down in the United States, their idea goes, but it might not be out. The present-future realities of global warming, nuclear annihilation, and divisive cultural conflict render the desire for religious authority more likely, in my view, which may help explain the dangerous rise of Christian nationalism. The authority of religion is therefore an ongoing contest for social power.[55] Zarathustra's prophecy is an astute wish, not a foregone conclusion.

The research of sociologists Michael Hout and Claude Fischer suggests that Chaves and Smith are right. According to their research, religion has fallen from relevance not because of its absence but because of its presence. It is a striking point. In Hout and Fischer's view, we are undergoing what Robert Putnam and David Campbell describe as aftershocks from the cultural earthquake of the 1960s.[56] In short, the 1960s scared conservatives. The hippies and social revolutionaries threatened to take their Jesus. So, they fought back. They created the Religious Right. Powerful figures like Jerry Falwell built the Moral

Majority. That social presence, in turn, created another fear and another response. The presence of conservative religion, which emerged as an aftershock of the 1960s, caused an increasing number of people to reject it. Religion, and Christianity in particular, became naturalized as a socially conservative force in the world. Religion has declined, then, according to Hout and Fischer, because of how it came to be regarded as a conservative presence that profanes liberal ambitions and politics.[57]

The recent decline in religion has been more than fodder for academic debate. It is more than a ripe conversation for the socially awkward lad sitting alone at a bar. It has incited real moral panic. Churches are concerned about the vitality of their presences. People who claim to be "spiritual but not religious" are often derided as individualists undermining the common good. They are like Robert Bellah's "Sheila."[58] They, that is, are perceived as superficial spiritual consumerists; unwittingly undermining the social good, they just want the freedom to feel good in the present and do what they want, come what may—and so they pick and choose practices and ideas from a plethora of spiritual traditions.[59] They buy a few crystals here and say a few chants there and bounce like bunnies from one religion to another.

Some writers and academics have pushed back on what they see as a destructive reduction of a promising historical trajectory.[60] Jeffrey Kripal suggests that "spiritual but not religious" folk are complex: that they are not a monolithic category and that their spiritual beliefs are remarkably diverse. For Kripal, however, people who consider themselves "spiritual but not religious" do have things in common. One is a passionate "moral protest." People who are spiritual but not religious do not lack a social commitment, in Kripal's analysis; their protest against religion *is* a social commitment. "They are horrified and disgusted," Kripal said during a lecture at Harvard, "with the way religious voices in the public have essentially promoted a kind of hatred with their own friends and peers."[61] Elizabeth Drescher's *Choosing Our Religion* is an in-depth look at the spiritual lives of the so-called "Nones." Brilliantly, it investigated the everyday spiritualities of people who are somewhere in the hazy realm of "spiritual but not religious." Drescher sees what Kripal does. She also found a moral protest and outrage, and a similar commitment to an imagined social world. At stake in the "none" or "spiritual but not religious sentiment," Drescher demonstrates, is a passionate distancing from harmful and unaccepting religious cultures. It is a good protest for loving action. At stake is a liberating rejection of a religion that is rejecting people, that is wounding them. Claiming to be a "none," Drescher writes, is a "queering gesture."[62]

rejecting religion (christianity) (and why it really matters)

Overwhelmingly, street kids in Seattle were religiously unaffiliated. Most did not like religion. Many hated it. Religion, they believed, instigated their social woundedness by creating a narrow-minded, judgmental, and wounding world. This world needed to be thrown off so that a freer and more caring one could emerge. Neither, though, did street kids care much for the word "spirituality." If you call them spiritual but not religious, they might reject and protest. Spirituality could be a maybe yuppie way of being human; it was an imperfect word to describe a true feeling. "Another box," a street kid named Heart told me. I asked a street kid named Where about his spirituality. He told me to go find another word. If I asked about *spirituality*, he said, I wouldn't find what I was looking for.

Recently, many scholars have cautioned us not to fall prey to a discourse that makes too much of the distinction between being spiritual and being religious. Really, Nancy Ammerman points out, for example, the categories are mutually constitutive, and few people are spiritual and *not* religious.[63] The modern mind is inebriated by dualism. I do not contend the complex interrelationship between being spiritual and not religious. As Robert Bellah points out in his ambitious work on human evolution, religious rejection is a historically religious disposition. Jesus and the Buddha became homeless in their rejection of religious worlds that caused unnecessary suffering, which their religious rejections promised freedom from through wisdom and spiritual care. These early "renouncers," Bellah argues, marked the beginning of the axial age.[64]

What my research demonstrates is that, on the streets, the rejection of religion really matters and that there is something more at stake than sheer rejection. Akin to Hout and Fischer's findings, the rejection of religion is clearly a rejection of the presence of conservative religion. Street kids are also, and more importantly, I think, distancing themselves from the social woundedness ravaging their lives. They are rejecting what has rejected them to help create a new world. They are trying to become free. The distancing from religion, as Snow and Anderson demonstrate, is also a way of salvaging the self. Engaging in religious distancing, or what I call *protest spirituality*, when you are in soul woundedness, is a matter of life and death. It is a creative way to survive an ultimately unlivable world.

I propose that protest spirituality is a form of attuned care; it helps a person and community become free, open, and let-be. Rooted in a philosophy of nonjudgment, attuned care is a spatial and material clearing of affective forces perceived to impose, violate, and reject. It is an intentional way of learning to accept people as they are rather than judging them by how one might think they should be. This point became especially clear to me one evening I spent on the Ave with Lucifer and Lilith. I told them that, the following morning, I was going to speak at Seattle University to faith-based organizations trying to help people who are homeless. I asked if they had a message they'd like me to pass on; specifically, if there was something that might help faith-based organizations (FBOs) better understand how to care for people like themselves. They became agitated. Lucifer told me to look the Roman Catholics in the eyes and tell them they cannot force people into their beliefs. "I'd rather rule in hell than serve in heaven," he said. Really, Lilith says, dismissively, 'heaven and hell are places that exist right now.' She points to the sidewalk and to her legs. I look slow at a tattoo of a bear, which is one of her "spirit animals." Lilith says that, out of respect, she wants religious people to keep away because they create hell for people here and now.

Religion, and Christianity in particular, is not just rejected in Seattle among the homeless on the streets. As I was finishing this chapter at a popular music bar in Capitol Hill, The Lookout, several conversations circled around religious rejection. It is also woven intimately throughout Seattle's history. In one of the finest and most powerful speeches written in Seattle history, for example, *Chief Seattle* (Si'ahl), the Indigenous leader who tried to broker peace for his people with colonists, rejected the hatefulness of the white Christian's God and warned that his people would remember their betrayal even after they died.[65] In 1871, Seattle's daughter, Kikisoblu, who had been renamed Angeline, or Princess Angeline, by early colonist Doc Maynard, erupted in protest over the violence caused by colonization in a gathering of "church ladies."[66] Gary Atkins's *Gay Seattle: Stories of Exile and Belonging* is a book about how gay activists rejected Christian heterosexism in the construction of spaces of belonging that then shaped the larger city itself.[67] The award-winning documentary *Hype!* shows the spirit of religious rejection in the context of the local music scene. Doug Pray's story about the grunge scene in Seattle during the 1990s is a cultural tale about how this music scene changed Seattle and did so with a spirit of religious rejection.[68]

Hold on. Purple is calling me. 'Just listen,' she says. 'Some crazy bitch just tried to baptize me in the name of the Father, Son, and Holy Spirit in front of QFC [Quality Food Centers]. I started speaking in tongues. I told her I was vexing her in the name of Satan for raping me spiritually. Can you believe that?'

3
The Wound of Human Being

Early on, I felt pity for those in the streets, but their relentless begging has forced me to change *my* habits, *my* attitudes. Panhandlers have taught me to suspect anyone approaching me on the street. 'Can I ask you something, sir?' a casually dressed man asks. Maybe he just wants to know the time. No. He wants access to my pockets. Tired of being hit like a money-access machine, I'm now deaf to people in the street. I'm not happy about that, but there it is.
—STUART BYKOFSKY, "NO HEART FOR THE HOMELESS,"
NEWSWEEK, DECEMBER 1, 1986

Please stop feeding the ave rats.
They are multiplying. Tonight they had tents pitched on the street so that people had to walk in the road to get around them. These people don't think they should have to work because they are "free thinkers" who will not succumb to "The Man" yet they rely on strangers to support them. They are rude, they catcall, they get angry and shout obscenities at people who don't give them what they want, in my experience usually cigarettes. Please stop giving them money. If they want to live life free of society's oppression they can go live in the woods. Let me here [sic] your thoughts on this topic Seattle. Thank you.
—ANONYMOUS SEATTLE RESIDENT'S POST ON REDDIT, CA. 2014

Anderson Cooper appears to be speaking with a St. Luke's client who's not destroying things or attacking anyone. I guess it would be too hard to get one of their tweakers who routinely terrorizes the neighborhood

to sit still and say rational things. Safe Seattle note: As we've said, the media are an essential part of the Homeless Industrial Complex. A corollary to that general principle is that the further away a media corporate office is located from the story its reporters are covering, the less accurate the reporting is likely to be, and we see that borne out

here, with a New York-based program ("60 Minutes") covering a homeless story on the opposite end of the country, in Seattle. 60 Minutes is practically guaranteed to get this story all wrong, as just *The New York Times* did with the LEAD story two weeks ago.
—FACEBOOK POST FOR ANTI–STREET HOMELESSNESS ACTIVIST GROUP SAFE SEATTLE, SEPTEMBER 13, 2019

The light is red. I am with a large flock of humans standing at the edge of the sidewalk on Broadway and E. Pike, looking. Green will move us forward. Everyone is going someplace. The streets of Capitol Hill are lined with promises of pleasure: a cup of coffee, a slogan for your woes, a delicious meal, a concert, a new shirt.

We walk on different shades of red, yellow, white, and purple. The evening is charged. The bodies next to me are an affective force. So am I. Music is coming from Neumos, a popular concert venue. The beats thud on my chest. With and without knowing it, we are penetrated by the forces in our environment. To be human is to be porous.

In 2015, Seattle mayor Ed Murray allocated nearly $70,000 to transform eleven crosswalks into pavement rainbows before Pride Week. The locations were chosen based on where heavy foot traffic occurs and where recent hate crimes had taken place. *The Seattle Times* published an article about the transformation. One woman, taking a selfie on a pavement rainbow, said: "You can't spread hate—spread love instead. With all the hate crimes going on, it sends the message that we're open." Someone else said the rainbows "reaffirm that we have a place in this neighborhood."[1]

I get to the end of the rainbow. Like most nights, "Homeless Freddie" is playing guitar. He strums his guitar, dances, and struts up and down the streets. His playing, he once told me, is a calling. Freddie said he plays to make money but also to serve people who are homeless. Occasionally, Freddie chastises the homeless individuals who hang around his pavement stage. "I am Freddie," he yells. "You must respect me. Behave, Damnit." When this happens, Freddie sometimes has violent conversations with his wife (who died a decade ago).

One afternoon Guerrero de la Libertad and I were walking on the streets, talking about God. We watched Freddie play. He seems to us a minister of sound for the streets, with the streets. He was standing in front of a picture of Freddie Mercury, the beloved frontman of Queen, which he had taped on a street sign above his small amplifier. Freddie touches Freddie with his palm, affectionately, says something neither of us can hear, and then turns toward the sidewalk to strum down his stage.

Today, Freddie is stumbling. He seems drunk. I fear a car might hit him. Looking at Freddie strum and stumble, Guerrero points and says, emphatically: "That's God. That's God in the city; it is God unfolding and becoming."

Freddie and I greet one another with a handshake and a smile. I stare at his brown fingers. Usually Freddie says: "I love you, man. I love you so much" and then asks for a cigarette. Tonight, however, he is too absorbed in the music. Street kids sit beside him with their backs against the wall. They are nodding their heads. They are passing beer and laughing.

In *The Cultural Politics of Emotion*, Sarah Ahmed explores how emotions move in the world through social encounters that shape the "surface of individual and collective bodies." Ahmed is interested in how emotions work to construct the way we think and relate.[2] She proposes that, as emotions move in the world, they stick to people and that their sticking gets people stuck: in thoughts, in politics, and in the complex, often unconscious ways we experience the world. Emotion, for Ahmed, is a weighty power that forces itself on the present. The weighty stuckness of emotion creates a dwelling, a relational state that people experience their being in.[3] The stuckness, moreover, is attractive; it is itself sticky. Being stuck may mean finding oneself as the source of a group's emotion. Ahmed's book questions how emotions stick and, in the process, create a world that gets people stuck in forms of attachment that discriminate against disempowered populations.[4] She also raises the question of how emotions can help people get unstuck and move them toward justice. "Justice involves feelings," Ahmed writes, "which move us across the surfaces of the world, creating ripples in the intimate contours of our lives."[5]

The laughter on the streets sticks. It hits me like a powerful, disruptive force.

I walk another block. I see Plato. He is walking his dog, Kali, who is named after the Hindu goddess of creative destruction. Her growl reminds me that I am like a guest on the streets: the streets are for me a place of loving and terrifying curiosity, not my home. Native once told me: 'Our paths crossed on the streets, but we did not share a path to the streets.'

Plato says he wants to introduce me to someone who recently moved back to "the Hill." We walk across a rainbow and reach the Comet Tavern. Heart is sitting beside the dumpster. "The Comet," as locals call it, is a historic Capitol Hill bar known for music, alcohol, and good energy. At the entrance is a sign. It depicts a fist in the air with a slogan: "No sexism, racism, ableism, homophobia, transphobia, or general hatefulness allowed. You will be asked to leave." Seattle, in many respects, is an affect against destruction for social justice. As

I demonstrated in the previous chapter, it is often experienced as a force of empowerment. Like the pavement rainbows, Seattle wishes to be a collective force to help people get unstuck—though, like most cities in the United States, it clashes with classist affects.

'This is Paul,' Plato says to Heart. 'He's the guy I was telling you about.' Heart looks at me and smiles. Heart moves his backpack to create space for me in his world and tells me to sit down. He was living in a tent in south Seattle last week, he says. He says he started to get stir crazy in the tent and felt "The Universe" calling him back. He said that the intersection we are sitting in, between Neumos and Comet Tavern, is a literal vortex. 'Somehow,' he says, 'the energy always pulls me back and traps me here.' 'Ain't that the truth,' Plato says.

Heart reaches into his bag. He pulls out a large sketch pad. As I flip through his art, conscious that we are both touching something tender and beautiful, on the page and inside us, I am drawn to an image that depicts people in a leaf-like prison. Heart calls it "trapped souls." Plato notices an obscure light on the image, which is removed from the souls who are trapped in the leafy prison. He says this is like what he was telling me a few nights ago when we shared a chicken quesadilla at a Mexican restaurant: how far God seems from the world sometimes, if there is a God.

fucked, stuck, trapped

Street kids often told me that they feel "fucked," "stuck," and "trapped" on the streets. The real experiential freedom on the streets is always, it seems to me, eclipsed by the cruel reality of street life. The laughter stops. It is overcome by a sorrow that makes one question whether and how life is worth living. Near the end of my fieldwork, I told a street kid named Burrito Bitch that I've heard a lot of people talk about feeling free on the streets and that I am thinking about what that really means.[6] We were sitting under a bridge. He found a used needle in the rocks. After struggling for several minutes to find a vein, Burrito Bitch injected the heroin in his hand, now bleeding, and put the question of freedom on the streets like this: 'The freedom you find on the streets is real, but it is a freedom that will eventually kill you.'

It killed Heart as I wrote this book. He died of an overdose, in the dawn, after finding housing for a few months, a few blocks from the vortex.

I met Burrito Bitch when he was spanging in front of QFC. His cardboard sign read: "Free Karma." Burrito Bitch didn't think that people who give him money would produce a spiritual ripple through time. To Burrito Bitch, at that time, spirituality was 'nonsense and bullshit.' Still, spirituality facilitated his spange. Spirituality rendered material goods that helped him stay alive and get well.

The sun was out and resting on his bare shoulders, on his chest. Stutter, with whom he traveled from Portland, joked that the sun isn't kind to him. He pointed to the red on his nose and around his freckles. "You're a ginger," Burrito Bitch said. "Yeah," Stutter said, laughing, "but I have a soul."

They laughed.

Burrito Bitch had been hopping freight trains. He rode trains from Texas to Los Angeles to San Francisco. My doubts about his romantic tale of homeless adventures evaporated when he showed me pictures of his travels on his Facebook page a year after we met. Proudly, he showed me an article written about him in a local Denver newspaper, which suggested that people like Burrito Bitch were drawn to Denver because of the progressive marijuana laws. Burrito Bitch had just been in Portland, which is his favorite city, he said, but had to leave because he got an arrest warrant. He came to Seattle because the people seem nice, the social services are good, and because he thought he might be able to get his ID before hitting the road again. More than two years after I met him, however, Burrito Bitch was still living on the streets of Seattle. He tried to reconnect with family and get into rehab, but the attempted reformations didn't stick.

He got stuck.

When I ask, Burrito Bitch doesn't gloss over what led him to the road. His mom died. His grandfather became terminally ill. He got fired from his job. He couldn't make enough money at the temp agency he started working at to pay child support. Burrito Bitch got into trouble with the law, and then he got banished from his aunt's house. His "home world," as I discuss in the previous chapter, became overwhelmed by the wound of rejection. His experience of the present collapsed into a paralyzing sense of impossibility. Some degree of freedom—from the weight of rejection, from a place where he might experience the care of being let be—emerged as a possibility. He heard it on a freight train headed out of town.

One day over lunch Burrito Bitch told me that his grandfather tried to push Christianity on him after his mother died. "It didn't stick," he said. He said that he imagines God is "out there" and that He is powerful and loving but that he can't believe that right now. He said it doesn't line up with the woundedness penetrating his soul. My question seemed to evoke and then change his theology. "I'm fucked," he says. "I'm fucked," he says. "I'm fucked."

Burrito Bitch tells me he is tangled in chains that even God can't get him out of.

As I demonstrated in the previous chapter, Lucifer and Lilith were some of freedom's champions on the streets of Seattle. For themselves and others, they helped make freedom a real experience by engaging various forms of attuned care so that people could be together and still let be. In the cold winter of 2018, the charismatic street family that had enticed Lilith turned on her. She and Lucifer became objects of derision. They were outcasts among outcasts. The police became stricter as businesses lost business. Lilith developed several grave wounds on her back. Though we encouraged her to seek professional medical care, Lilith refused until the pain became unbearable. She did not want to be seen as a weak person, receive care from an abusive structure, or give up the promise of self-sufficiency. 'I have been trained as a caretaker,' she often said, 'so I can take care of myself.' A few evenings before she and Lucifer took a Greyhound bus back to Michigan, she asked if I remembered her telling me that, for her, homelessness is a choice. 'Well,' she said, 'now it is not a choice. Now I need help and to get the fuck out of here.'

They were lucky. Most of the street kids I spent time with did not have a home away from the streets they could go back to. I think of Rosie. Rosie came to Seattle seven years ago. 'It was,' she jokes, 'just supposed to be a three months' vacation.' Rosie met a man in a chat room. After she lost her job, Rosie's chat room romantic encouraged her to come stay with him in Seattle. It sounded like fun—like a new beginning. And better than living with her father. As it turned out, however, her lover was living with five of his family members in a small motel room in a rough part of town. After a few nights, Rosie couldn't stand to be inside. She hated the noise, the smell, and the lack of space. Rosie started hanging out on the streets of downtown Seattle. In time, she befriended street kids. They liked each other, had fun, and could get by with the social services available for young adults. 'With the street kids,' she said, 'I felt safe and free and accepted.' She said they had her back, that they protected her, and that they became like family.

At first, she said, living on the streets was like a party. She said she had a genuinely good time and that she'd never take that time back. But then she hit age twenty-five and was no longer able to use the many services available to young adults experiencing homelessness. She became pregnant with another street kid's baby. 'Good luck after you're twenty-five and pregnant,' Rosie said, 'then you're really fucked. Then you must go to adult shelters and it's a totally different world.'

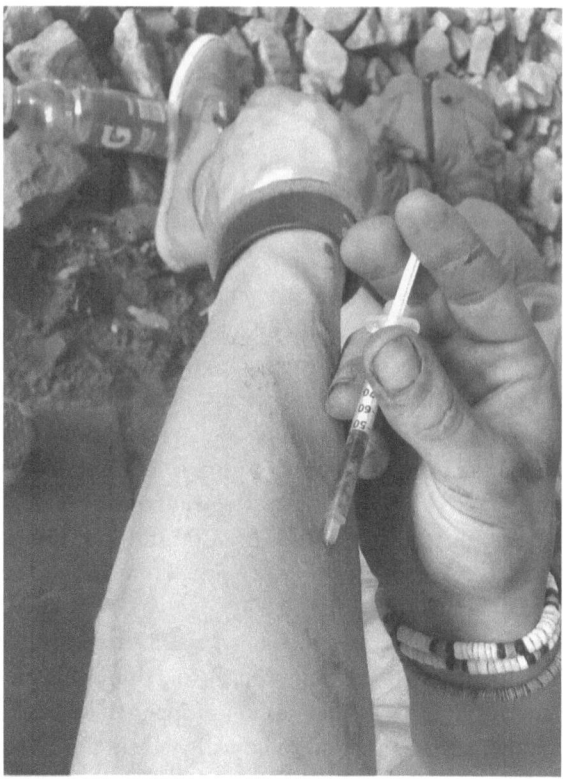

ordinary affects

In 2007, Kathleen Stewart published *Ordinary Affects*. It is an attempt to understand the living, pulsating, erupting presences in the world. Stewart laments that our conceptions of the world tend to impose a view that obstructs attention from what is alive with affect and irreducible to thought. "The notion of a totalized system, of which everything is always already somehow a part," Stewart writes, "is not helpful (to say the least) in the effort to approach a weighted and reeling present."[7] While not ignoring "named systems," *Ordinary Affects* is a question about how to pay attention to the systems we always inadequately speak about with a view to affective forces, as they happen, rather than leaving them "looking like dead effects imposed on an innocent world."[8] The point of *Ordinary Affects* is to slow down the observant pace of the ordinary. It aims to notice the forces that impact the world before giving them a name.

In 2011, Lauren Berlant published *Cruel Optimism*. Berlant is also interested in how the world is imbued with forces that affect how people live. Berlant is searching for a way to describe how the world impacts people and helps constitute their relationship to it through the raw force of ordinary affects. For Berlant, the present moment is first lived affectively.[9] We feel the world before we think it. In *Cruel Optimism*, the present world is made of crisis and precarity. Human subjects, they write, are "overwhelmed, forced to change, and yet also stuck."[10] Another affect theorist, Brian Massumi, refers to the configuration of the affective present Berlant describes as an "immanence of catastrophe."[11]

Cruel Optimism is a question about how we perish when we live in an ordinary that is imbued with affective forces that constantly threaten our survival.[12] Precarity is an overwhelming and multidimensional force within the present. In the erupting presence of precarity, Berlant thinks, people struggle to hold on to life. Everyday life is lived in search of optimistic attachments that help a person hold on to life but end up being cruel because they may also undermine flourishing.

Ahmed, Stewart, and Berlant are working within what scholars have called "the affective turn." The affective turn can be traced to the seventeenth-century philosopher Baruch Spinoza, who was read and rejuvenated through Gilles Deleuze. For Spinoza, the human person is a creature that is affected and affecting. The human, in contrast to the prevailing view of his time promulgated by Descartes, is not a body separate from the mind. Working from Spinoza, Deleuze put the interconnection between mind and body this way: "What is an action in the mind is necessarily an action in the body as well, and what is a passion in the body is necessarily a passion in the mind. There is no primacy of one series over the other."[13]

For Spinoza, human and nonhuman forces surround the subject and help constitute one's *potentia* (power to act). The question about how to build an ethical world, which is Spinoza's underlying interest, is how to increase the power of collective joy over and against collective sadness. For Spinoza, joy increases one's power to act. Sadness, on the other extreme, diminishes it. Spinoza is working with a relational ontology that collapses the notion that we are isolated individuals and disembodied minds. People act when the affects around them, which come from both the human and the nonhuman world, are related and imbue people with a positive force to act.[14]

Affect theorists taught me how to become attentive to immanent forces on the streets. In other words, they offered me a way to question how people were being affected in everyday life on the streets and how that helped constitute their relationship to the world and power to act. I found Ben Anderson's concept of "affective atmospheres" especially helpful. For Anderson, ordinary life is imbued with a complex network of forces that are experienced as *weight* and *heaviness*. These affects help constitute an atmosphere that fosters or diminishes human action. Anderson cites a speech by Karl Marx to illustrate the point. In the speech, Marx described the weight of capitalism as a 20,000-pound force that oppresses working people even though they did not name that force "capitalism" or "economic injustice."[15] Affect theory, Donovan Schaefer writes, is a theory of power.[16]

Ethnographically, I began to think of this mode of research as an *ordinary attention to the affective atmosphere of the streets*. In sum, ordinary attention to affective atmospheres pays attention to "moments of force": it queries what people are being affected by and, to use the concept I cited from Sarah Ahmed earlier, "stuck" in. I wanted to know what forces people on the streets believed stuck to them and, as a result, increased or inhibited their power to act and become unstuck from the streets. I wanted to know what made people joyful and sad and what affects were banal. On the one hand, this concern is fundamentally ethnographic. Ethnography is a question about how the people being studied live and experience their world, and I wanted to know what is sticking to people on the streets and how they are trying to become unstuck.

the affective atmosphere on the streets

The reasons that people are stuck in homelessness may seem overwhelmingly clear. Affordable housing is difficult to find. Income levels are inadequate to support everyday life. An illness can render one homeless—or homeless again. Most people living in the United States do not have the funds to cover a $1,000.00 emergency and fret about how to pay to stay alive if they were to lose their job.[17] People who are homeless may need permanent supportive services if they become housed, which cities may be unable to afford and facilitate skillfully. Even if one is securely and humanizingly housed, living inside can engender an isolation that exacerbates mental health challenges. It is easy to become homeless, street kids would often tell me, but it is tremendously difficult to find a humane, stable, and affordable dwelling place.

This chapter illuminates another force that contributes to a person's stuckness on the streets: everyday affects. I focus on the stickiest affects that street kids talked about: the socially wounding force that was spoken about with more frequency than affordable housing, drugs, and mental health. I call this affective force *the look of worthlessness* from *the wound of human being*.

the look of worthlessness

It is raining on the Ave. It is a dark, November afternoon. I am outside Starbucks, chatting with a few street kids. Clear walks up to us and says he needs a smoke. He says 'some dick' just stole the tip jar from the coffee shop down the street—then ran straight toward Clear and handed it to him. 'I am paranoid as fuck,' Clear says. He thinks everyone is looking at him; he is frozen and shaking.

Hitch and Shaman cross the street. They walk up to us. Shaman asks me how my birthday went. 'Real nice,' I say. I ask if they've seen Native, whom I'd been looking for. 'Jail,' Hitch responds curtly. Hitch says someone saw him in the back of a police car by Jack in the Box. I go on Facebook and read Native's last two posts to learn what might have happened. The first one reads: "FUCKING HURTN." The last one reads: "YOU WISH THE WORLD WAS CLEAN BUT I AM IN LOVE WITH HOW IT IS DIRTY."

Hitch and I walk to Safeway to spange. When we get to Safeway, Hitch realizes there is ranch dressing all over his brown jacket. He is mad. He likes this jacket. A friend gave it to him. It keeps him warm. 'I am going to find the person who did this to me,' Hitch says, almost yelling, 'and I am going to punch them in the *fucking* face.' I wonder if Hitch thinks he might have fallen into the dressing himself. Now, he says, people will think he is a 'cracked out homeless person' as opposed to a 'decent homeless person' like he is. Now, he says, people will not give him money. 'Might as well just go back to my tent,' Hitch says.

Hitch tosses his blue bandana into a puddle of rainwater. I am struck by the gentleness of the toss. He pushes the bandana into the puddle, drowning and soaking it. Hitch picks the bandana up and uses it to wipe the dressing off. He repeats the ritual multiple times. 'Nothing,' he says, grieving and tender, 'will keep me warm like this jacket.' I notice that the rainwater is getting some of the ranch dressing off but spreading it to other parts of his jacket.

'Fuck,' he says. 'More than anything,' Hitch says, 'I hate the smell.'

I tell Hitch that I have a gift card to a secondhand clothing store down the street. 'If you want to get another jacket,' I say, 'we can get you one. Then I can take this one home and wash it.' Hitch is unwilling to go to the store, initially, but I convince him otherwise.

The secondhand clothing store is popular among young adults in Seattle. Unlike a more traditional thrift store, like Goodwill, this place is chic. Hitch and I find the rack with jackets. I suggest that he try on a jacket. He looks at me with disgust. His lips quiver. Hitch turns away from the workers at the registers and whispers aggressively: 'Look at me,' he says. 'I have dirty clothes on. They'll get upset. They don't want some street kid trying their clothes on. Come on, Paul. Fuck, man!' I didn't notice their gaze, but it was clear, through the emotion surfacing on his skin, that Hitch thought their eyes were stuck on him.

A week later, Hitch got "run off" the Ave. He got in a fight with Reaper. He said Reaper kicked his face while he was asleep for "talking shit." Reaper claims that Hitch tried to steal his new shoes while he was asleep. Sleep, a precious human need that influences one's power to act in the world, is difficult to experience when you are homeless. It is a hardly met need.[18] Reaper and his friend Mad beat Hitch up. They told him that if he comes back to the Ave, they will kill him.

Several months passed before I saw Hitch again: at a Starbucks in another neighborhood. I was writing fieldnotes and looking out the window with a view of the streets when Hitch came in for hot water and free internet. He sat down and told me that he is going to Portland. He is excited, he said, to have another adventure and shake Seattle off. Maybe, he said, he will meet a girl. He tells me about how he once met a girl on an adventure and how they stopped at a beach along the Oregon Coast and made love all night in her car. We drink the black tea he made from the mason jars in his bag, which is genuinely the best-tasting tea I've ever had, and Hitch tells me about more adventures. He is happy when he thinks about becoming free and unstuck from the streets of Seattle.

The following week, I got a text from Hitch. 'I want to die,' it read. 'I am for real,' it continued.

He calls me. 'Hello?' He tells me that his brother promised to get him a bus ticket to Virginia but that he didn't come through. 'Fuck him, anyway,' Hitch says.

Hitch tells me how angry he is that people look at him like a piece of shit. He says he cannot take it anymore, cannot take another yuppie looking at him like that. He goes to bed looking like a piece of shit, he says, and then he wakes up looking like a piece of shit. People won't even let him sleep in front of an abandoned building. 'Like trash,' he says, 'everyone wants to sweep me away.' Hitch calls this look—the way he sees the public seeing him—the look of worthlessness. He says that sometimes he wants to buy a gun and mow down everyone who looks at him with the look of worthlessness.

When I asked street kids about the hardest thing about being homeless, that was the most common answer I got: how people look at you like you're not human anymore; how the "shitty" way people see you penetrates your body and is shot into you like heroin. The look of the human world often imbues street kids with dehumanizing, disempowering affects. It helped create an emotion that stuck and inhibited their power to get unstuck from the streets. It undermines their power to act.

In interviews, I would ask people what the streets smelt and sounded like. If you could liken your experience on the streets to a smell or a sound, I'd ask, what would it be? "Piss" was a common answer. Everyday life, street kids often said, smelt like piss. 'Like piss and dumpster juice,' December once told me. Tiger Hoods told me that his experience of the streets smells like a porta-potty. 'Go on,' I said. 'What do you mean?' 'Urine,' he said. 'Just urine. That simple. It's one place you don't want to stay for too long. If you stay there for too long,' he said, 'then every other sense will attract and stay on people. If you can't get the smell off you, then people are going to learn to judge you by what you smell like.'

Tiger Hoods says he is trying to get the smell of urine off him. 'I am working on bleaching everything I have,' he says.

On a walk through the streets of Capitol Hill, Heart told me that he doesn't understand why people who are homeless aren't given the basic respect of a smile and a decent look in the eyes. Heart is saying 'hello' and 'I love you' to strangers as we walk up the Hill. He is crying. 'It fuckin' hurts,' he says. 'It makes me want to cry, it kills me, it makes me want to rage.' Heart says he has 'this love inside him, that he has a love grenade, this thermal love detonator.' He wants to 'set it off and blow everyone's mind so they will wake up and stop living like capitalistic robots.'

Samantha feels the look of worthlessness most strongly when she steps into a coffee shop. 'It feels like everyone immediately looks at me like a piece of shit junkie who isn't even a person,' she said. 'Like they think I am going to shoot up in the bathroom and take up a table. Like fuck,' she says, 'I am just trying to have a coffee and a bagel and look at my phone like everyone else.'

The look of worthlessness is not just a looking at you that becomes a look looking within you; it is also a looking away. 'What hurts more than anything,' Lucifer told me, 'is when people stop looking at you because they feel sorry for you or think you're shit. You can feel it,' Lucifer said, 'when someone is trying *not* to look at you.' Lucifer said that, sometimes, the human species makes him want to hitchhike to the woods and never see a person again. 'Just quit the human race,' he said. I ask him what he thinks people should know about their eyes and their thinking and their looking. I say a new knowing might create a good change. Lucifer isn't optimistic. 'I think it's basically impossible,' he says, 'unless you live through it. It's fucked up, dude,' he says, 'but it's true. There are some things people won't let themselves see.'

I met Zarathustra in a doorway. He said I could sit down if I 'didn't fuck with him.' He said it's his birthday today and that he hates 99 percent of humanity. He said he is about ready to give up on all humans. On the streets, strikingly, I came to realize, human persons are often experienced as affects of destruction that engender an experience of worthlessness. They become a wound. The look of worthlessness becomes a social wound of human being, in other words: coming from everywhere and nowhere all the time. Street kids live under the weight of disempowering, sticky looks in their affective atmosphere. On the streets, Sartre's dictum from No Exit is a powerful force in the affective present: "Hell is other people."[19]

the committee to end homelessness in king county

In March 2005, the Committee to End Homelessness in King County was formed.[20] It was part of a national campaign for local governments designed by the National Alliance to End Homelessness and the United States Interagency Council on Homelessness.[21] Along with the City of Seattle, the committee made a bold promise: within ten years, they would virtually eliminate homelessness from King County. The committee found it unconscionable that, in a county as rich as King County, more than eight thousand people would be homeless on a given night.

The committee did remarkable work. It brought together an array of organizations: the Metropolitan King County Council, 85 percent of the cities in the county, and dozens of social organizations. One of their platforms, the Funders Group, was recognized by Harvard's Kennedy School of Government as one of the Top 25 Innovations in Government. In addition to creating a diverse platform for organizations to work together to end homelessness, the committee helped over 5,000 people avoid homelessness through emergency services. It made King County/Seattle the third-highest provider of housing for the homeless in the United States. By 2011, it helped over 40,000 people transition out of homelessness and helped create more than 5,000 new affordable housing units. It also increased public awareness of homelessness and fed the political will to eliminate it.

Tragically, by March 2015, despite millions of dollars spent, homelessness had risen dramatically. The annual count, which is notorious for being a conservative measure of homelessness, revealed that homelessness had gone up by about 20 percent. Ten thousand people were now homeless in King County, with more than 4,500 of those sleeping on the streets. The increase gave Seattle one of the highest rates of homelessness in the United States. In the media and public discourse, the committee's effort to end homelessness was dubbed a failure and an embarrassment.[22]

As to the reasons for failure, the committee itself cited a lack of interorganizational collaboration, insufficient data about what's effective in getting people housed, rising inequality, and a lackluster commitment from state and national governments. Resilient in the struggle, the Committee to End Homelessness in King County rebranded itself "All Home."

A few months later, as the public outcry continued to grow, Mayor Ed Murray declared a state of emergency on homelessness. Seattle followed Portland, San Francisco, Los Angeles, New York City, and the state of Hawaii. The declaration freed millions of dollars in Seattle's budget to respond to the crisis. It gave the mayor "emergency powers." If necessary, Murray said, for example, he would bypass strict permitting rules to open habitable living spaces for unhoused people. The state of emergency also petitioned state and federal governments to provide more funding, as they would to a natural disaster. Murray said that over forty-five people died on the streets of Seattle the year before and that more than three thousand children in Seattle's public schools were homeless. He emphasized that while the city could do more, it could only do so much. He decried the amount of money Seattle had received from the federal government, which had declined steeply since the 1980s. Barack Obama, a proponent of using the federal government to respond to homelessness, was president of the United States. A year later, however, in January 2017, Donald Trump would become president and take a radically different approach.

At the end of Mayor Murray's speech, a reporter asked a pointed question. He asked if Murray was worried that the increase in services and spending on homelessness would attract more people who are homeless to Seattle. Murray said the last thing he wanted was for the city to ignore the needs of the homeless in Seattle. "To simply say we're not going to fund people starving on the streets . . . I just can't go there."[23]

Murray was known as a curious Catholic. His response to homelessness was motivated by his faith. In 2017, *the Seattle Weekly* published a story entitled "Why Ed Murray Can't Quit the Catholic Church." What's curious to people in Seattle is that Murray is a gay man in a staunchly secular city who made Catholicism central to his public identity. Catholicism and politics don't usually go well together in Seattle. Radical mayors in entrepreneurial cities like Seattle make big business nervous. In an interview, Murray said that he sometimes wonders whether he should give up government, become like Francis of Assisi, and live with people who are homeless.[24]

A few months after he declared a state of emergency, Murray gave another speech about homelessness. He called it "Homelessness Address to the City." Murray spoke from Mary's Place, a homeless shelter for women and children to which Amazon donated millions of dollars. Murray spoke about the local problems associated with homelessness and a new vision to help bring affordable housing to every neighborhood. Again, Murray emphasized that people are dying on the streets in record numbers and how many homeless children there are in Seattle schools. Death and child suffering evoke affects of compassion that can be politically mobilized. He also drove another point home: homelessness is not just a Seattle problem. Murray said ending homelessness will require national change and more federal funding. He concluded the speech by citing Dorothy Day and her frequent reference to Dostoevsky in *The Brothers Karamazov*: "Love in action is a dreadful thing compared to love in dreams."[25]

Seattle's love for the homeless is not quite real or not quite good enough, Murray seemed to suggest. It is not getting people unstuck and housed. During his speech, two people were shot in a homeless encampment notoriously referred to as "the Jungle." The incident made *the New York Times*. Murray rushed to the Jungle and wondered aloud about whether he could have done more.[26]

Murray's promising political career came to a heartbreaking end when he was accused of sexually abusing a former street kid in his apartment in Capitol Hill during the 1980s. Murray denied the allegations but, ultimately, was forced out of office. Public disgust stuck to him; there was little affect for a judicial pause or public forgiveness to help rehabilitate a person in power, unfortunately. Murray was replaced by a more business-friendly Democrat in Jenny Durkan, who continued, by public and private demand, to make homelessness central to city governance. In 2022, after Durkan declined to run for a second term, Seattle elected Bruce Harrell as its fifty-seventh mayor. Harrell, whose capacity to be mayor was questioned because of his support of Ed Murray, campaigned with a tougher stance against street homelessness, for which some say he was elected.[27]

seattle is dying

Through the COVID-19 pandemic, during which the number of tent encampments in public view grew significantly, Seattle's collective response to homelessness wearied. New affects of discontent had been generated. Compassion fatigue pulsed through the city. The best evidence for the increased discontent is in a popular and controversial film aired by KOMO News, *Seattle Is Dying*.[28] For some, *Seattle Is Dying* watched like a wakeup call. For others, it felt like big business propaganda and cruel authoritarianism. To be sure, the film fanned a flame into a raging fire.[29]

Eric Johnson, the producer of *Seattle Is Dying*, wondered if the title was too dramatic. In the end, he decided otherwise. "Seattle," Johnson said, "is rotting from within."[30] *Seattle Is Dying* claims that Seattle is being destroyed by homelessness. The film portrays homelessness as a "sickness" contaminating business, safety, and public well-being. It documents the sickness by showing images of people experiencing homelessness on the streets using drugs and experiencing mental health crises. The film argues that homelessness cannot be solved until the city allows police officers to inflict harsher punishment. It proposes that a reasonable solution to homelessness is banishing people who are homeless to a rehabilitative prison on an island.[31] In the film, homelessness is reduced to street homelessness. No structural issues—such as lack of affordable housing, inadequate income levels, and insufficient health care—are cited as problems contributing to homelessness. One is left with the distinct impression that people on the streets are crazy addicts living in filth who need to be deported and rehabilitated by the criminal justice system for Seattle to be healed.

Seattle Is Dying scared other cities. Not long after *Seattle Is Dying* came out, a film called *Curing Spokane* hit Spokane's virtual airways.[32] It shares the script of *Seattle Is Dying*. Unflinchingly, it argues that homeless persons carry a social disease that is destroying business, beauty, and well-being. The film suggests that one should be afraid and intolerant. It is an affective argument against so-called liberal compassion. The future vitality of Spokane, and the well-being of its citizens, it claims, are at stake. *Curing Spokane* proposes that the remedy for the disease of homelessness, which it also reduces to street homelessness alone, is refusal and criminalization.

Both *Seattle Is Dying* and *Curing Spokane* shared the Trump administration's script on homelessness. In September 2019, the president's Council of Economic Advisers published a document titled "The State of Homelessness in America." The document begins by blaming failed liberal policies for the problem of homelessness. More specifically, it cites overregulation of the housing market, tolerant cities making street homelessness more acceptable, the number of available homeless shelters, and specific characteristics of homeless individuals such as substance abuse and mental health problems as the reason for the problem of homelessness.[33] The previous July, as he officially kicked off his reelection campaign with the slogan "Keep America Great," Donald Trump did an interview on Fox News with Tucker Carlson. In the interview, Trump referred to homelessness as a "disgrace" that is "ruining our cities." He said that police officers are getting sick just walking on the streets near people who are homeless and that people who are homeless probably like living in their "filth" because they have "mental problems." Trump blamed "the liberal establishment" for the "terrible thing that is taking place." Trump also said that, when he first got elected, there was a problem with street homelessness in Washington, D.C. He said it hurt the reputation of the United States for world leaders to visit the president of the United States and look at people who are homeless. Trump took care of "the situation," he said, and "ended it very quickly" by removing people who are homeless from the streets. He did not say what happened to the people he removed from the nation's capital and, seemingly, Carlson did not ask. Trump said the government might need to intercede in liberal cities and "take the [homeless] people and do something." He said the government probably shouldn't be doing that kind of thing, really, but that the problem of homelessness is unprecedented. He said liberal cities need to realize that they are "destroying our way of life."[34] Two months later, Fox News ran a series of videos and articles decrying the liberal approach to homelessness. In one video, the conservative provocateur Dan Bongino referred to liberalism as "a cancer, a forest fire" and said it "destroys everything it touches."[35] On Christmas Day, just a few months after "The State of Homelessness in America" was released, Donald Trump threatened California's governor, Gavin Newsom, on Twitter. Trump tweeted that if Newsom did not fix the problem of homelessness the liberal policies in California created, the federal government would step in and take control.[36] He told Newsom, who is notorious for a debonair persona, to lay off the hair gel and get to work. Though Joe Biden's election and subsequent efforts to address homelessness differed sharply from Trump's—admonishing those who blame people who are homeless for their situation and making the government responsible for a hoped-for end to homelessness—the affective atmosphere Trump cultivated around homelessness as president remains an affective political force.[37]

The affective degradation and criminalization of homelessness is also central to Trump's 2024 reelection effort, which is underway as I write. On Truth Social, for example, which Trump founded in 2021 after being banned from Twitter and Facebook, he characterizes people experiencing homelessness as violently deranged insurrectionists who've stolen cities across the United States, making them "unlivable, unsanitary nightmares." Trump claims that it will save taxpayer money and be helpful to outlaw urban camping punitively—and "relocate" people who are homeless to inexpensive parcels of land. For Trump, the absence of people who are visibly homeless will make cities livable and beautiful for people who work. In this Trumpian vision, which, terrifyingly, he says he will do everything possible to make real, Trump frames "the underlying issues" of homelessness not in terms of social inequities like unaffordable housing and inadequate health care but as personal disabilities like addiction and mental health.[38] This book makes precisely the reverse case: the lack of affordable housing and the inadequate health care system are violent social wounds that cause homelessness, overwhelm human capacity, and result in mental health and addiction crises.

In *Shelter Blues*, the anthropologist Robert Desjarlais refers to media-driven representations of homelessness as promulgated by *Seattle Is Dying, Curing Spokane*, and Donald Trump/Fox News as "the potent imagery of homelessness."[39] The potent imagery of homelessness transforms people who are homeless into siphons of the beauty and morality of public order. They are cast, Desjarlais writes, as "negative figures" that "offend a spectator's sensory faculties."[40] The kind of media presence rendered justifies a houseless person's dehumanization and forceful removal from public space. It charges the look of worthlessness with affective power. As *Seattle Is Dying* illustrates, there is a vibrant and well-funded public campaign in Seattle dedicated to shepherding a feeling public into a story that people who are homeless are criminal addicts who should be punished and shipped away if they do not clean up their trash and sober up. It is an affective discourse that aims to shape how people who are homeless appear and how they are felt, consciously and unconsciously. The campaign wants the public to experience homeless persons as ugly diseases to the social order that can be cured through rejection: for people who are homeless to be experienced as a force getting Seattle stuck in crime, instability, and decay—away from the promises of beauty and prosperity. As I have shown, it is also a national discourse that the Trump administration championed through Fox News. The campaign against homelessness is only the latest iteration of a historic struggle over how to define homelessness in the public experience to motivate a coherent response. While religion has historically been a defining presence in the struggle over how to define and respond to the "deserving and undeserving poor," its power to influence the debate has weakened. Today, with notable exceptions in figures like Ed Murray and William Barber II, the affective struggle is being fought on mostly secular ground.[41]

everyday life on the streets:
finding connections in a holding environment

Street life is monotonous. Usually, when street kids wake up in the morning, they are forced out of public view. Upon waking up, street kids likely struggle to find relief from a serious addiction. The most common addictive substances on the street were "black" (heroin), "clear" (meth), "blues" (crushed fentanyl), and alcohol. By contrast, weed and cigarettes seem common and innocuous as oxygen. If one is fortunate, there will be enough of whatever substance one is addicted to left over from the night prior. If not, one must begin searching for a way to "get well." On the streets, most people consider their addiction a medical problem that they treat with the substance they are addicted to. Hence the reason people call using a substance "getting well" as opposed to "getting high." After a while, Samantha told me, no one is really getting high—you just try to avoid the excruciating symptoms of withdrawal so that you can make it through another day. Since local cliques among street kids are often formed in relation to the substance one is addicted to, the pursuit of "getting well" is rarely done alone. Drugs create, maintain, and break relationships. Most street kids also struggle desperately for sobriety and feel like failures when they are unsuccessful and inadequately supported, which is another affective weight that they feel fucked by and stuck in.

Cell phones are vital on the streets. Hardly is there a more important commodity. Cell phones allow a street kid to go on social media, listen to music, and cultivate human connection. Cell phones occupy a street kid's time and provide a remedy against the material and existential threat of boredom.[42] A critical part of street life consists of "plugging in" once the day begins so that one's electronic device maintains a charge. Plugging in is usually done at coffee shops, libraries, and public outlets in parks. Since cell phones are often lost and stolen, it is common for street kids to be in a perpetual struggle to maintain or keep one. The COVID-19 pandemic, which caused coffee shops and restaurants to close or limit dine-in services, seriously undermined the possibility that street kids could plug in to their virtual worlds.

"Hanging out" is another integral component of daily life on the streets. Street life is about finding a place to pass the time with other creatures, human and nonhuman. Good presences keep the internalized terror generated by the look of worthlessness at bay. Popular hangouts include street corners, parks, coffee shops, libraries, and day centers. More than merely providing a place to pass the time, hangout spaces engender care. Since most street kids come from hurting nuclear families, the relationships they form with one another may be considered closer than biological family. Some scholars refer to this social phenomenon as "fictive kinship," but most street kids would find the term "fictive" disrespectful since they experience street bonds as more real and true than their biological ones.

Most street kids told me that they felt more connected to the human world when they became homeless. I found it surprising that their homelessness could provide a cure for the social isolation wounding them. As I have shown, street kids often found home and family for the first time when they became homeless. If a street kid gets off the streets, it is common for them to come back to experience the connections formed on the streets. That was the case with May. May came to the Ave almost every day after she found an apartment because the streets, she told me, are where her friends are. Becoming housed may be frightening precisely because one might lose the familiar community formed on the streets, which one must inevitably seek again to continue building a life worth living.

Relational separation is an obstacle to housing people who are homeless. A woman named Daisey told me that she lost her mind when she got housing because of how isolated she began to feel from the community she had formed. Loneliness made the terrifying voices in her head louder and crueler, she said. Still, the relationships formed on the streets are not as healthy and stable as an optimist might be inclined to imagine. Relationships are deeply fragile on the streets. They can be life-threatening. When I asked street kids who they could most trust on the streets, almost without exception I heard: "No one but myself." Street kids were more likely to trust animals and electronic devices than humans. The human world is enveloped by deep distrust and abiding suspicion. Human relationships are necessary for survival, but they are also profoundly risky. It is an underappreciated courage to stay alive on the streets and merely relate.

No street kid I spent time with wanted to be on the streets permanently. As I described, it's easy to become homeless but tremendously difficult to get off the streets. It's not for lack of desire. Most street kids want a life off the streets doing meaningful work in a stable dwelling. For some, however, getting off the streets appears to be an impossible task. It is hard enough to get through another day. If a street kid is actively trying to get off the streets, they may have several appointments to juggle. Daily, one may need to go to drug treatment, medical appointments, and meetings with social workers. Most street kids found this juggling arduous, confusing, and unsustainable. A street kid named Soil told me he is never busier than when he is homeless.

The road out of homelessness is also often unclear. Finding sustainable and experientially livable housing is often like a mirage in the desert: promising and inspiring, maybe, but perhaps not real and worth taking seriously. For this reason, the pursuit of life in a permanent dwelling is often experienced as a threatening but necessary hope for a life worth living. It may become a survival strategy to refuse this kind of hope. A street kid must be careful when thinking about the future. Thinking of the future might produce an affective experience that generates a sense that life off the streets is not actually possible and that being on the streets is permanent. I found that a street kid's worst fear is often of becoming a kind of homeless person who is unfashionable and almost completely destitute. This line of thinking can be like a train to a hell where there are no other people. Despite their wishes and best intentions, most street kids

I spent time with feared that they were "stuck" on the streets and doomed to live under the cruel affective weight of the look of worthlessness, not to mention the real threat of being murdered or dying of an overdose.

Street kids in Seattle are suspicious of institutions. In my experience, they were likely to think that institutions claiming to care are vultures waiting to feast upon and profit from their suffering. While most street kids do not think the world is completely empty of good people, they feel that the culture they live in is imbued with people in institutions that are exploitive, ineffective, and uncaring. The bigger the organization, the worse it probably is. When push comes to shove, however, and despite an impressive commitment to self-sufficiency, street kids take advantage of the institutional resources they need to survive. If a street kid is deathly ill, for example, they may go to the hospital. After they are released, however, they will probably protest that they received inadequate care because of their homeless status (and sometimes, though not always, they will be right). It is for this reason that hospitals and medical professionals can be experienced as wounding presences that must be avoided.

Donald Winnicott was a psychoanalyst recognized for his work with infants and their mothers. In *The Child, the Family, and the Outside World*, Winnicott demonstrated that how a mother holds her infant is arguably the most significant feature of a child's development. Motherly holding is essential for a child to establish a positive relationship to the world. Adequate holding meant being attentive to the child. It also meant demonstrating affection. The holding is about more than physical touch and a gravitational hold. Essential is a real experience of warm tenderness and affection. If warm tenderness and affection do not stick to a child, Winnicott argued, the child is likely to experience mental and emotional challenges later in life. How a child enters and begins to dwell in their home world is therefore contingent upon how they are held.

Knowing that a mother could not hold her child perfectly, Winnicott coined the term "the good enough mother." The "good enough mother" describes a mother who holds her child in a way that is good enough.[43] Good enough means meeting the child's basic needs for affective experience and, ultimately, individuation. Winnicott recognized that a child needs other kinds of holdings as well. He argued that a child needs to be held by a good enough environment.[44] In other words, a child needs more than the mother's holding for healthy development to occur. We are radically dependent creatures, Winnicott believed, upheld by various forces in our environment. A child needs ecological holding. The world one lives in is a holding environment. It performs a series of actions on a person that hold them in place. People hold on in a world, but they are also held by a world. The holding in one's world is an assemblage of affective forces that really matter.

I propose that the streets of Seattle function as a unique holding environment. Despite the social woundedness that constitutes everyday life, and the overwhelming *weight* from the look of worthlessness that street kids experience, a complex assemblage of human and nonhuman forces holds a person in place and makes life possible. In *Sidewalk*, Mitchell Duneier speaks of a similar force operative on Sixth Avenue in New York City. He refers to it as a "sustaining habitat."[45] Everyday life on the streets is a question of making connections within a holding environment or sustaining habitat. It is a question about plugging in to get an affective charge that will empower one to live through another "fucked" day. These connections are both necessary and fraught. As Berlant would suggest, they may be cruel: they help one achieve what is necessary to keep living but may also pose a threat to that fragile living.[46]

The rest of this chapter will illuminate an integral but overlooked dimension of the holding environment on the streets of Seattle. I show the way many street kids struggle to experience what I call *good affects* in a spiritual universe. The struggle helps street kids come to believe that life is not overcome by human destruction, the look of worthlessness, and a paralyzing sense of stuckness. It also helps street kids come to know that there is a benevolent spiritual force in the universe that is holding their life in place, even if, as the next chapter describes, this force is impersonal. Here, I will demonstrate that this affective spiritual pulse in the universe is sought through three common and interrelated spiritual street practices: manifestation, dumpster diving, and spanging.

spirituality as rendering affective goodness and changing the charge of the universe

Isis doesn't live by clocks. "You'll just have to find me." She and her boyfriend, Osiris, had been traveling. I was surprised to see new street kids in town. Many street kids leave town in the winter for a warmer climate. Nor did I expect to spend so much time with Isis and Osiris. I thought they were just passing through.

Isis is wearing pink cat ears. Osiris has blue cat ears on. He is also wearing a yellow tail with black spots. It falls along his pants and down to his white shoes. He is tall. Isis says that they've come to Seattle to "house up" for a while. Osiris's brother is deathly ill, she says, and they are going to take care of him. Osiris nods as he colors his shoes with a blue sharpie. 'I couldn't let him die alone,' he says.

They go by the names of the Egyptian gods Isis and Osiris because together, they say, they symbolize death and rebirth. They tell me that their bond demonstrates that life can emerge from death. 'Our story is a tragedy turned positive,' Isis says.

I ask about their cat outfits. Isis says they represent their "spirithood." A cat pissed on them both around the same time, she says. They took it as a sign from The Universe that they were meant to be together. Plus, Isis likes cat energy. She says they have 'the power to relax and stay the fuck out of shit and literally be chill as fuck when shit's going down.'

I marvel at how she smiles and laughs. She tells me that life is what you make it. It reminds me of something Reaper once told me: 'The streets can be the best experience in your life if you make it that way. Or the worst. It's up to you.' Isis says that what's different about her is that she 'doesn't pay to live in a prison or a box.' I ask if a house or an apartment is a box. 'Fuck yeah,' she says. 'Living inside kills my creativity.'

The last time she was living inside, she says, she would ponder suicide on the back porch every night. 'Actually, though,' she says, 'it's suicide to be indoors.' Isis says that when she lives inside she doesn't see her 'homies coming up to me every ten minutes and asking for a cig or a hit or whatever. That kills me,' she says.

I look down at her fingers. "Immortal" is tattooed on them. 'It's for protection,' she tells me. 'People will know if they try something on me,' Isis says. 'They will look at my fingers and read it and won't even do it.'

She just got another tattoo. Isis pulls her blue jeans up and shows me her ankle. It's a semicolon. It represents suicide and a collective wish to keep living, she says. 'He has one, too' Isis says. Osiris rolls up his sleeve and shows me the semicolon on his arm.

I ask Osiris if he feels the same way about living inside. 'Kind of,' he says. He says he doesn't want to be inside and get forced to do things. Osiris says that's the upside of being on the streets. 'You have freedom. On the streets,' Osiris says, 'I have choices and can be creative. I can play music, draw, and write.' Like many street kids, Iris and Osiris are planning to start a band.

Osiris ran away from home when he was fourteen. Being on the streets, he says, was fun for a time. When he wanted to get off the streets, however, he felt stuck. He had no ID, no GED, no work experience, and no secure address. He was strung out and he couldn't get a job or afford a place to live.

Osiris looks at Isis. 'This time it will be different,' he says. He is trying to persuade Isis that it will be okay to live inside. 'We will get a place of our own,' he says. 'It will be different.' 'Free,' she says.

'I know it can be really hard to be homeless,' I say. 'How do you keep going?' Osiris says the only way to survive the streets is 'to have fun and to walk around and entertain yourself.' Isis says it helps to spange. Today she is spanging for a new hat. The point of spanging is material, but it is more than that. I came to see that the point is also to render a spiritual connection that changes the affective atmosphere of the streets and fosters a connection to The Universe.

Osiris says he is a pagan. He tells me that after a while, being in the city is bad for your energy. He says he must 'get out of here and away from people to really be spiritual.' He'd also have to go into the forest and get more mushrooms. Osiris reaches into his backpack and pulls out a large bag of mushrooms. 'It's okay,' he says. 'I am basically a shaman.'

'Yeah,' Isis says. Now she is coloring on her shoes. 'People can be hella bad for your energy. You gotta get out, meditate, eat a mushroom, and listen to music. Get chill as fuck.'

Isis is wearing a cross around her neck. I ask if she is a Christian. She says she believes in Christianity—and everything. Osiris interjects. 'Jesus was a prophet but not the son of God,' he says. 'That's evident from the Old Testament.'

I ask if they pray. Osiris says he calls on 'the powers of the earth, not the powers of the gods.' The question, and the word "prayer," it seems, struck a nerve. It imbued him with the force of religious rejection. 'I am a shaman,' he says, 'not a fucking Christian.' He needed to make that clear to me and the affective world around him, which is holding him.

Isis says she calls upon wiccan gods. 'What for?' I ask. 'Protection, strength, healing, and manifestation. A lot of manifestation.' I am intrigued by the word "manifestation" because it's come up a lot.

'What do you manifest?' I ask. 'Music, creation, and inspiration,' she says. 'When?' I ask. 'All the time,' she says. 'And especially while spanging.'

'Tell me more about manifestation,' I say. 'It's energy,' she says. 'It's directing and spiritualizing.' Osiris agrees. 'It's push and pull,' he says. 'If you push toward something it will push back. There's this thing called the tenfold law in The Universe,' he says. 'That's what pagans call it. With wiccans, it's three. Anyway,' he says, 'that's not the point. The point is that what you do will come back to you—tenfold.'

'Like karma?' 'Yeah, like karma.'

I ask if there's karma on the streets. 'There's karma on everything,' Isis says. 'Street karma, drug karma. Karma,' she says, 'is that when you lose weed, you get ten times more in the morning. Lose a baggie,' she says, 'find a baggie.'

Manifestation is not an exact street science. It does not come from one sacred text everyone is reading, studying, and debating—other than one's own experience in the world. People spoke about manifestation in different ways and with varying degrees of sophistication.

Shaman demurs when I ask him to write a short book about street manifestation. 'Really,' he says, 'there are as many ways to manifest as there are people.' We are sitting on the steps of the Vineyard Church on the Ave. He is trying to manifest a bus ticket to Eugene. The Ave is starting to wear on him, he says—'the cold, the drama, and the bullshit'—and, plus, he has a spiritual connection there. 'There are some rules, though,' Shaman says. He says that it is usually better to manifest in groups. 'There is more power and force in numbers,' he says. Shaman also says you can't think too much about what you want to manifest, or if it's working. Obsessive thinking, he says, gets in the way. 'It's better to trust that The Universe will provide,' he says. 'And say thank you when it comes.'

Like many street kids, December and Burrito Bitch practice manifestation in dumpsters. 'One trick,' December told me, 'is to not be selfish about it.' She is more likely to manifest something if she isn't trying to manifest for herself alone, she said. 'You never know,' she says. 'A homie might need something I come upon.' Burrito Bitch and I once dumpster dove in the garage of a grocery store in Capitol Hill. We tried to manifest a large bucket that he could play like a drum. 'When I am playing music,' Burrito Bitch told me, 'I almost feel human again. Like I am almost not homeless or something.' We didn't find a bucket that day. There, as Burrito Bitch says, was no "dumpster score." Still, the practice of manifestation helped him think he'd have a way to get well and feel human again later. The courage of faith in drug karma is particularly critical when one is experiencing the excruciating pain of withdrawal. 'There are better dumpsters up the hill,' he says. 'I usually have better luck up there.'

Clear considers himself "residentially impaired," not "homeless." For Clear, "homeless" is a word that will get the weight of the look of worthlessness stuck on him. One's identity is an affective force, too. Clear has been residentially awkward since his mother died when he was thirteen. 'Fuck it, then,' he said. He rode freight trains around the country before ending up in Seattle. Clear considered going back, he says, but then he reflected on all he had done wrong and there just didn't seem to be a point. 'I felt stuck,' he says.

Clear considers himself a very spiritual person but says that he is not religious. He says religion is about fearful allegiance to a deity. It's about mind control and cruel obedience, he says. Being spiritual, on the other hand, he says, means being aware of the otherworldly influences that surround you. Clear thinks that you cannot understand things like spirituality, really, but that you can acknowledge, appreciate, and broaden your perspective. 'Interestingly,' he says, 'I used to be skeptical about spiritual things, but being on the streets changed all that. There's just too many things going on behind the scenes,' he says. 'The fact that you can't prove them,' he says, 'doesn't make them unreal.'

I ask him what kind of things go on behind the scenes. 'Energies and vibrations of The Universe,' he says. 'Spirituality,' Clear says, 'is about aligning with the energies of The Universe. It is about harassing them,' he continues, 'and manipulating them to realize what you desire, the wish you put into The Universe.' One way to do that, Clear tells me, is through manifestation. He gives me an example. Once, in front of 7-Eleven, Clear was terribly hungry. He hadn't eaten for a day. Clear said to himself, 'I am hungry.' He then said aloud to his friend: 'I am going to manifest a cheeseburger.' Moments later, Clear says, someone gave him a cheeseburger. It's times like that, Clear says, that he feels connected to a world behind the scenes and knows he can manipulate the powers of The Universe and change his current circumstance. Clear refers to the Ave, where he spends most of his time, as his "karmic circle."

Manifestation is practiced in virtual space as well. Samantha practices it regularly on her blog. Online, Samantha describes herself as "another junkie living with the lows of highs in a city I can't escape and a heroin addiction that feels likewise." Samantha told me that her blog is an attempt to put "good energy" in The Universe. She posts things she considers beautiful: women, waterfalls, and comfortable beds in chic apartments. She posts information about how to take care of people in the drug culture: how everyone should carry naloxone, for example, which is a medicine that quickly reverses the effects of an opioid overdose, and how much better it would be if Seattle had a safe site where people like her could use heroin without fear and harassment. Occasionally, like when she struggles to make enough money to get well, Samantha will post a "money dog." A money dog is a way to manifest money. 'It's ridiculous,' Samantha told me, 'but sometimes it actually works.'

The last post I read on Samantha's blog was about how she spent all last night and this morning looking for a vein to shoot heroin in, how her hands and pants are covered in blood, how all her bones feel like they are going to break, how the nearest bathroom is a mile away, how she fears that she is going to shit herself, how she's afraid that she won't see her future, that she'll be another sad and meaningless junkie statistic, how she asks her higher power to get her out of this mess, find a home again, and be able to look in the mirror and not see her eyes and face sunken in.

I tried manifestation for the first time in front of Walgreens. I was with Cleopatra. I told her I was going to manifest ice cream. She laughed. Searching for the meaning behind the tickling always seemed to stop the laughter. Cleopatra and I sat still and silent for ten minutes. We didn't ask for anything or think too hard—we trusted The Universe. People moved past us like ripples in a steady river. Some ten minutes later, someone gave me a cup of cold Boba tea from an ice cream shop, a block away.

'Close enough,' Cleopatra said, chuckling. 'The Universe does not always give you *exactly* what you want.'

Lilith manifested smiles. Before I met her, I'd often walk by Lilith and Lucifer. I heard her saying things to people walking by like 'Have a nice day,' 'You are beautiful,' 'Enjoy the sunshine,' and 'Smile, it's a gorgeous day.' When Housies, people who are securely housed, gave her money or stuff, she'd thank them, enthusiastically. I thought Lilith's kindness was a shrewd way to trick yuppies into giving her money. But Lilith wasn't fooling. After Lilith left the Ave and had been recovering with her parents in Michigan, she wrote me a letter. Part of the letter was about the difference the practice of manifestation made in her life on the streets. She wrote that, when she lived on the streets, she trusted The Universe to give her all the love she needed with "the entirety of her being.' She had real faith in a power greater than herself that really mattered and made a difference in her everyday life. The Universe, she wrote, did not let her down. It often became manifest in a "nice smile" generated by her "love infection." "Even though I was poor," Lilith wrote, "the nature in humankind came forward to me and I did my best to pass it on. It was enlightening," she concluded the letter, "to trust so deeply in the nature of our existence and be caught by the love web of that delicate structure."

On the other side of town, in Capitol Hill, Rainbow manifests smiles as well. Sitting on a street corner, usually near The Comet that Heart referred to as "the vortex" that The Universe called him back to but also got him stuck in, and where he died, Rainbow asks Housies who pass by if she can "have a smile." At first, she says, Housies usually think she asked for a smoke. When she corrects them, she says, they often smile. 'And then,' she says, 'like a chain reaction, smiles start going off.' She begins counting them, she says: '1, 2, 3!' 'It's so beautiful,' Rainbow says. Rainbow told me that, on the streets, she collects smiles and then holds them in her soul so that she can gather and feel them when she wakes up in the morning and begins to feel crushed by the weight of her woundedness.

Rainbow and I did our first interview in downtown Seattle. We drank coffee at Barnes & Noble. Before we left, Rainbow took me to a book with a poem in it that, she said, expresses her spirituality beautifully. It is called "Ballad of the Water of the Sea" by Federico Garcia Lorca. I notice that the poem is about how the sea offers itself to a troubled youth as a smile. When we rushed out the door, she spilt her coffee on the floor. Rainbow pointed to the ground. 'Look,' she said. 'Don't you see it?' The spill, she said, formed a smile on the tile.

In 2023, under a bridge a few miles from Barnes & Noble, Rainbow overdosed and died.

faith in the goodness of the universe

Freud begins *Civilization and Its Discontents* with a quandary. In response to a previous book, *The Future of Illusion*, which argued that religious belief arises from an infantile longing for a protective father against the cold hand of fate, a friend penned a grievance. The grievance unsettled Freud. Freud's friend agreed with his assessment that religious belief is an illusion but thought Freud failed to account for the true source of religious sentiments. The true source of religious sentiments, Freud's friend suggested, is in a peculiar feeling that humans throughout time and space share, and which religious organizations have seized, named, and routinized. The feeling, Freud's friend said, in Freud's retelling, is a subjective experience of a connection to a limitless, eternal, and unbounded energy. The real root of religion, they claimed, is "oceanic feeling."[47] Freud could not locate oceanic feeling in himself, and he could not agree with how it was being interpreted (or that it is in fact the *fons et origo* of religion). At the same time, however, Freud could not disagree that a profound experience of oneness with the world does occur in other people.[48]

Freud's friend is among many to suggest that oceanic feeling is the deep, abiding source of religious sentiment. Friedrich Schleiermacher famously referred to religion as a "feeling of absolute dependence."[49] Rudolf Otto suggested that religion is derived from what he called encounters with "the numinous," which are felt experiences of mysterious terror and awe that are wholly other, and which transcend the mind's rational capacity.[50]

Social scientists have long demonstrated the differences that spiritual emotion and affect make in the world. Emile Durkheim showed that the emotional power generated in religious ritual is the glue of the social fabric.[51] He also worried what would happen if sacred symbols, which hold and transmit religious affects, went away. Max Weber proposed that the emotional dread over eternal punishment shaped the early colonies, helped build the economic engine of modern capitalism, and fashions the iron cage we bang our heads against.[52]

The world pulses with affect. Different worlds have different pulses and different affects that constitute an affective atmosphere. Unavoidably, we live in multiple unique and peculiar affective atmospheres. As Spinoza had it, affects impact our power to act. There is no one affective atmosphere; there is no one emotion that sticks. On the streets of Seattle, however, the pulse of the world is imbued with relentless dehumanization. Like a drug, this pulsing affect breaks violently through the surface of the soul and wounds people with what Hitch refers to as the "look of worthlessness."

The dehumanizing look from the housed population toward the unhoused is a force that fills the affective atmosphere that street kids experience. The affect shapes what street kids experience as most real in and outside of themselves. It becomes an affective *weight* that can be traced from the streets to local and national media—and to the former president of the United States, Donald Trump. The look of worthlessness is not the only emotional force that constitutes a street kid's affective atmosphere but, according to street kids themselves, it is one of the most powerful. That affect gets people further stuck on the street and in experiences of homelessness. I call this affect *the wound of the human being* because the human itself can represent destruction. For many street kids, tragically, the mere sight of a human being can conjure affects of disempowerment that threaten survival and weaken their power to act.

In their stuckness, street kids struggle to make connections to something good that can keep life in place. Those connections are found in other street kids, in electrical outlets that power personal devices, in institutional services, in animal companions and the nonhuman world, and in drugs. Critically, however, street kids also seek connections from diverse spiritual realities they often name "The Universe." Most street kids reject religion because it is perceived to be violent and disempowering and because religious distancing is a cure for their intimate wound of multifarious rejection. While religion is rejected by most of the street kids I spent time with, a spiritual connection to The Universe is not. Most street kids in Seattle believe that the world is alive with benevolent spiritual forces laboring for one's good. Connecting to The Universe is an integral and often overlooked dimension of the holding environment on the streets. The connection helps street kids find a *good affect*, change the pulse of their affective atmosphere, and come to believe that there is a Force of Good in The Universe that is not overcome by human destruction, the look of worthlessness, and the wound of the human being. This connection helps street kids continue to believe that life is worth living, tend their soul wounds, and live in an almost unlivable world.

Connecting to The Universe takes faith: that life is not reducible to the social woundedness one is experiencing and that there is Something Good. On the streets, faith is affirmed when material items are found in the dumpster, when random goods are manifested, and even when someone smiles. Without these good affects, life would (and does) lose a sacred affective center, causing one to collapse into the violent forces that constitute social woundedness. Connecting to The Universe also takes courage. It is risky to trust that there is a transcendent force living and to believe that the world hasn't suffocated

Something Good. Spiritual practices like dumpster diving, spanging, and manifestation keep a cruel weight of cosmic loneliness away.

Faith in The Universe is also a vulnerability. This vulnerability became clear to me one day in front of a local grocer in Capitol Hill. Nearly a year after I met her, Isis came up to me while I was speaking with Train. By this time, her boyfriend, Osiris, had taken a Greyhound to another city with another girl. She was desperately holding on to their relationship and the possibility that he'd come back. He was stuck on her.

'Hey homie,' she said, 'is there any chance you could go into the store and buy me some soup? I am dope sick as fuck and need nutrition.'

Train rolled his eyes. He detests it when people who are homeless ask for money like that, without a spange. 'What a leach,' Train whispered, distancing her from himself. I hurt for Isis as I watch her pretend not to be wounded by Train's violent whisper. The look of worthlessness comes from the housed and the unhoused.

'Still,' I say, 'she needs help.'

I went into the store, smelt different soups, and purchased the one that smelt the best to me: chicken tortilla. I came out and handed Isis the soup, happy that I might make her happy. Isis opened the lid, looked at the soup, and threw it down. It splattered on the sidewalk. Isis broke down and cried and yelled: "Fuck you, Universe!" She fell to her knees and began to cry. Isis told me to never get her something that she doesn't like. She left cursing herself, and The Universe. 'Fuck my life, I am a piece of shit. Fuck my life, I am a piece of shit. Fuck you, Universe! Why do you always do this to me?'

4
The Wound of God

"where can we find ourselves?"

An evangelist is passing out Christian tracts on the corner of Third and Pike. He is staring blankly at a mostly uninterested, hurried world. A few feet from him a homeless woman is looking up at the sky and smiling, trying to balance her body on one leg.

I took a tract before crossing the street to watch the evangelist and the homeless woman from a concrete stump outside Starbucks. A young street kid sits beside me. She is wearing brown UGGs and purple pajama pants. She asks me for a dollar. 'That's how much a cookie costs at McDonald's,' she says. 'What the hell,' I think. I search for the quarters at the bottom of my backpack. I find them. She thanks me and takes the quarters from my palm. A yellow cab almost hits her when she crosses the street. 'Slow the fuck down,' she yells.

I look at the evangelist's tract. The front reads: "Eternal Life is a Free Gift." Underneath the words there is a white gift box topped with a red ribbon. Tied to the ribbon is a name tag; it is blank, white, and awaiting a name. In one short sentence, the tract describes how to save your soul: "If you receive Jesus Christ into your heart, by trusting Him to save your soul, you will become a son of God and spend eternity in Heaven." The tract also spells out the consequences of refusing the gift: "The wages of sin are death. Failure to repent will result in an eternity in hell."

Down the street, Prophet is yelling: 'God is a puppet of the white man. Fuck God,' she yells. 'Christians talk about Jesus, but they don't do shit. God and Jesus enslaved my people.'

Sidekick listens. She tells me that Prophet is mad at God. Prophet, she says, is unaware that the Jews were enslaved before Black people. Sidekick is Jewish and unsure what God is up to. She believes in God but hasn't heard much since she ended up on the streets. Sidekick left her house in eastern Washington when her husband refused to believe the CIA wiretapped their basement. She packed up her things and took a Greyhound to Seattle. 'He called me crazy,' she said. 'That's betrayal.'

I ask Sidekick if she knows God's will for her life. She shakes her head, says no. 'Sometimes it's better to put the question on hold,' she says. 'I know to be grateful,' she tells me. 'I wake up and I smile at people.'

The workday is over. There is hardly an inch between people on the sidewalk. Tall buildings and tower cranes crowd the sky and tell a story, I think, about what has come to really matter to Seattle. Brash horns and unapologetic sirens fill the soundscape. Construction workers walk home with their hard hats in hand, in yellow and orange uniforms. Tonight the wind is strong. I watch a man in a pressed shirt put a jacket on.

Apocalypse walks past me. His dog, Golden Boy, is beside him. 'Apocalypse,' I say. Incidentally, Apocalypse is the reason I came to downtown. I had been looking for him. The last time I saw Apocalypse, he had found several love letters in a dumpster behind an apartment complex. I read them aloud late one night in front of a coffee shop. The letters were written by a man in a prison cell. They were about his vision for a new beginning and a good life. 'I am a new man now,' he wrote. 'With Allah's help I will take care of you and our child. Please understand that I am a changed man.'

Apocalypse looks distraught. He didn't have the letters. He says he has been looking for a woman. She has black hair, he says, and a dog. She has tattoos on her neck. 'Right here,' he says, pointing to his own neck. 'And here.'

Apocalypse asks me if I've seen her. 'I haven't,' I say. He looks at me, I think, like I might be hiding her.

I offer Apocalypse a cigarette. On the streets, nicotine is a glue that binds people together. Smoking laces the present with a force that keeps people connected. It also keeps the haunting presence of annihilation at bay.

Apocalypse pulls a lighter from his pocket. He lights the cigarette. He looks around and sighs. 'At this time of day,' Apocalypse says, 'I just want to disappear. Come on,' he says. 'Let's go.'

We walk up Third Avenue, squeezing through the crowd. 'Let's find a quiet place,' he says. 'Where do you think we should go?'

I suggest Native Park. The downtown park overlooking Puget Sound may not be a quiet place, I think, but it will at least have a view of a quiet place.

On our walk to Native Park, we approach Christ Our Hope Catholic Church. I ask Apocalypse if he's been inside. 'No,' he says. 'But do you want to go in?' 'Yeah,' I say, 'it's a quiet place.'

In addition to being the quiet place Apocalypse is looking for, I imagine that going inside the church might conjure what Harold Garfinkel described as a "breaching experiment." Garfinkel thought that unrecognized features of everyday life are illuminated when the steady flow of routine is disrupted. In street culture, going into a church or a religious institution is likely to violate a common norm that, I thought, might produce a helpful understanding of the streets and how spirituality matters here.[1]

The church sits below a housing unit for 240 people who were formerly homeless. The building goes up seven flights. A receptionist for the housing facility sits behind a large desk at the entrance. I enter the church, but Apocalypse and Golden Boy stay in the lobby.

Inside the church, I light a candle underneath a painting of Mary, the mother of Jesus. I sit down and say a prayer. 'Help me, Mother, to understand to love.' The pews in this church are made of wood but they do not creak when you sit on them. There is no one else inside the church, but it is not empty. With muted force, the cacophony of downtown sound fills the space. I prayerfully gaze at a statue of Jesus on the cross and feel overcome by the sound of a jackhammer digging into the blacktop.

I wonder where Apocalypse is. I walk to the fountain in the middle of the church. I read the biblical passage from the book of Isaiah written along the rim: "When you pass through the rivers, they will not overwhelm you." I dip my fingers into the fountain and cross my forehead and my neck with what I perceive to be holy water. Not just my feet, Lord, Peter cried, but my entire body. Yes, Lord, I pray. Yes, Lord.

Tonight, it is hard to do research on the streets and try to understand the people who live here. The woundedness on the streets is wounding me. I want Aslan to emerge from the fountain and take me to Narnia in springtime. I want to look up at the cross and hear angels.

And I think part of me does hear something like angels singing somewhere.

Apocalypse and Golden Boy walk in. An oppressive force strikes him. 'Whoa,' he says. Apocalypse asks what the rules in the church are. I imagine all the rules there are and what might go wrong if said rules are violated. 'There aren't any,' I say.

Apocalypse looks at the fountain, the stained-glass windows, the wooden pews, and the image of Jesus on the cross. I wonder how he is experiencing what he is looking at. I observe how he interacts with the space. Apocalypse sits down in the back of the church. He leans against the marble wall behind him. Golden Boy lies down beside him, sighs, and closes her eyes.

Apocalypse fixes his gaze on the image of the crucified Jesus. He turns around and investigates the marble. Apocalypse touches the marble, caresses it. 'Funny,' he says, 'how many different things they can be. I fell in love with almost each one of you.'

Apocalypse is known for using acid, so I imagine he could be on a trip. What he is experiencing may be the result of the mental health challenges he struggles with. Or perhaps, I think, the presences he is interacting with are real.

Apocalypse turns to me as I sit on the wooden pew, facing Jesus. 'I have a question,' he says. 'Where can we go to find ourselves?' I am uninterested in my answer to this question. I prefer to know where Apocalypse thinks we should find ourselves.

'I really don't know,' I say. Apocalypse pushes back. 'I am really asking,' he says. 'We need to find ourselves.'

Looking away from me and into the marble, Apocalypse says: 'You may not know it, but we are pure soul.' For a few minutes, I listen to a discourse—a kind of homily from the back of the church, as I think of it now—about love and the spiritual nature of human personhood.

Apocalypse sits up. He turns away from the marble. He smiles. To my great relief, Apocalypse does not appear to be having a bad trip or a harmful psychotic episode. He seems peaceful, grounded, and coherent.

'There is a Great Something here,' Apocalypse tells me. His fingers caress the marble and move down it, slowly. 'It gave me a message,' he says. Apocalypse says the Great Something told him to find four companions to help him find himself. Apocalypse looks away from the marble and then at me. He invites me to be one of his companions.

'Will the church allow it?'

Apocalypse is not looking for an ethnographer-companion. He wants someone to live with him and Golden Boy on the streets and go on the pilgrimage the Great Something compelled him into. I tell Apocalypse that I'd like to continue hanging out with him. My indirect refusal is interpreted accurately: he understands that I have rejected his invitation and that I will not be the companion he desires.

Apocalypse looks back into the marble. He asks me, or perhaps the Great Something, if the woman he lost will be found.

'Go with Paul,' he tells Golden Boy. Golden Boy sits at my feet. She cushions her head against the wooden pew, against my feet. Apocalypse gets up. He leaves Christ Our Hope without saying goodbye.

An hour later, after fretting through downtown in search of him, I found Apocalypse in front of McDonald's. Sitting down with his back against the concrete wall of the McDonald's on Third and Pike, Apocalypse was bereft. He had not found his beloved. Before going home, I gave Apocalypse his dog back and bought them both a cheeseburger.

The preceding chapter explored how street kids in Seattle hold on to a life worth living in the grip of soul woundedness by cultivating an empowering spiritual connection to The Universe. This chapter focuses on what street kids mean when they talk about The Universe and if the concept of God is salient in their lives. It queries how street kids imagine God and what difference that makes. It demonstrates that, on the streets, God concepts are diverse, ambivalent, and contested. It also demonstrates that there are nevertheless coherent and meaningful patterns to people's God concepts that make a difference in everyday life. God concepts sustain purpose against the haunting threat of meaninglessness and empower people to pursue personal fullness in the struggle to get off the streets. This chapter also queries why the Christian conception of a personally loving God fails to matter for most of the street kids I spent time with. I propose that the Christian conception of God fails because of its oppressive connotations, the larger epistemological changes that have placed us in what Charles Taylor describes as an "immanent frame," and because the unloving social conditions of street life render the "problem of presence" Christians face across space and time difficult to resolve.[2] I conclude with a brief discussion about what really matters to most street kids: discerning a purpose off the streets from The Universe or a higher power within to find a life worth living. The story of Apocalypse is a story that symbolizes one facet of our culture's relationship to God and the pursuit of human fullness.

god(s) in america

God—or, rather, the gods of public perception—has been a central character in world history. Consider the role of God in the history of the United States. Many Europeans were driven to the "new world" to freely worship the God they believed compelled them to leave home. The mostly Puritanical notions of God inherited from European theology, which asserted that God was the author of the social reality within which people were obligated to live faithfully, were central to the development and maintenance of the colonies.[3] Many believed that the new world was a new Eden given to them by God to manifest his destiny. Belief in this God justified genocide against Indigenous people. It also caused people to live in dread over a God who would send them to hell if they strayed from a predestined, narrow path. Max Weber argued that anxiety over eternal salvation, which had to be worked out in one's domestic life, was the spark that lit the flame of modern capitalism.[4]

Belief in God also helped undo a major pillar of the American economic system: slavery. In his understanding of God, Abraham Lincoln found a courage to fight the Civil War despite the South's violent insistence that slavery was divinely decreed.[5] Later, a minister from Atlanta who believed he was called by God to help lead the American people to a new promised land would work through nonviolent direct action to get civil rights legislation passed. Without his belief in God, the work of Martin Luther King Jr. is hard to imagine.[6] Since the rise of Jerry Falwell and the Moral Majority in the 1970s, moreover, the religious group most likely to report having a direct relationship with God—that is, evangelicals—has been one of the most powerful political forces in the United States.[7] Evangelical politics is an expression of faith and a protection against the secular world they think threatens it.[8] Today, Christian nationalists paint into the world with their minds a violent God who they believe calls them to manifest their theocratic visions with, if need be, spiritual and physical violence.

As I demonstrated in the first chapter, the persistence of belief in God in the United States would have confounded the founders of social science. Many reasoned that, as the currents of modernization continued to wash over the world, people would give up religious thinking in exchange for scientific thinking.[9] The future of the world, they theorized, would be unbound from religion. Secular. Despite secularization theorists' predictions, however, God remains alive and well for most people in the United States. Friedrich Nietzsche's Zarathustra appears to be a victim of wishful thinking.[10]

In *America's Four Gods*, Paul Froese and Christopher Bader demonstrate that the vast majority of Americans—approximately 95 percent—believe in God and that belief in God is one of the most significant influences on human action.[11] Despite overwhelming belief in God, however, Froese and Bader demonstrate, there is considerable disagreement about what God is like. The specific kind of God one believes in, they found, influences different kinds of human action. Americans may not be at war over whether God exists, but "we might," Froese and Bader suggest, "be at war over who God is."[12]

Froese and Bader found that Americans hold wildly diverse understandings of God. "There are," they report, "as many kinds of God in America as there are people."[13] Notwithstanding the diversity in what I call *the divine imaginary*, which is a social constellation of the diverse ways it is possible to imagine, name, and relate to God, Froese and Bader found that Americans generally conceive of four different kinds of God: an authoritative god, a benevolent god, a critical god, and a distant god. The differences between our four conceptions of God concern levels of divine engagement: that is, people differ quite significantly less on whether God exists than on how they think God interacts with the world. The pressing question is about what difference God makes, not whether God exists. People who believe in an authoritative god see God as engaged and judgmental; people who believe in a benevolent god see God as engaged but nonjudgmental; Americans who believe in a critical god see God as disengaged but judgmental; and Americans who believe in a distant god imagine that God is both nonjudgmental and disengaged.[14] What is striking is that, despite the tremendous diversity in the divine imaginary, Froese and Bader found that almost all Americans feel that a personally loving God engages the world.[15] Even those who believe in a distant god—the smallest group aside from atheists, who make up only 5 percent of the respondents in their study—believe that a cosmic force of love is active in the universe.[16] We are, it seems, strikingly, an eternity from the cries over hell that helped build the nation. By and large, people of faith do not cry out to be saved from eternal fire. Instead, they cry out to be loved here and now. *USA Weekend's* 2010 report put it well: "For Americans today, God, quite simply, is love."[17]

The purpose of Froese and Bader's study was to get a general understanding of how the average American imagines God and determine what difference that makes. The limitation of any generalizable study is that local worlds can get lost in them. As I will demonstrate, one local world lost to their study, which will challenge the way we understand American spirituality, is the experience of street homelessness.

God concepts are developed and experienced in relation to the social world one is living in. As Ana-Maria Rizzuto explains in her psychoanalytic study of God concepts, following Freud's insight, the gods we believe in are constructed from the "warp and woof of everyday life."[18] An adequate understanding of how people understand God, therefore, requires close attention to a person's immediate social world. While no ethnography has foregrounded spirituality among people experiencing homelessness, many ethnographies treat spirituality anecdotally. Those studies suggest that God concepts matter to people and that many persons experiencing homelessness experience God as lovingly engaged in their lives. David A. Snow and Leon Anderson, for example, found that belief in God can help "salvage the self" from the destructive conditions of street life.[19] Without belief in God, Elliot Liebow found, many of the women in the homeless shelters he studied would not be able to survive their homelessness.[20] In *Shelter Blues*, Robert Desjarlais describes a woman named Alice who reads the Bible for up to sixteen hours a day to cultivate an awareness of a numinous presence that shelters her from the streets.[21]

Not every study has found that belief in God among the homeless bears a demonstrably positive effect. Teresa Gowan found that some homeless men in San Francisco experience their homelessness as God's judgment for their sins.[22] In her view, belief in this God perpetuates a discourse—which she dubs "sin talk"—that internalizes social injustice as a personal responsibility and distracts people from altering the unnecessary social conditions that produce homelessness in the first place.[23] Though, as I will show, this line of thinking is virtually absent from the street kids I spent time with, I often heard it among older homeless persons in Seattle. These persons thought their homelessness was retribution for their sins, yes, but they did not think that God wanted them to remain homeless. They also did not think God had abandoned them. Many said that God was putting them through a test and that God would eventually see them through it. 'God never gives us nothin' we can't handle,' Tito told me in Pioneer Square. This dynamic divine imaginary can be destructive and salvific at once.

To be sure, there is no one experience of homelessness. Different people experience homelessness differently. The historical time in which one experiences homelessness will shape the experience of homelessness. So, even, may the specific street. In Seattle, I learned that different neighborhoods help create a different experience of homelessness. Worlds of homelessness are not the same, so we cannot expect a divine imaginary to remain constant across space and time.

One salient question that motivated my research is whether the personally loving God the majority of Americans believe in survives the streets of Seattle. That question is an animating query of this chapter. While the previous chapter demonstrated that most street kids pursue an affective and transcendent force of good in The Universe through spiritual practices unique to street life, this chapter further queries what that force is like and whether street kids would name that force God—and, if not, then why not.

god talk

When I went to visit the Vineyard, a charismatic Christian church on the Ave, one Sunday morning during my fieldwork, a street kid disrupted the service. As the worship leader strummed his guitar and sang, a street kid walked into the church. He stood at the back and condemned the leaders at the Vineyard for being 'wolves in sheep's clothing.' He said that the rest of the church needs to know about the harm the pastors have done. Promptly, and quite gently, he was asked to leave. The pastor informed the church that they had been trying to help this young man and that he is suffering from severe mental health challenges. Uncertain about who he really was or where he went, we began singing again.

I came to find out that the Vineyard had gotten to know this young person through a ministry they call "God Talk." God Talk was an early morning Sunday service designed specifically for street kids. It offers street kids free breakfast and a conversational space to talk about God. Almost every street kid I spoke to about God Talk said they only went for the free bagels and coffee. Almost no one I spoke to said they went to talk about God. Most street kids felt that the Vineyard created the service to try to convert them. Since I never attended God Talk, I cannot say whether the Vineyard was trying to convert street kids, and I did not personally get that impression from the good people at the Vineyard. As for myself, I invited street kids into a kind of God Talk as well. I tried to create a space where they could let themselves be and share whatever they honestly thought about God, a higher power, or The Universe. 'It's interesting to me,' I'd just say. 'I want to listen and understand.'

Not everyone had much to say about God.[24] For a small number of the street kids I spent time with, that is, God did not seem to be worth talking about. Consider Skate. I asked Skate what he thought about God when we sat down for a cup of coffee on the Ave. 'Total bullshit,' he said. When I asked him to elaborate, he simply repeated: 'Total bullshit.' May had a similar but more gracious response. 'God has been good for my Catholic mother,' she said. 'For me, though, God isn't plausible. I think God is a human idea people use to make themselves feel good.' Zarathustra made a similar comment one afternoon in front of Starbucks. 'I really don't believe in an entity like that,' he said. 'It's people who create the world, not God. Everyone is capable and responsible for creating their own universe.' Rage, who was 'on the run' from the police for 'selling a lot of drugs and really, really hurting someone,' told me that people need to stop thinking about God. Solemnly, as we walked off the Ave and wandered between the trees on the University of Washington's campus to avoid being seen by the police, Rage told me that there are few things more hazardous than thinking about God. 'God is the most dangerous question anyone could ever ask,' he said. Rage told me that it has been scientifically proven that 'pondering God' makes people clinically insane. 'People commit suicide over God,' he said. 'Hundreds and hundreds of people every year.'

I don't know if anyone on the streets died by suicide because they thought too much about God, but spirituality could seriously exacerbate a street kid's mental health challenges. One evening, on the steps of the Vineyard, for example, Shaman told me that he needs to stop thinking about spirituality. 'I think thinking about spirituality is making me crazy,' he said. Shaman was one of the most spiritual people experiencing homelessness I spent time with, so his comment struck me as a change worth taking seriously. A few weeks later, Shaman went to a psychiatric hospital. Three days after that, he came back to the streets thinking he might be Jesus Christ and I might be one of his twelve disciples. God Talk certainly creates a different affective atmosphere when you are talking to a person who thinks he is God.

In what follows, I will summarize the two most common conceptions of this transcendent presence that came up during the God Talk I facilitated: (i) a negligent but purposeful creator and (ii) an immanent force experienced through a connection to a good but impersonal connection to The Universe.

aliens, ant farms, and a purposeful creator

December said she isn't sure if God exists. 'I have thought a lot about this,' she says. We are sitting on the sidewalk on the Ave. Our backs are against the glass wall of an abandoned Radio Shack. In purple and yellow and blue and red, she is coloring her notorious tag into her sketch pad: "Fuck the Ave." 'There must be *something* out there,' she says. 'How could all of this come from nothing?' 'But,' she goes on, 'it seems cruel to let people know that you are real but then allow them to experience so much suffering. If *something* exists,' she says, 'then maybe it's an alien in the seventh grade who created us for his science fair project. Now he hasn't seen it—he hasn't seen us—in eons. It's like we are collecting dust in his parents' attic.'

Red described experiencing a similar conception of God. We were in the sun at Cal Anderson Park. 'If there is *something* out there,' he says, 'then it's out there. I am close to saying there is no God but once in a blue moon—like when I am at the end of my rope—something crazy good happens and it keeps me thinking that maybe *something* is looking out for me.' His wife, River, interjects. 'It'd be an awful waste of space if *something* ain't out there. For me,' she continues, 'this planet might be an ant farm in a giant alien's bedroom.' River laughs. She says maybe God-the-giant-alien shakes us up occasionally to 'fuck shit up.'

'It'd be an awful big waste of space,' she repeats, as her laughter subsides, 'if there's no one in charge. Well, not in charge,' she says, 'but if there isn't a creator. There's gotta be *something* that gave us the privilege of being alive. Life didn't come from nothing.'

'There's got to be *something* out there,' Reaper told me. In a coffee shop on the Ave, Reaper said that 'scientists who think we evolved from monkeys and fish are fucking idiots because if that were true it would still be happening.' Whether whatever is out there cares for Reaper personally, however, is another story. Reaper said he used to pray. He said he cried and prayed for his suffering to go away, sometimes all through the night. Reaper said that he asked God, as he came to understand God at the evangelical church he and his mother went to, for more than a few fleeting moments of happiness in an otherwise excruciating life. But God, Reaper says, never came through. Lasting happiness never fell upon him, lifting him up out of his suffering. 'Whatever is out there,' Reaper says, 'doesn't give any fucks about me. So, I ain't going to be its cheerleader. I am going to stay in my lane as a human and it can stay in its lane as a deity. This might be my spiteful side,' Reaper concludes, 'but I see God like a child with an ant farm.'

Of course, not everyone had a strikingly neglectful image of God. Over a pot of coffee at Denny's, Plato told me that he would like to believe in a personal and loving God. 'It just doesn't seem possible, though.' For Plato, there is too little love and too much suffering for that to make sense. 'Maybe it's like a creator,' he said. 'I mean,' he corrects himself, 'maybe the creator is like a painter who created a beautiful painting.' As he speaks, I admire the conceptual painting he is creating for us. 'It's like he makes it, sells it, and then moves on to the next one. Does he adore the painting? Sure. Maybe he even has pride in it. But love? Absolute love? I'm sure he doesn't want to see his painting absolutely go to shit or be destroyed,' he says, 'but honestly if it happened then could the artist move on to another painting? There may be some suffering there, but will it destroy God?' he asks rhetorically. 'No.'

Plato is a Taoist. We met at Starbucks near the beginning of my fieldwork. Someone walked up to him and asked if he had any meth to sell. Plato was just drinking coffee, looking out the window, and reading the *Tao Te Ching*. Plato became furious, yelled and swore until the person left. 'How do people see me?' he asked.

Plato likes talking about spirituality. He speaks eloquently about the possibility of God as he pours another cup of coffee at Denny's. 'Now,' he says enthusiastically, 'I think we create the universe like God does, but through our choices.' 'What,' he asks me, 'is God besides what we do? We have all these choices. Perhaps,' he says, 'God gives us our life and then says, here you go. It's yours.'

'So, I don't know.' Plato says he could come up with another analogy but that it won't get close to what he is trying to say. It was common for people on the streets to preface their remarks about God with qualifications like 'but I don't know' or 'it's really a mystery.'

Plato says he has one last thing to say. He says that his sense of God comes from a feeling, not a fact. He says he doesn't know what to call the feeling but that he feels it when he sees people smile, when he sees an elderly couple holding hands, when he hears a child laugh, or when he is starving and someone gives him twenty bucks out of nowhere. 'But there is another feeling, too' Plato says. 'What really scares me,' Plato says, 'is that there might be no purpose. Like all this trying to be good and do the right thing is, in the end, for nothing. Like there is no deeper purpose to it. I hate to admit it,' Plato says, 'but I am afraid to believe there isn't *something* out there.'

The relationship between belief in a possible creator—that there is a *Something* out there—and a real experience of creaturely purpose was one of the most striking themes that came up during God Talk. In street cosmology, God was regularly imagined as a creator who created the world for a purpose but was not actively engaged with their creation. This *maybe God* is distant and mostly disengaged. That belief, however, seemingly obscure and pithy, perhaps, really mattered. As Plato explained, the possibility that there is *not* a Creator—or *Something* out there—opened the terrifying possibility that life might not have a purpose. Believing that there is an original purpose imbues one's symbolic universe with a meaning that helps one believe that life is still worth living. At the same time, the possibility of God evoked unsettling affect.

Native referred to The Great Something in The Universe as "Creator." He told me about his Creator late one night at a Mexican food restaurant on the Ave. Another street kid had wandered in to use the bathroom. 'Any black?' As he took the heroin out of his pocket, Native said that, without his Creator, he'd be dead. 'Simple as that,' he said. 'Any clean needles?' the street kid asked. 'Creator,' Native said, 'keeps me going when the world is raining swords.' While he does not know precisely what it is, Native believes Creator is keeping him alive for a purpose. He said he has had 'too many dances with death' to deny that. Native wishes Creator did not make it so hard to stay alive and experience a good life, but he knows that is not realistic.

Found, one of the first street kids I met in Seattle, created an insightful link between an abstract creator and the experience of purpose. Found was showing me a terrible wound on his foot. We were taking turns playing his guitar near Pike Place Market in downtown. As I strummed the guitar, Found told me that he is afraid to go to the doctor. He said he is worried that a doctor will look at his wound and say his leg will need to be amputated. 'That will kill me," Found says. 'I can't be homeless without legs.' Found said he is worried that the doctors will judge him and 'not do shit for me anyway since I am homeless.' When I asked Found about God, he become animated. 'I don't know what it is,' he says, 'but *something* is keeping me around for a purpose.' Found tells me a story. One night, he said, he went to sleep in a dumpster. He said it was raining, that he was 'hella dope sick,' and that the dumpster seemed like the safest place to sleep. The next morning, Found said, he woke up to the dumpster being picked up by a dump truck. He screamed and clawed and, somehow, he got out of the dumpster. That he got out in time, Found said, was a miracle. In his mind, it is evidence that Something is keeping him around for a purpose. While he thinks Something is keeping him around for an undisclosed purpose, however, Found does wonder from time to time if Something's keeping him around is 'a cruel joke.'

'Look around,' he said.

Color and I spoke about God for the first time on the light rail. We were headed from downtown to Capitol Hill. Color said what Found and so many other street kids did. He isn't sure what God is, but he knows that there is a *something* out there because Something keeps him going. Color says he is a scientific person. 'Given the number of dangerous situations I have been in and the number of drugs I have taken,' he says, 'even to the point of trying to overdose, the fact is that I should be dead. I think that Something has intervened in my life.' Something kept Color more than physically alive. It has also kept him emotionally alive. Color told me that, when he thinks about God, he thinks about a time he was going to kill himself for all the terrible things he had done. Late at night, when he was strung out and alone in a squat house, a powerful emotion came over him. He called it "forgiveness." 'Fear melted away,' he said. 'I felt total mercy, love, and complete acceptance. I knew I wanted to keep living and help others keep living, too. Forgiveness,' Color said, 'gave me sympathy for the devil.'

Old Steve is a street father on the Ave. Like a street mother, a street father is someone who takes care of someone new to the streets and becomes like family. His world has fallen apart many times. After his mother died and he got out of the military, Old Steve came to Seattle on a boat from Hawaii. 'Something is holding things together,' he told me one night. 'If there weren't,' he said, 'we'd have blown ourselves up a long time ago.' Old Steve says God is like a gambler with an infinite number of dice. 'It's like God places a bet, blows, throws us onto the table, and then sometimes it doesn't work out but sometimes it does. But at least God threw you into the world, you know, and at least God's there.'

an impersonal, immanent, enlivening presence in the universe

Hitch and I are at a park off the Ave. It is evening. We are eating beans and chicken. Two hours ago, Hitch and I were at the Food Bank. We stood in line for an hour to get beans and chicken for a "Hobo Barbeque."

'Hitch,' I say, 'do you believe in God or a higher power?' 'Definitely a higher power,' Hitch says. 'It's hard to describe,' he says. Hitch says his higher power is warmth and passion building up inside him. He says it's a force that makes him feel alive. 'I feel it most in the woods,' he tells me, 'and least when I'm in the city.'

I ask Hitch if his higher power is also a god. 'I can't say that,' Hitch says. 'God sounds too Christian.' Hitch doesn't receive personal messages from a deity, he says, but he does, on occasion, feel a power from The Universe that becomes alive in him. 'It makes me feel open' he says. 'Open,' he says again, 'free, and brave.'

Filth and I spoke about God as we drank cheap vodka before going into the courthouse. 'Do you believe in God?' I ask. 'I am Native American,' Filth says. 'What do you mean? I cannot believe in the white man's God. I don't believe in the Christian God,' he says, 'I will tell you that. What is God, anyway,' Filth says. 'I believe in the force of life that lives in nature and that makes a home in me. I believe what my people have always believed.'

Lucifer and Lilith were among the first street kids to help me understand the salient God concept Hitch and Filth describe. This God concept is different from the abstract, aloof, and possibly negligent creator. For these street kids, there is no definitive and separate entity in the world named God. There is no external force that operates in the world like a person, even at a great distance. There is, however, an inseparable power in The Universe that people can align themselves with. The effect of this alignment with a transcendent force in The Universe is an empowerment of one's personhood. What really matters about having a higher power is that a connection to it helps one tend their woundedness and feel more alive. It makes possible a life worth living and perhaps loving. When Lucifer 'gave his life to the original Lucifer' in a meditation, for example, he said that he aligned himself with a force in The Universe that gave him the power to become free from the arbitrary religious woundedness ruling his life. He didn't talk to Satan like a friend or a lover.

'I don't believe in God,' Lilith told me one day on the Ave, 'but I do have a higher power.' Lilith said that she feels closest to her higher power in nature. 'Like when I am lying back and floating in the lake,' she said, 'and I can feel the water line around both sides of my body. I feel it,' she continued, 'when part of me is submerged and the other part of me is in the sun.' Lilith is also warmed by her higher power and least likely to experience it on the streets. 'It's hard to connect to my higher power when I am sitting down on the Ave and buses constantly go by and I can't hear anything but noise,' she says. What she really seeks from her higher power, Lilith told me, is a peace to help her appreciate the wonder of being alive.

Sometimes, Lucifer and Lilith consider themselves gods. 'I am in control of what's going on,' Lilith told me, 'not an external God. If I am the one who needs to do something,' she says, 'then I am the one who needs to do it. I don't rely on something out there.' 'We are all gods,' Lucifer interjected. When I ask him to take a picture of what he means by that, Lucifer tells me to take a picture of him and Lilith on the trash can they often sit down on. Call this picture 'trash gods,' Lucifer says. 'Yeah,' Lilith says, 'we are trash gods.'

'God is me,' Strawberry said. 'It is you.' Strawberry feels closest to her higher power when she plays the mandolin and hula hoops. 'I felt it in my hula hoop last week before I went inside my friend's apartment,' she said. Strawberry's friend didn't want to live anymore. He called Strawberry to help him overdose on heroin. He wanted to die cuddling with her on his bed, listening to Nirvana. Strawberry hula hooped in front of his apartment as she moved through fear and debated whether to go inside and help him kill himself. She did go inside, she said, but her friend decided not to die.

Cleopatra thinks we are all gods, too. She came into Red Couch Café one afternoon on the Ave as I was writing fieldnotes. She was barefoot. Her feet were wet with blood. Cleopatra said she'd been using meth again, that she hadn't slept in days, and that she'd just been walking and walking in search of home. 'Let me see your phone,' she told me. 'I will take a picture of how I see God.' I handed her my phone. Cleopatra took a picture of her bloody feet and told me that she reminds herself of Jesus on the cross. 'God is so close,' she said. 'God is telling me: love yourself, girl. Love yourself no matter what.'

Tiger Hoods and I spoke about his higher power one evening inside another local café on the Ave. He was upset because someone living on the Ave is, he said, sexually abusing a teenager. Tiger Hoods recently found a can of mace on the sidewalk. Right now, Tiger Hoods told me, 'my higher power is telling me to mace the perpetrator and run him off the Ave. My higher power says that you cannot live on the streets and give a kid dope to get in their pants. My higher power calls that rape,' he says. Tiger Hoods has taken it upon himself to protect people who are vulnerable on the streets. 'Since the police won't protect us,' he told me, 'we have to protect ourselves.'

Normally, Tiger Hoods says, he experiences his higher power when he is around his daughter. He said his higher power lives within his daughter and motivates him to be a good father. Being a good father, Tiger Hoods told me, means avoiding the police and staying out of jail. Tiger Hoods said that, recently, his gut told him that he shouldn't take the 49 bus to downtown. His gut told him to take the light rail instead. Tiger Hoods found out later that there were police officers on the buses. 'If I had taken the 49,' he said, 'I probably would have gone to jail for the dope I had on me.'

Guerrero de la Libertad found her higher power when she took five hits of acid one night at a party. She was lying down in the snow and thinking about killing herself. She hated that she hated everyone and that everyone hated her. 'I was living in a nightmare' she said. Lying down in the snow, Guerrero heard a voice. It spoke to her from inside her own mind. 'The Voice,' she said, 'asked me why I came here.' Guerrero, fearfully, told The Voice that she didn't know why she came here. 'My friends gave me a lot of drugs,' she told The Voice. Guerrero asked The Voice its name. 'The Voice said it was me. It said it was me coming from every place I've ever been and every creature that has lived.' Guerrero said that The Voice, which she thinks of as her higher power, asked her why she cares so much about what other people think. The Voice told her that she needs to love herself before she can love anyone else. It also said that, no matter what, she needs to keep going.

Samantha says she prays, but that she isn't sure what she prays to. 'I don't consider it a god,' she says. 'It is not like a person at all.' Samantha tells me that she is not sure 'how the world was created and all of that. I do have a higher power, though' she says. 'It's a really strong force.' Samantha says she is open to her higher power being anything other than 'a man in the clouds.' What she knows for sure is that her higher power is kind and good. That it cares for her. Samantha believes her higher power helps when she is dope sick, when she needs to make some money on the street to get well, and when she is about to give up. It guides her life. Samantha told me a 'preacher man' once offered her a free hotel room for several nights while she was spanging in front of an ice cream shop in Capitol Hill. 'He said he wanted to show me how much God loves me,' she said. At first, Samantha didn't trust the preacher man. She worried the preacher man's offer might be a ruse. She feared he might be a sex trafficker. 'Something in my gut told me it'd be okay, though,' Samantha told me, 'and that I could trust him. I don't know,' Samantha said, 'but I had a peace about it.' Samantha said she is glad she took the offer. 'I hadn't slept that well in more than a year,' she said. More than anything, Samantha told me, she feels closest to her higher power when she is with her dog. Samantha says that she would not be alive without her dog. Samantha says her dog gives her something to love and something to love her.

What can be gleaned from the God Talk on the streets? First, God matters. God evokes real concerns street kids think through. The degree to which God matters, however, is a question. Second, there is no one way to describe how people talk about God on the street. The God language people use is contested and negotiated. It also, as I will demonstrate below, changes. For many,

moreover, the word "God" is refused and "higher power," "Creator," or "The Universe" is used instead. Some reject "God" precisely because of its Christian connotations. Most street kids do not have a strict, fundamentalist understanding of whether there is a God or a higher power and what it is like. When God is discussed, it is often hedged with "well, maybe I am wrong" or "it's really a mystery." Third, street kids, for the most part, do not believe in a personally loving God. If there is a person-like entity that exists outside a person, it is thought to be a creator who abandoned creation, operates with a dismissive relationship to it, or only intervenes through acts of life-saving care in extreme situations. Fourth, when discussed as a higher power or impersonal but benevolent force like The Universe, God was spoken of as an immanent power that is alive in the human person. One's higher power brings a sense of fullness that makes life worth living in the grip of soul woundedness.

the christian god lives

Of the fifty or so street kids I got to know, a small handful used unambiguously Christian language to describe their spirituality. As I discussed in the first chapter, rejecting Christianity is often experienced as a kind of personal and social salvation. Religious rejection is like a baptism into the possibility of new life. Soil was the only self-professed Christian I got to know. When I first met him, however, he was not a Christian. Soil was resolutely hostile to Christianity, in fact. Soil had just left a tent encampment for people experiencing homelessness because it was being hosted at a Christian college. The students, he said, were trying to convert him. 'Fuck that,' Soil said. 'I'd rather sleep on the streets than in a creepy Christian environment. My freedom,' Soil said, 'is everything to me.'

One day, on a walk through the streets of Capitol Hill, Soil told me about a band he likes. He said the band has a song about burning Christian churches down to the ground. Soil said that Christianity deserves to have its churches burnt down because it has committed egregious crimes against humanity. 'I'd burn down a church if the right opportunity presented itself,' Soil told me. The unfettered anger I saw in his eyes indicated to me that he was serious. Like most street kids, Soil raged against a machine that generated his woundedness, and which he imagined Christianity to operate. This raging, which I call protest spirituality, is a form of care on the streets, a way street kids distance themselves from their social woundedness, and how people clear the numinous realm from oppressive affects.

Soil has been on the streets for more than ten years. Today, he feels stuck. Being houseless used to feel free—but no more. Today, the streets of Seattle are like a prison. The figure of Seattle as a place of freedom appears like a mirage in a desert now. I remember the first time Soil told me he is stuck in Seattle. He had just lost his dog, Hercules, without whom, he told me, he'd rather be dead. We were sitting across from each other in a public library in Capitol Hill. We were staring at an injured pigeon from the window. Soil hadn't slept, he said, in three days. Soil said he is going to quit heroin 'once and for all.' A green worm wiggled around in one of his boots as he told me that he wants to get off the streets and 'just have a normal fucking life.'

One day, years after I met Soil, I was walking around downtown. I prayed like I often did when I'd start my fieldwork: to be freely open to the present. I imagined swimming in Lake Washington and asking Aslan, the lion roaring at the center of my spirituality, to roam away from me and stay in the water so that I might make room to apprehend and become transformed by spiritual difference. Within a few minutes, I ran into Soil. He had Hercules. 'Soil,' I said. Soil and I walked to Target where he was planning to spange. On our way there, Soil told me that he became a born-again Christian. I thought he was joking. I thought back to the time Shaman told me he had found Jesus. 'Really?' I asked Shaman. 'Yeah,' Shaman said, 'look. I found him in a dumpster.' Shaman smiled as he pulled a small figurine of Jesus from his pocket.

But it becomes clear that Soil is not kidding. He is somber. It looks like someone shot him in the heart with a dart of love. 'I am not exactly sure how it happened,' he says. Soil begins to think. He wonders aloud. He said he had been watching videos online from Seventh Day Adventists. 'That must have had something to do with it,' he said. 'Ah,' Soil goes on. 'I know what it must have been.' He stops in the center of downtown Seattle, almost a block from Target. Soil says he was deeply influenced when he watched videos of the Notre Dame Cathedral in flames. It made him realize, he told me, that we're in the end times. 'Look around you, man,' he said. 'Isn't it obvious?'

Watching the cathedral burn, Soil said he became more aware of how people are wounding God with their sinful behavior. 'We're so ungrateful, selfish, and sinful' Soil said. 'We are wasting the only life God gave us.' Soil also said that he realized that he is running out of second chances and that his eternal soul is at stake. 'I don't want to go to hell, man,' Soil said frankly.

'So,' Soil said, 'I gave my life to Jesus Christ.' Doing so, Soil told me, engendered a remarkable sense of warmth, grace, and surrender. Soil said that for the first time in a long time, he felt love. I felt a new warmth on him. He had a discernably different affect. Soil's conversion also transformed his life. He stopped using heroin, removed himself from what he considered an enabling homeless encampment, and began working with an anti–street homelessness organization called Safe Seattle. Today, he is on a mission to 'save the streets from drugs.'

the problem of presence

In a 2007 article, the brilliant and kind sociologist Christian Smith asked why Christianity has survived for two millennia and what makes it "work" for people. Given all the challenges and problems it has faced over the years, he wanted to know, why do so many people in the world continue to put their faith in it? One reason, Smith argues, is because of the degree to which Christianity meets basic emotional and mental needs that humans have. In Smith's view, Christianity helps people *feel*—not just know—that their lives are meaningful, that they belong, and that they are unconditionally loved.[25] Central to Christianity's capacity to meet these basic human needs is the *belief* in a personal and loving God and a set of *practices* that engage this belief and make it emotionally convincing. Christianity works, in other words, because people feel that a personal and loving God is alive in the world and because this imbues them with significance, belonging, and love.[26]

Smith's article answered why Christianity works; it did not, however, answer *how* it works. The empirical question of precisely how Christians come to feel, in their everyday lives, that a seemingly immaterial God is real and that the world is charged with meaning, connectedness, and love, is open. In recent years, several anthropologists have explored this question. Matthew Engelke refers to the challenge of how a seemingly immaterial God becomes real to people as a "problem of presence." His book, *A Problem of Presence*, is an ethnographic study in Zimbabwe on a group of Christians referred to as the Friday Masowe apostolics. The peculiar feature of the Masowe apostolics is that they do not read the Bible. In fact, they consider the Bible a sacrilegious document. It is forbidden in services and, according to their prophets, best used as toilet paper. There are several reasons why this is the case. One reason is Africa's colonial history and the degree to which the Bible was used against them as a weapon of political subjugation. Their approach to the Bible, however, Engelke contends, is not reducible to that. Another reason they reject the Bible is because they desire a live and direct faith. The Bible, in their view, deadens and disorients faith. Unlike the presence of God, the Bible can tear, fall apart, and be destroyed. Words on a page can suffocate the real breath of God. The Bible traps Christians in the past and prevents them from experiencing God in the present. Unlike other Christian groups for whom reading the Bible is integral to their relationship with God, in this expression of Christianity it is a hindrance.[27] But the problem of presence does not go away. How the Friday apostolics respond to it is the subject of Engelke's book.

His argument is complex. It requires a degree of nuance that I cannot provide in this chapter. In short, Engelke's argument is that their rejection of the Bible creates the possibility for experiencing the presence of God in different ways. For this group, the voice of their prophet is considered the True Bible, and sound, experienced within "a community of practice," is one means through which the presence of God is resolved. This experience of God through sound transpires within a sophisticated and locally constituted performance and interpretation (which frequently causes problems for their neighbors).[28]

In *When God Talks Back*, Tanya Marie Luhrmann asks how charismatic evangelicals in the United States resolve their problem of presence. "The problem of presence," in her words, "is that an immaterial God cannot be seen, heard, smelled, or felt in an ordinary way, and so worshippers cannot know through their senses that God is real."[29] Luhrmann's ethnography at various Vineyard churches led her to the conclusion that charismatic evangelicals resolve their problem of presence through a series of sophisticated practices that teach them to pay attention to their minds in particular and concentrated ways, and in that process learn to hear the voice of God talking back to them. These practices involve experiencing God in the private space of one's mind, relating to God as a person, and experiencing oneself as unconditionally loved. At the Vineyard, it is in the mind that one waits for God to speak; it is there that one learns to encounter God as real and present. The real problem with the problem of presence is sustaining faith in the midst of doubt—when the divine evidence apparent to one's senses seems to contradict the notion of a personally loving God. Luhrmann contends that faith takes work—hard work.[30]

For Americans, and people in the West more broadly, the problem of presence is qualitatively different. In contrast to Africa, fewer people in the West are convinced that gods are real and that they make an observable difference in the world. Our lives in the West are less shackled to the gods and their religious traditions. Arguably, this makes it more difficult to resolve the problem of presence and come to believe that there is a personally loving God at the center of the universe. Charles Taylor, in *Sources of the Self* and *The Secular Age*, helps us understand why. For Taylor, the question of meaning that confronts the human person is inescapable.[31] It is a question that one must answer to achieve selfhood.[32] For Taylor, the intrinsic pull toward meaning is the result of the human person's innate craving to be in contact with the good.[33] Practically, however, meaning is discovered on the basis of finding one's weight in the world where, Taylor writes, one experiences a sense of power and fullness.

That the world is imbued with innate meaning is no longer axiomatic. Here, Taylor sees a distinctive feature of the modern age. The modern self stands before a horizon that, as Nietzsche put it, has been soaked up.[34] Today, in other words, one is confronted with the agonizing possibility that there might not be an underlying meaning and purpose in the world. There are people for whom the universe is now cold and without intrinsic meaning. Further, we are aware that the quest for meaning can end destructively. A human person meaning something good, in other words, we see, can create destruction. The modern challenge, as philosophers like Albert Camus have put it, is to confront the problem of meaning as the absurd hero: to leap not into the arms of God, as Kierkegaard thought, but into the ultimate meaninglessness of the world with acceptance, joy, and wit. Meaning is made from below, Camus thinks, not given from above.[35]

Taylor argues that our existential situation has changed because our "background framework" for the world has changed. He contends that human persons need a background framework to make sense of the world. Existentially, a background framework is like oxygen: though we cannot see it, our lives depend on it. To be without such a framework is to be spiritually senseless.[36] Following Wittgenstein, Taylor reasons that our background framework is like a deep picture that holds us. The background picture that we have today is unique. It has developed through a profound existential struggle with cosmic meaninglessness. We are less certain about where to stand among the multiple frameworks available. Many are uncertain which framework may best adjudicate where one can find the place of power and fullness.[37] The sense of meaning which modern humans face is, for Taylor, a challenge that people in previous generations did not experience. While people today are threatened with a sense of meaninglessness, it appears that the stakes in finding meaning are raised. One could argue, that is, that the threat of meaninglessness has made the pursuit of meaning more meaningful. As Alasdair MacIntyre has it, the human person is on a quest of seeking.[38] Like Apocalypse in Christ Our Hope, many of us do not know where to find ourselves—even in a religious institution where, for almost two thousand years, much of the Western world built its existential home.

In *A Secular Age*, written eighteen years after Taylor published *Sources of the Self*, Taylor continues exploring the peculiarity of the human quest for fullness. A *Secular Age*, however, is focused more specifically on the question of God. Taylor's tome is a question about how the Western world went from a nearly axiomatic belief in God five hundred years ago to a world in which belief in God is no longer assumed. While people still believe in God, to be sure, belief is now a choice—and a choice, at that, which requires hard work.

God, to people in a secular age, does not hold the power They once did. The pursuit of meaning—and of a fullness that brings power to act in the world so that one may have a life worth living and loving—does not bring them to Their door. In fact, it is likely to bring them to directly outside it. Today, there is an apocalypse taking place inside the church that many people are running away from to save and create their spiritual lives. It may not always be this way, it is important to note, and the existential reality could change drastically. How this epistemological transformation occurred is the subject of Taylor's nearly thousand-page book. I cannot do his argument justice here. What is important to recognize, however, is Taylor's overarching argument that the human struggle for fullness took an inward turn that "buffered the self" against the "porousness" it needed to make it possible to believe in external gods. The inward turn disenchanted the world; it drew the human pursuit of fullness into an "immanent frame."[39] Now, Taylor demonstrates, the ship we are on in the universe travels through an impersonal ocean. Many do not seek a divine wind. Scientists make our compasses, not priests. The land we are looking for is one in which the human person can flourish without godly collars on. In the immanent frame, fullness is found within the human person's pursuit. We search for and find mysteries inside ourselves. The story of disenchantment is not merely one of loss, however; it is also a story of gain. As belief in God declined, a "rage for order" took its place. This rage for order, which Taylor refers to as Reform, brought on an exclusive humanism that sought an end to human suffering. To end suffering and promote human fullness, Taylor thinks, we unshackled ourselves from the gods and the religions that gave birth to them.[40]

For most street kids, the notion of a personally loving God is not salient. The absence of the personal divine lover can be explained because Christianity is perceived to be a source of oppression: that which vanquishes the possibility of love. Christianity is experienced as wounding rather than healing. It is the object of Rage. There is a second reason. A personally loving God is not salient because the "conditions of belief" in the Western world have changed; through a long, epistemological struggle, as Taylor demonstrates, our world functions in an immanent frame.

In my view, another salient reason street kids reject a personally loving God is related to an insight from Ana-Maria Rizzuto in her acclaimed book *The Birth of the Living God*. For Rizzuto, God is sensible only when a person's understanding of God is created with the warp and woof of their everyday life.[41] If God does not align authentically with the experience of one's real life, God will not be experienced as real. Often the streets do not suggest traces of a personally loving God. People who think about God on the streets might imagine something negligent like a teenager for whom the world is an old, dusty science project in the attic, an artist who abandoned the beauty they created, and a gambler who rolls human dice. I found it striking that, when I asked street kids what most loved them, they would usually struggle to find an answer. This research question about the personal salience of love created the longest pause; it seemed to confuse and wound the people I spent time with. The diverse realities of everyday life on the streets, I came to understand, can be described as unloving. While there is real, transformative love on the streets, the social conditions and personal experiences are dominated by unlovingness and heartbreaking, disorienting absences of love. The social woundedness people experience on the streets is damning evidence against the personally loving God most Americans believe in. On the streets of Seattle, and perhaps in neighborhoods around the world, it is perhaps truer to say that experiences of divine love have been soaked up from the universe, not meaning. Given the ubiquitous hunger human persons experience for a love greater than oneself alone, and Christian history's unwavering promise that divine love is real, powerful, and accessible in the present to meet that intrinsic need, the street kids I got to know live wounded, I think, with something we might call the *failed promise of God*.

5
The Wound of Love

for fear of wounding her

River is calling me from a psychiatric hospital. Last week, Red died of an overdose. She held her husband in her arms as he stopped breathing; she watched as his face turned blue. When the paramedics got to their unsanctioned encampment, where they were living homeless, she was pulling the hair from his scalp and weeping violently. The gravity of the situation, she said, broke her into tiny pieces.

Red was desperate to get off the streets: he was in treatment, applying for housing, and looking for work. 'I don't know what else to do,' he said. Red was sick of fighting on the block every day, of being drunk all the time, of sleeping outside. What he really wanted to do, Red told me a few weeks before he died, was get his life back.

Red was deeply loved. His death was a tragedy. I could feel grief for his life on faces, see it in eyes, hear it in voices. Rainbow cried into her palms as we shared a plate of fries at the Comet Tavern. 'I can't believe I lost another brother,' she said. 'It fucking hurts, Paul. Look,' she says, 'the streets are killing us.'

I pick up River's call. I gaze out the murky window of the public bus I am riding to downtown Seattle. I ask how things are. 'It's like I am trying not to believe it,' she says. 'Red's death—fuck, my life—feels like a bad dream.'

A few weeks later, after she got out of the hospital, I met River at Cal Anderson Park. We sat on the table where she and Red and their street family sometimes felt at home in the world. 'I fucking broke,' she told me. She kept

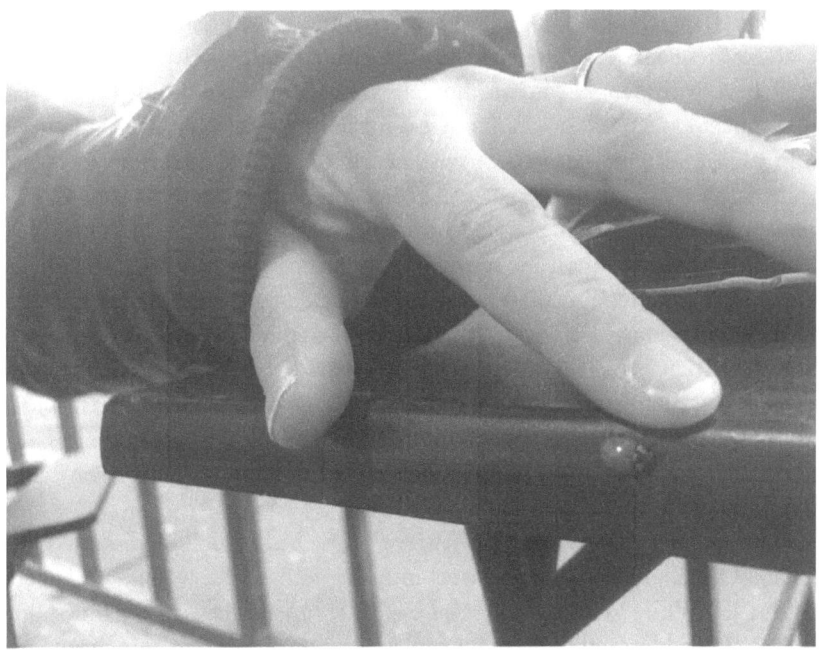

saying it: 'I broke. I fucking broke. Write this down in your book: I fucking broke. Tell people I broke.'

I ask River if spirituality is important to her right now. 'It's always important,' she says. River reaches into her bag. She looks for her Bible—the Bible Red made fun of her for reading before sleep. 'I can't think too much about spirituality right now, though. It's too real.'

A few nights ago, River had a dream. 'Maybe it was Red,' she says, 'or maybe it was God. *Something* told me to get the hell off the streets. And be happy. Whatever it was wants me to be barefoot and pregnant in the kitchen.'

I ask River what she needs. 'Just your company,' she says. 'Promise me,' she says, 'that you won't be one of those people trying to fix me?'

She, though we say goodbye, is holding on to our conversation.

'I love you, Paul.'

For fear of wounding her, of taking any of the air she is grasping for, I am reluctant to say it back.

This chapter is about homelessness, suffering, and Christian spirituality. It is about the relationship housed Christians who call themselves "street ministers" have with people who are homeless. I ask three questions. First, what difference do people who are homeless make in the spiritual lives of housed Christians? Second, *why* do people who are homeless make a difference in the spiritual lives of housed Christians? Third, what difference do housed Christians make in the lives of people who are homeless?

While I intend to query the spiritual relationship between housed Christians and people experiencing homelessness in a broad, global context, the answers to these queries are derived mostly from ethnographic fieldwork I conducted with Christian "street ministers" who are securely housed at an organization called Operation Nightwatch. At stake in this chapter is a reliable perspective on the relationship between street ministers and people who are homeless. An adequate response to River is also at stake: a deeply life-giving way of saying to her, if not with words, then somehow: 'I love you, too.'

This chapter will move in three steps. First, I describe Operation Nightwatch (ON) and its practice of street ministry with people who are homeless in Seattle. While focusing on ON, I explicate other Christian organizations in Seattle and beyond that practice related forms of spiritual care. I propose that street ministers at ON, and some housed Christians more broadly, have a spiritual relationship to people who are homeless. In this spiritual relationship, people who are homeless motivate a housed Christian's desire for God and make possible their practice of love. In this historically significant expression of Christian spirituality, people who are homeless are, to use a manner of speaking that mystics throughout history have employed, and which I will elucidate below, "wounds of love."

With the second step of this chapter, I explain *why* people who are homeless motivate a housed Christian's desire for God and make their practice of love possible. I do this by drawing on the work of the contemporary social scientists who study Christianity that I discussed in the previous chapter. Here, I propose that Christians have a "problem of presence" that people who are homeless help resolve. I also show that many Christian theologians have helped solve the problem of presence because of the degree to which they write about how God might be found, experienced, and pursued in their relationship to the suffering poor.

Finally, with the third step of this chapter, I consider the difference a housed Christian's spiritual love makes in the lives of people who are homeless. I demonstrate that the meaning and belonging that street ministers cultivate is likely to help some homeless individuals but devastate others. I show that loving in unloving social conditions is a profound and often unknown risk. The peril of loving in unloving social conditions raises a question about the efficacy of love and how one's love for people experiencing homelessness might become more loving. For a housed Christian's love to become more loving, I propose, one must help change the unloving social conditions in which people experiencing homelessness live. If that does not happen, I fear that homeless individuals can be experienced as little more than a means by which many housed Christians save themselves from the poverty of disbelief, meaninglessness, and lovelessness.

operation nightwatch

ON was founded in 1967. It began when a pastor from a small church on Mercer Island named Bud Palmberg heard that a young man from his church had run away from home. Concerned that he might begin traveling with hippies, Bud traveled to Seattle's skid row one night after choir practice. The suffering that Bud witnessed that night changed his life. The seeming dearth of love, evidenced by rampant homelessness, drug addiction, and prostitution, called out to him as if from the mouth of God. People on the streets, he began to think, need a minister just as do people in church. Every week after choir practice, even after he had found the young man, Bud returned to skid row.

Since the streets were large and dangerous, Bud recruited others. One problem was that none of the ministers he knew wanted to minister on the streets. Undeterred, Bud picked up a copy of the Yellow Pages. "You get some pretty strange guys when you look in the Yellow Pages," Bud recalled in an interview, "but the strange ones were the only ones who were willing to go."[1] In time, a group of strange ministers were on the streets of Seattle's skid road every night from 10 p.m. until 4 a.m. Their purpose was simple: to accompany people on and off the streets and help them remember, or perhaps discover, that God loves them and has a plan for them. There must be no judging or preaching, though, Bud told everyone.

Not everyone on the streets experienced the street ministers' presence as loving or wanted them around. Some worried that the street ministers were undercover cops. Since it was the height of the counterculture movement, some didn't want anything to do with people who resembled "the establishment." The first year was difficult. Several street ministers were held up at knifepoint, there were visits to the emergency room, and Bud was thrown through the glass windows of a porn shop.

Despite the trouble, they kept showing up. And they kept growing. Today, ON is an impressive organization doing immense good, playing an integral role in the response to homelessness. ON provides a warm meal every night at 9 p.m. to over two hundred people who are homeless, runs a dispatch center that helps people who might otherwise sleep on the street find shelter, and operates an apartment complex that houses twenty-four low-income seniors. Its annual budget exceeds one million dollars. And, after all these years, ON still practices street ministry.

street ministry

While ON played an integral role in the development of street ministry in Seattle, it is part of a broader ministerial phenomenon. Similar forms of spiritual care, also referred to as "spiritual accompaniment" and "ministries of presence," are practiced by organizations in Seattle, across the United States, and all over the world. Other organizations in Seattle that practice some form of street ministry include Seattle's Union Gospel Mission, New Horizons, Mental Health Chaplaincy, and Street Youth Ministries Seattle. During my ethnographic fieldwork in Seattle, I interviewed people at all these organizations. I also got to know Rick and Ben, street ministers at Operation Nightwatch at the time, on a personal level. To help me understand what it means to be a street minister and provide spiritual accompaniment to someone who is homeless, they invited me to minister on the streets with them as a volunteer and then, years later, offered me a full-time job as a street minister.

During my time with ON, I identified five practices associated with street ministry. The first practice is prayer. Prayer, Ben told me, is the foundation of street ministry. Before street ministers go to the streets, they join hands and pray. The content of their prayers varies. Generally, it consists of asking for God's guidance. Street ministers, for example, might ask God to lead them to the right people on the streets. The intent is to become open to God's Holy Spirit so that, through the street minister, God can love people who are homeless with a personal love.

After prayer, street ministers show up. Showing up is the second practice of street ministry. It is about being there and making one's presence known. It is vital not just to show up, Rick and Ben told me, but to show up consistently. Showing up is how a street minister builds trust with people who are homeless, which can be remarkably difficult.

The third practice is greeting people who are homeless. As it turns out, it can be problematic to greet people who are homeless. Ben told me that many people develop invisible armor to protect themselves on the streets. Their armor makes them guarded, he said. Saying hello might be experienced like picking the lock on one's front door. To overcome this challenge, Ben offers survival items from a backpack he carries around. Rick brings Little Caesar's.

Building a relationship with people who are homeless is the fourth practice I identified at ON. Central here is listening. For street ministers, listening means creating space for someone to share what they are going through. In this space, it is imperative that a street minister be nonjudgmental, be compassionate, and surrender to a Listening Power greater than oneself.

Sometimes a street minister will pray for a person who is homeless and give them a prophecy. To speak prophetically at ON is not about telling someone their future. It is simply telling someone that they are loved by God and that God has a plan for them. In an interview, Ben told me that sometimes people become so overwhelmed by this prophecy that they begin to cry. He said that love gets turned off on the streets because of the armor people develop to protect themselves. When there is a chink in the armor, he said, which can come by way of a prophecy, it can be overwhelming.

Divine love is what really matters to the street ministers at ON. The street minister is like a channel for this love to flow through. Ben and I spoke for the first time on a park bench at Cal Anderson Park. I asked Ben what he'd like to know from my research: if he were me, that is, what he'd like to find out. Ben told me that he'd want to know how people come to believe something untrue about themselves: why people on the streets believe they are unlovely and unloved and without purpose. Five years later, as I prepared for a talk at a national gathering of street ministers in San Francisco, he reiterated this guiding question.

street stories

After a long night of street ministry, Rick and Ben often return to the office. If they have the energy, they may sit at a desk, reflect on their time, and write a story. The goal is to bring the presence of the homeless people they have gotten to know to the larger Christian church, and to the world, so that people who are homeless can be better loved. The relationship street ministers work to establish with people who are homeless is intended to be a humble model for other Christians' relationships with people who are homeless. Street ministers believe they are telling a story not just about people who are homeless but about God. Their stories are therefore invitations to a transformative encounter with a living God. Storytelling is what I consider the fifth practice of street ministry at ON.

In 2015, a book of Rick's stories was published. It is aptly titled *Street Stories*. By and large, it is a book of frustrated laments. The laments are ecclesial, institutional, and personal. Rick laments how inadequate the Christian church's response to homelessness is, for example: how many churches have the physical space to shelter people who are homeless but don't. He laments how other institutions, like the city of Seattle, seem, despite their rhetoric, to lack the political will to solve the problem. Rick laments personal greed and pride: how many housed people hoard unneeded belongings while people without houses have almost nothing. He laments his own ministry on the streets as well and how, at times, he feels swallowed by cynicism. In *Street Stories*, Rick fashions himself as a street minister who gives banal blessings and who feels compelled, perhaps in delirium, to dream an impossible dream. *Street Stories* is an honest, beautiful, and painfully prophetic book from a pioneer in spiritual care with people who are homeless.

"Ronnie Kisses Me" is a quintessential street story. Rick tells it not only in *Street Stories* but also at the places where he is invited to speak. It goes like this. "Ronnie" is an unhoused person in Seattle. Because he causes so much trouble, Ronnie is barred from most shelters in Seattle. One night, parting a large crowd, Ronnie approaches Rick. He comes up close to Rick and asks him if he is beautiful. Uncomfortable and lying, Rick tells Ronnie that he is beautiful. Ronnie gets even closer. With a "big, crooked grin," he kisses Rick and then leaves, going out into the night. Rick recoils. Ronnie's lips have a disgusting taste of homelessness on them. The experience overwhelms Rick with a presence that is undesirable. When Ronnie is gone, however, "in the night," Rick realizes the experience was "a God moment."[2]

The meaning of the stories, Rick told me, changes over time. In his book, Rick writes that Ronnie's kiss helped him realize how ugly and unloving he was being. He wanted to keep Ronnie and his problems at arm's length. Ronnie's kiss taught him that loving God and other people means embracing what is perceived as ugly and uncomfortable. It is a lesson we can all learn. The story ends with a prayer to God: "Help me love everyone with Your uninhibited joy."[3]

In a video online, the meaning of the story is different. Rick says that Ronnie's kiss changed the way he sees people who are homeless. After Ronnie kissed him, Rick said, he no longer sees suffering on the faces of people who are homeless. Instead, he sees their hopes and joys; the hopes and joys everyone, homeless or not, has for their lives.[4]

Most of the Christian organizations that provide spiritual care to people who are homeless that I observed in Seattle tell stories in this way. In 2009, Craig Rennebohm, founder of Mental Health Chaplaincy, published a widely acclaimed book, *Souls in the Hands of a Tender God: Stories of the Search for Home and Healing on the Streets*. Craig's book begins this way: "We begin not in the sanctuary, but on the street. Here in the most unexpected and obscure places, we discover the Spirit at work in the world, *the touch of God that holds* every moment of life with infinite care."[5] The next year, in 2010, Ron Ruthruff, a former director at New Horizons, published a book titled *The Least of These: Lessons Learned from Kids on the Street*. An endorsement suggests Ron's book is "about how the ministry to young people has broken and shaped Ron's heart for God and for proclaiming the good news in hard places" and how the streets function as a seminary that reveals the face of God.[6] Other books, written by authors from outside Seattle, include *Sometimes God Has a Kid's Face* by Bruce Ritter and *Practicing Presence: Insights from the Streets* by Phyllis Cole-Dai. Ben, the street minister I got to know most intimately, is writing a book about how becoming present to people on the streets can help deepen a person's relationship with God. Here is one poem that Ben shared with me about how the practice of street ministry creates the possibility of experiencing church. While I find this raw and gritty poem itself beautifully written, what I find more beautiful still is the authentic spiritual work that made Ben's experience a real, prophetic possibility that can help transform dehumanizing images of people experiencing homelessness and nourish a more loving love.

> Right there in the park, it was kinda dark, conditions a little
> Stark.
> Instead of rings on the pastor's fingers, it was rings of coke
> On dude's nose.
> Wailing sirens were the Gospel choir,
> Accompanied by squealing tires.
> Lady lifting her hands in praise, maybe a manifestation,
> Maybe just drug-induced haze.
> But we had church.
> A reading on the Good Shepherd,
> We were far from the ninety-nine.
> Homey walking by offerings 'bottles,' the communion wine,
> A half-eaten granola bar the body of the Divine.
> Prayers for deliverance, safety and peace,
> Let's go down and say hello to the least.
> Come one, come all, the big and the small,
> Come to where grace and love meet the fall,
> Cross the street to the other side of the tracks,
> Come on down and we can have church.

In my view, this street ministry literature constitutes a historically unique genre in the history of Christian spirituality. There is no one way to read this literature, and there is great variance within it. Yet it seems to me that most stories embody a central dynamic related to the absence and presence of God.

On one hand, the stories evoke an absence of God. That absence is articulated in the suffering that people who are homeless experience. On the other hand, the stories evoke a presence of God. God is identified with people who are homeless. In their suffering, God's presence is framed as a question of love. Responding to that question with love is framed as a means of loving God and realizing one's Christianity. The interplay between the absence and presence of God among the homeless motivates a housed Christian's relationship with God and makes their practices of love, which the Christian religion tells itself it is meaningless without, possible.

wounds of love

"The wound of love" is a motif that runs through the history of Christian spirituality. Since the third century, Christian mystics have used it to describe the experience of being uniquely and transformatively touched by God.[7] The touch is described as a wound because of what happens in a person's soul. Divine love, the supposed fount of human desire, becomes immediately, beautifully, and terrifyingly present. In this state, the experience of God's presence seems to disappear: where once there was a fulfilling touch, now there is a painful absence. This wound of love engenders a painful and yet beautiful longing. With God, the wounded person becomes the shepherd of their wound. It is kept, cultivated, and cared for through prayer and acts of love in the material world.

The spiritual experience of divine wounding is described by Christian mystics throughout history. Interestingly, however, the material symbols that facilitate the wound can be strikingly different. The precise way of God's wounding is historically peculiar. Consider Origen of Alexandria, who is the first person in the Christian tradition to use the motif. Origen believed that Scripture, and the Song of Songs in particular, wounded him with God's loving power. In the third century, Origen writes: "Indeed, the soul is led by a heavenly desire and love when once the beauty and glory of the Word of God has been perceived, he falls in love with His splendor and by this receives some dart and wound of love."[8] Julian of Norwich's book *Showings* provides a second example of a Christian who wrote about her experience being wounded with God's love. Like many Christians in the medieval world, Julian believed that images of Jesus's suffering wounded her with God's love.[9] Teresa of Avila's *The Interior Castle* provides one of the most poetic and beautiful renderings of the wound of love. Teresa describes the wound of love as "exquisite" and "something precious" that "one would not want to be cured from."[10] For Teresa, it is the figure of the unknown, whom she later identifies as God, operating within "the deep interior parts of the soul" that whispers a penetrating wound.[11] In our contemporary moment, Wendy Farley writes compellingly about the wound of love. For Farley, to be human is to live wounded with a desire for infinite love and wounded in our capacity to embody and realize love's power.[12]

Today, people who are homeless are, for some housed Christians, wounds of love. While I did not hear anyone explicitly refer to homeless individuals as "wounds of love," I believe the phenomenon is functionally similar and historically congruent for two reasons. First, the relationship some housed Christians have with people who are homeless is spiritual. It is a spiritual relationship because it is a material site where Christians indicate that they find, experience, and pursue God. Their relationship with people who are homeless transforms themselves and their relationship with God. Second, it is precisely the alternating experience of God's presence and absence that establishes, motivates, and enriches the relationship. The relationship is not described as merely transactional; it is imbued with captivating experiences of the divine.

the suffering poor: a place of divine encounter in christian spirituality

At the heart of Christianity is a story about a powerful and loving God. Belief in this God threads the garment of Christianity identity. There is a problem with this story, however: it comes apart at the seams when people suffer. For this reason, Christians have long queried: If God is powerful and loving, why is there so much suffering? Is God not powerful enough to prevent people from experiencing homelessness? Is God not loving enough? This line of thinking is referred to as traditional theodicy: it worries itself with explaining suffering, and it has failed.

I consider traditional theodicy a failure because it is, by and large, considered rationally untenable and ethically unsound.[13] In the face of radical suffering, there aren't good answers for why people suffer, and the bad answers that are available too often make the problem worse. While many Christian theologians agree that radical suffering can no longer be explained, however, they do think that it can be transformed. That has been a main challenge facing Christian theologians since the collapse of traditional theodicy: not to explain suffering but, rather, to transform it.[14]

The collapse of traditional theodicy has changed Christian theology. This change is important to observe because it has made an empirical difference in the world. Theologians speak about God. In doing this, theologians give people language to relate to God and develop their own spiritualities. In the next section of this chapter, I review the work of two influential modern theologians: Dorothee Soelle and Gustavo Gutiérrez. I demonstrate the degree to which they speak about God in relation to the suffering poor. I also propose that this manner of speaking has increased the likelihood that Christians will report having spiritual experiences with the suffering poor. That, then, will be one answer to the question of why people experiencing homelessness may wound a housed Christian with love.

Dorothee Soelle

Though less well known than her German contemporaries Jürgen Moltmann and Johann Baptist Metz, Dorothee Soelle left an indelible mark on Christian theology. *Suffering*, written in the aftermath of Auschwitz and the subsequent "death of God," is her most popular work. Much of Soelle's work is an attempt to change the way Christians imagine God. In her view, the conception of God as an omnipotent being needed to change.

For Soelle, there are two problems that result from belief in divine omnipotence. The first problem is connected to God. She argues that it creates a god whose power is vindicated through human powerlessness.[15] The second problem concerns the effect this god has on individuals. Essentially, this divine imaginary engenders a willingness to suffer and an unwillingness to ask questions about suffering. Ultimate desire is constituted as submission to an alien power. "Why God sends affliction is no longer asked," Soelle writes. "It is sufficient to know he causes it."[16] People become powerless at the hands of an all-powerful God who uses suffering as a disciplinary tactic. No protest against suffering is expressed. "In this particular thought-world," Soelle continues, "the idea does not surface that one should battle suffering and eliminate its causes."[17] Not only does this God alienate a person from themselves, God also alienates them from other people. "What this Christian theism has succeeded in producing can be characterized as 'insensitivity to human misery' and thereby 'contempt for humanity,'" Soelle argues.[18] The result is that people end up worshiping their executioner and glorifying their powerlessness.

In effect, Soelle disentangled suffering from God. She argued that suffering and God go together like oil and water: not at all. This theological position doesn't mean that suffering cannot serve a positive function. To desire a life without suffering is to desire death. What matters is one's relationship to suffering and whether that relationship produces love. "Suffering," Soelle contends, "makes one more sensitive to the pain in the world. It can teach us to put forth a greater love for everything that exists."[19] For Soelle, this requires transforming suffering into a purposeful activity through a kind of mystical openness to it. "It is the mystic sufferer," according to Soelle, "who opens his hands for everything coming his way. He has given up faith in and hope for a God who reaches into the world from outside, but not hope for changing suffering and learning from suffering."[20]

Suffering can be transformed, then, when it teaches one to love. The transformation of suffering, however, according to Soelle, is contingent upon the poor and those suffering most brutally from abuses of power. Christians are called to their suffering. For Soelle, it is, in a real way, where Jesus is being crucified in present time. It is where Christians can hear God's mourning voice teaching them how to love. "The poor are the teachers," Soelle wrote in a later book, *Theology for Skeptics*. "From them, not from those who have possessions, make decrees, or hold power, we learn what it means to believe in God."[21]

Gustavo Gutiérrez

Gustavo Gutiérrez is a world-renowned theologian and Dominican priest. He is regarded as a founder of liberation theology in Latin America, which is one of the most significant theological movements of our time. For Gutiérrez, liberation theology must be rooted in a concrete spiritual experience with the poor. Like Soelle, he argues that the suffering poor teach us how to love and therefore how to be Christian in the world today.

In *We Drink from Our Own Wells*, for example, Gutiérrez is fundamentally uninterested in the question of how an all-powerful and loving God might permit suffering. Instead, what is at stake for Gutiérrez is an adequate response to the death-dealing poverty in which vast majorities of people in Latin America live. What is at stake is a transformation of the situation that people living in poverty are in so that they may have the option to choose life. Further, what is at stake is the response to Jesus's call in the form of the church's solidarity with the poor in their pursuit of life in the face of death in Latin America. That is, the very possibility of the Christian life is at stake.

The response Gutiérrez develops begins with three rejections. First, he rejects "idealized poverty" in which the suffering of impoverished people is used for pastoral, theological, and spiritual purposes. Gutiérrez calls for a spirituality that is grounded in the real suffering of real bodies whose lives hang in the balance. Second, Gutiérrez's spirituality rejects two prevalent forms of Christian spirituality widely practiced in the church: one that leaves the world behind in the pursuit of God and another that focuses on the interior life of individual Christians. What Gutiérrez seeks, in *We Drink from Our Own Wells*, is a synthesis between contemplation and action.

Gutiérrez is known less for his work on spirituality than for theology. The distinction is, for him, however, a vital one. For Gutiérrez, theology is a discursive reflection on spiritual experience. It is secondary. Spirituality, on the other hand, is about a particular experience of Christ. It comes first. It is what motivates Christian action and what good theology depends upon. Successful liberation theology, therefore, and an adequate response to the real suffering taking place in Latin America, hinges on spiritual experience. It is the well from which we drink.

While Gutiérrez believes in a universality of spiritual experience, he argues that the experience of Christ is always particular. "At the root of every spirituality," he writes, "there is a particular experience that is had by concrete persons living at a particular time. The experience is both proper to them and yet communicable to others."[22] For Latin Americans like Gutiérrez, to encounter the poor is to encounter Jesus. To follow Jesus is to be in solidarity with the poor in their pursuit of life. Needed for liberation theology, therefore, is a spiritual experience in which one encounters the face of the poor. Gutiérrez writes: "To be followers of Jesus requires that they [Christians] walk with and be committed to the poor; when they do, they experience an encounter with the Lord who is simultaneously revealed and hidden in the faces of the poor."[23]

The last point is essential. Jesus is revealed in the poor, but Jesus is not commensurate with the poor. The entities do not collapse into one. Indeed, the encounter with the poor is contingent upon an experience of God's "gratuitous love." A real encounter with the poor is not possible without this liberative love beyond human power. A living experience of gratuitous love, which enables one to love purely, and not force an alien will upon someone, is what it means to love authentically and without force. Gutiérrez again: "The other is our way for reaching God, but our relationship with God is a precondition for encounter and true communion with the other."[24]

It is clear that Soelle and Gutiérrez are not interested in explaining suffering in relation to a powerful and loving God. Instead, their concern is with how suffering can be transformed and replaced with love. It is also clear that both Soelle and Gutiérrez argue that suffering can be transformed and replaced with love in the context of a spiritual relationship with the suffering poor. Since the death of the theodicy project, this has been a strong characteristic in modern Christian theology. To a considerable extent, their theology suggests that God can be discovered, experienced, and pursued in the context of a relationship with the suffering poor. The poor reveal where love is lacking, and therefore where God is, and this lack is used to motivate and materialize Christian love. For many Christian theologians today, the experience of suffering is not a problem in relationship to a powerful and loving God. It is a solution.

christianity: why it works and its problem of presence

In the last chapter, I proposed that Christians have a problem of presence. The problem of presence is how Christians sustain belief in a seemingly immaterial God. I also demonstrated that Christians have resolved their problem of presence through culturally meaningful practices. Christianity has worked—and continues to work—because Christians have found salient ways to make belief in a loving God real and because this embodied belief is intrinsic to the needs people have for love, meaning, and belonging. Among a small group called the Friday Masowe apostolics in Africa, as Matthew Engelke's ethnography *A Problem of Presence* demonstrates, the problem of presence is resolved through their rejection of the Bible and acceptance of God within a polyphony of sound that is interpreted within a community of practice. In Tanya Marie Luhrmann's ethnography on charismatic evangelicals in the United States, Luhrmann demonstrates that the problem of presence is resolved through a series of sophisticated practices that place the experience of God within the human mind. Based on my fieldwork with street ministers in Seattle, it seems to me that people who are homeless help some housed Christians resolve their problem of presence. People who are homeless, in other words, help make Christianity work. In the context of a relationship with someone who is homeless, which many theologians posit as spiritually vital, Christians come to experience that a personally loving God is real, active in the world, and emotionally convincing.

Of course, people who are homeless do not *invariably* help Christians resolve their problem of presence. No doubt countless Christians have lost their faith by witnessing the abject suffering that people who are homeless experience. Notwithstanding, the sentiment that people experiencing homelessness help make Christianity work is captured well in an April 1964 article by a founder of the Catholic Worker Movement, Dorothy Day. "The mystery of the poor is this," Day wrote. "They are Jesus and what you do for them you do for him. It is the only way we have of knowing and believing in our love. It is an act of faith, constantly repeated."[25]

Some may read this chapter and suggest that street ministers and other housed Christians are instrumentalizing people who are homeless: using them, that is, for their own spiritual advantage. That assumption would be a mistake. The street ministers I know are deeply concerned about the danger of making their work about themselves. They describe the problem as being like a temptation to sin and counsel that humility is a grounding disposition for street ministry. Beyond reason and their human frailties, the street ministers I know desire to make a positive and lasting difference in the lives of people who are homeless. They want by grace their love to be loving. In the final section of this chapter, I reflect on the difference a street minister's spiritual love for people who are homeless makes. And in the concluding chapter, I join them in struggling with the question of what it will take for their love to become more loving. I begin here with a story about Daisey, a woman living on the streets of Seattle.

daisey (and the limits of christian love on the streets)

Daisey is sitting in a busy street corner in Capitol Hill. There is a yellow dog in her lap. Homeless Freddie is playing guitar. With several young adults who are homeless, I am sitting against a wall: we are listening to the music, watching people walk by, and asking people for their spare change.

'Why did you have to go to jail, Wit? Why did you have to leave me alone?' I overhear Daisey ask this question aloud, through fits of tears and rage, to herself, or Something Out There, over and over again.

The police say Wit hit Daisey. They arrested him for domestic violence and put him in jail. Daisey and Wit claim that is untrue. They say they like kinky sex and don't have a place, being houseless, to be human like that together.

On that same street corner, Daisey practices magic. She describes the old, uneven patch of concrete as if it is holy ground; she talks about her finger as a wand that casts spells. The last spell she cast was meant to dispel two men. They were fighting over her, she said, and she wanted them to go away. Sometimes, for at least a little while, the magic seems to work.

Today, she is casting a spell on the table we are eating on at Chipotle. We are doing an interview because Daisey is upset and, knowing that I study spirituality on the streets, wants to tell me something that happened recently.

A few mornings ago, Daisey remembers, as morning sunlight moved onto the streets, a brown sedan drove slowly past her. Then it turned around, drove back, and parked right in front of her. Startled, Daisey watched the driver roll down his car window. Smiling, the man told Daisey that Jesus loves her. Then he drove away again. In protest, she raised her middle finger in the air and spoke softly under her lips: "Asshole."

Later that night, something more upsetting happened. Her boyfriend, she said, became possessed by a demon. Daisey told me she didn't think it was a bad reaction to the meth they smoke together. What happened, she said, was different, unique, and scary: he spoke in tongues, his eyes changed color, and he tried to rape her. None of those things had happened before. When Daisey tells me this story her body appears like a teakettle about to whistle, as though she were a steel container needing to expel what's been boiling inside.

What really frightened Daisy was not the stranger's remark about Jesus's love or the sexual assault. What frightened her most, she said, had to do with what both events, happening so close together, might signify about the voices she hears.

Daisey thought she had it all figured out: the voices she hears, which she thought were Satan and God, fighting a war for her soul, were not real. With some psychiatric care, she came to experience them as parts of herself that need medical care. Today, she is no longer sure. She is afraid that the voices might be real and that 'The Universe is sending me a message or something.'

In the absence of adequate institutional care, many people with serious mental health problems are homeless. Precise numbers are hard to establish, but conservative studies indicate that around one in every four homeless individuals suffer in this way. For some of these people, spirituality is deeply beneficial.[26] One reason spirituality is helpful for people with mental illness is that it can help people make meaning out of difficult situations. Meaning, as David A. Snow and Leon Anderson found in their ethnography of people experiencing homelessness in Texas, is as rudimentary a human need as food and shelter.[27] There are others, however, for whom certain kinds of spirituality, and the meanings they evoke, can be devastating. Daisey's experience is one example. In her case, being told that she is loved by God, something street ministers at Operation Nightwatch and other housed Christians frequently do, meant something different from what was intended. Unwittingly, sharing a prophecy about divine love contributed to a frightening psychological experience.

Suffering, we must remember, is not a tame animal. It can feed on the things we'd least expect.

A sense of meaning, however, is not the only difference a housed Christian's spiritual love might make in the lives of people who are homeless. I remind the reader of River, with whose story I began this chapter. The one thing she said she needed from me was my company. Explicitly, she said she didn't want me to be 'one of those people' trying to fix her. It is one of the most common sentiments I observed during my fieldwork. Many people who are homeless pine for positive human relationships. The need to be in personal and loving relationships does not usually go away on the streets. Housed Christians who provide spiritual care to homeless individuals often meet this need. It is part of the tremendous good they do. Overlooking the good that street ministers do renders our efforts to combat homelessness inept. Street ministers provide personal, beautiful, and humanizing presence in a crushingly dehumanizing context. They open a door to a real reality where hope dwells within and transcends the overwhelming weight of soul woundedness. As I walked the streets of Seattle with Rick and Ben, I frequently saw the unhoused people they hang out with come alive with the joy that arises from being in relationship with them. I experienced this joy, too, when I became homeless in 2023. Wherever I was, Ben made time to just be with me. His love, which he says is not his own, held me tenderly in the world when I neither felt at home nor had one.

Building relationships with people who are homeless, however, creates risks. As I described in the first chapter, most people who are homeless have painful wounds stemming from broken relationships. Many walk a fine line between life and death. Another perceived betrayal, or broken relationship, can be like a wind that pushes someone over that line. Zarathustra wrote this on Facebook after Red's death: "I told myself that I'd end tonight by either going to a psych ward or putting a bullet in my head. Fuck life. The next friend who betrays me may very well get killed."

Christianity is more than a leap into the absurd; it is an opening of the heart.[28] Christian spirituality may require emotional labor that is risky for people who are living under tremendous distress in unloving social conditions. Asking someone to open their heart, therefore, might cause unexpected harm. The summons to become open to love, be it numinous or human, is a solemn and hardly known peril when the social infrastructure needed to support, protect, and nourish that open heart is nonexistent.

Conclusion: A More Loving Love

a girl on a bridge

'There's a girl on the bridge,' he says. 'She threw a can of beer in the river. I think she might jump.'

Love is engraved on the bridge. "Pat Loves Erica" is written in pink and purple chalk. In yellow and blue is an imperative: "Love Earth." A heart is drawn in black sharpie next to the word "more."

Love is hanging on to the bridge. Several "love locks" dangle on the bridge's support cables. Lovers write their names on a padlock, latch it onto the bridge, and throw the key into the river.

Some have merely written their names: "Jesse," "Suzanna," "Jungle Boy." An image of a penis is etched in spray paint. A small bomb is drawn into the word "revolution."

She is wearing torn blue jeans, showing her olive knee, and a black jacket. A beanie covers her forehead. She has green eyes. On the bottom of her chin there is acne, red.

'Excuse me,' she says aggressively, 'do you have any drugs?' 'I don't,' I say. 'Well fuck it, then.'

A kind of wounded gravity pulls her to the ledge. Her hands clutch the concrete safety wall. Solemnly, like it might be the last time, she looks down at the river.

I am on my way to a coffee shop to work on this book. I am also on the phone with Ben, the street minister from Operation Nightwatch. We are talking about an event we are organizing at the University of Washington, which will

CONCLUSION: A MORE LOVING LOVE

query the difference faith-based ministries make with people experiencing homelessness in Seattle.

I tell Ben about the girl on the bridge. 'I will call you back,' I say. 'Just have a conversation with her,' he says. 'Be present.'

I walk toward her and wonder where she is. Though she is standing in front of me, I don't know where she is.

'I am going through spiritual warfare,' she says. 'It's real even if you can't see it.' 'I am so sorry,' I say. 'What can I do to help?'

'If you *actually* want to help,' she says, 'then call my *fucking* mother.' 'Tell her,' she says, convulsing, 'what she is doing to me.' Her mother, she tells me, is using heroin again.

She leans over the bridge, takes frantic breaths. Mucus drips from her nose. 'Don't misunderstand me,' she says, 'if she hadn't kicked me out of the house for using drugs, I wouldn't have become homeless and learned who I really am. I love my mother.'

She wipes the mucus from her nose and lips and walks toward me. 'Why aren't you calling her? Fuck you,' she says. 'You don't care. I am going to jump.'

'Okay,' I say, 'what's her number?'

She walks back to the concrete safety wall, lifts her left leg over and then her right. She sits down. Her feet hang free. I look past her feet and onto the river, past the river and onto my neighborhood of Peaceful Valley.

'I am so sorry,' she says. 'I am so sorry.'

'Will I be okay?'

I dwell in her question, unknowing what to say.

No longer asking, she demands that I bless her suicide: 'Tell me that I will be okay!'

I think she will be okay, but I don't want her to die. In hope and fear of the world to come into her, I say: 'It will be okay if you stay. You will be okay. Everything will be okay.'

Again and again, she tells me that she is sorry, that she is so sorry. Again and again, I tell her she is forgiven, that all will be well.

I look toward the street, past the other side of the railing. It is a cold December afternoon in Spokane. I moved here three months ago to get presence-making distance from the streets of Seattle. Being here, I thought, would help me be there and bring you with me, dear reader: so that we might see the streets of Seattle more clearly and discern how to take contemplative, loving action.

Snowflakes fill the air, fall to the ground, and melt. Cars drive past. A man on a bike speeds up to us. I mouth silently the words, 'help, help,' but he isn't looking at me. Everyone I see is moving too fast to notice us.

'You're not calling her,' she says, 'so obviously you don't care. She needs to see what she is doing to me. Call her right now or I am going to jump.'

I say, 'I would feel safer if you stepped back off the ledge. I am scared,' I say. Seeing me afraid punctures her and calls a different part of her forward.

She steps off the ledge: '5 . . . 0 . . . 9 . . .'

Two police officers arrive. One officer reaches out to Henrietta with his hand, seeming gentle and kind. When she reaches back, he grabs her hands, forcefully, turns her around, and puts her in handcuffs.

'Get off me,' she yells. 'Don't do this. I don't want this,' she cries. 'Stop.'

She says the officer made her touch his dick. 'Fucking pervert,' she yells. 'He is sexually harassing me. Someone help!'

'Jesus,' she cries over and again, 'please help me.' 'I think, sweetheart,' the officer says, 'that this is his answer.'

vision mirror

Henrietta Snow. When the police came to the bridge, they asked for her name. She spoke her name confidently with her soul wounds and like she knew its power: 'Henrietta Snow.'

A few weeks later, I went online to see if she had a digital presence.

I found her Facebook. Most recently, Henrietta had posted a music video. The video is called "I'm a Mess." It is by pop artist Bebe Rexha. In the video, Bebe plays a woman distraught, grieving love's absence. Here's the refrain:

I'm a mess, I'm a loser
I'm a hater, I'm a user
I'm a mess for your love, it ain't new[1]

Though "a mess," Bebe assures herself that everything will be okay. It will be okay, she says, because she loves herself and her therapist says there is a bright side. It will be a good, good life. Bebe repeats this refrain as she's wheeled into a psychiatric hospital on a stretcher.

In another post, Henrietta invites people to her newly created YouTube presence. 'I love you guys so much,' she wrote. 'I just made my first YouTube channel. Feeling fragile, but you keep me going. I'm not letting this dream slip away. I'm not afraid of a thousand eyes if there's five hundred smiles.'

I watch Henrietta's video. It's called "Vision Mirror." She looks almost identical to Bebe Rexha in "I'm a Mess."

Henrietta says that she created the channel to recover from mental illness and addiction. She says it's been her dream to create this digital space and that her dream kept her alive. 'So here I am.'

'It's the beginning of the journey,' she says. 'I want you to join me.'

Henrietta promises that we'll do good things together: color, read stories, sing. 'We will have a good connection,' she promises.

The wall behind her is bare except for a line of Christmas lights and a piece of paper. There is in front of her a mirror. On her lap there is paint and a pack of stickers that she purchased from Walmart. Henrietta quips, smiling, that she's 'ballin' on a budget right now.'

In our first video together, Henrietta says, we will create "a vision mirror." Transforming her mirror will help her see herself. Looking in the mirror with intention and our presence will manifest who she really is.

The first three stickers she puts on the mirror are *thankful, friendship,* and *grateful*. She is *thankful* for the realization that, when one door closes, another one opens. That she can be the key in a room full of locks. Knowing you are a key, she says, is better than staring at a door as though you can never open it. *Friends*. They are essential. Sometimes she can be a lone wolf, which is one of her "spirit animals." Still, it's important for her to have a pack. *Grateful*. It's in a moment. That's where it lives. And it's not the same as *thankful*. Thankfulness comes after gratitude. Or maybe it's the other way around. Anyway. What she knows for certain is that gratitude is the opposite of fear. And that it's like faith.

She pulls out a vape pen, inhales, and says she quit smoking. She bends close to the camera and asks if we saw down her shirt. 'Remember modesty girl,' she says, laughing.

Henrietta soaks her fingers in rose gold paint and moves them onto the mirror.

'Fuck,' she says. 'I ruined it.'

Henrietta takes a hit, inhales, soothes herself and puts *love* on the mirror. 'For me,' she says, '*love* is the only language, the only law.'

Henrietta sticks *dream* on the mirror. She tells us that she promised to make her *dream* come alive. 'It will be hard,' she says, 'but it's possible if you help me.' We, the people she cannot see but hopes will be there, keep her going.

Henrietta says she is a very spiritual person. She is spiritual, she clarifies, but not religious. 'I am a rebel,' she says. 'And I am not irrelevant.'

The camera is like a bridge.

Henrietta asks us a question: 'Will you forgive me if I share myself like this? Right now, I am so fragile. Ah,' she sighs. 'I think I was made to understand, but not to be understood.'

Henrietta pulls the paper off the wall, which is a page from a coloring book with a mirror drawn on it. She reads a quote beneath the mirror: "Restoring treasures to their former glory is his passion."[2]

Henrietta places her hand on her heart, softly. She tapes the page back on the wall and smiles.

'Is the audio okay? Am I coming through? Can you guys hear me? I am going to put this here,' she says. Henrietta places *create* on the mirror. *Create* is next to the gold blotch that, she feared, ruined her project. It is next to *love*. Looking in the mirror she sees herself and reads: "Create love."

a spiritual practice of loving social power for the violently uprooted

In this book, I wondered about the spiritual lives of young adults experiencing homelessness. I tried to render a reliable account of what spirituality is like on the streets, what difference it makes, and why it's important. In chapter 1, I described ethnography as a quest for an adequate understanding of the Other's presence for love that invites faithful practices of unknowing.[3] Ethnography, however, is not ultimately a question about the ethnographer. Though the ethnographer's self-implication is inescapable, I have been practicing an ethnography that is interested in understanding different creatures who are suffering unnecessarily in different local worlds for a more loving love. Though I look in my own mirror to see the Other, I labor to show you glimpses of Henrietta's mirror. I want you to imagine what it's like to see into Henrietta's mirror and be alive in her. I want you to understand, feel, touch with loving fingers her social wounds that are soul deep. Henrietta, Henrietta's bridge, and Henrietta's mirror are at stake. In Henrietta and her mirror there is a story for us to live together in a spirit of friendship about people who live homeless and on the streets.

In this final chapter, after having rendered the presence of the human and nonhuman creatures I got to know in the preceding chapters, and how they tend the social wounds that wound them soul deep through spiritual practices to cultivate a life still worth living, I hope to facilitate what Elizabeth Liebert calls "contemplative action."[4] Contemplative action looks at the Other slowly and lovingly to love the Other more lovingly. It wants to ease the Other's suffering and grow their happiness and love in the world. While appreciating the diverse notes we each must play to respond to homelessness, so that everyone has a home, always, I play here one small note. This note, which I pray becomes attuned with your note to create a more loving love, freely, hopes to transform how we become present on the streets in our own everyday lives. I propose accessible, adaptable ways of being on the streets together that create efficacious love within ourselves, our relationships, and our political economy. What is at stake in this chapter is the cultivation of a spiritual practice that aims to materialize the loving presences that people who are homeless are already pursuing, a practice I call *a spirituality of loving social power for the violently uprooted*. For this spirituality of loving social power to become more real, I propose that, on the streets in our own everyday lives, we tend our interior landscapes, creatively deepen our friendships with human and nonhuman creatures, and engage in nonviolent direct action to manifest an Economic Bill of Rights. I also invite the global Christian church to create monthly, interdenominational meetings in candlelit silence that gather Christians across and into their differences for one year: to simply be lovingly present with each other and listen compassionately to what others are going through.

People who are homeless suffer from absences of love. Homelessness is fundamentally a collective failure to help love become present in the lives of others. Loving ourselves and each other on our streets—where often we carry, and wound with, the subtle, uprooting hatreds our present world is plagued by—is a direct response to homelessness. Love generates love in and across

various dwelling places. Conversely, hatred is a ubiquitous, contagious everyday practice that uproots us from ourselves and each other—and creates homelessness. I invite creative, authentic practices that transform our streets into places for a more loving love, where we walk slowly and wish for our own happiness, smile sincerely at a stranger and make time to listen to their story, and nurture the political will for national and international economic revolution. I begin (again) the construction of a spiritual practice of loving social power for the violently uprooted by turning to a friend in history: and a further invitation that we experience history as one of love's companions in the present.

jesus and the person whose back is against the wall

Howard Thurman is one of the most important and least recognized spiritual teachers of the twentieth century. Born of two former slaves, Thurman served at Morehouse and Spelman Colleges, Howard University, and Boston University. He founded the first interracial, interfaith, interdenominational church in the United States—the Church for the Fellowship of All Peoples in San Francisco. Thurman was friend and minister to prominent civil rights leaders such as Martin Luther King Jr., James Farmer, and Jesse Jackson. He is considered an ideological architect of the nonviolent presences within the civil rights movement. It is said that King carried in his pocket a copy of Thurman's most popular book, *Jesus and the Disinherited*, and would read it before a demonstration.

Jesus and the Disinherited was written in 1949. It is a response to a question that made a home in Thurman: "What does the religion of Jesus have to say to the man [sic] whose back is against a wall?"[5] By "the man whose back is against the wall," Thurman is referring to people who "are poor, disinherited, dispossessed."[6] He is decidedly uninterested in what the religion of Jesus tells the person whose back is against the wall to do for others, but concerned with what balm the religion of Jesus has for the wounds on one's back.[7] For Thurman, the need for an answer that really makes a difference is paramount. He wrote: "The search for an answer to this question is perhaps the most important religious quest of modern life."[8]

The question thrust itself into Thurman in the fall of 1935. It wounded him and became a companion that he held and tended. Thurman was on a "pilgrimage of friendship" with American students in Ceylon. After giving a talk about the relationship between Christian theology and civil disabilities in the United States, Thurman was invited to have coffee with a school principal. The principal, a Hindu, invited Thurman for coffee because he was perplexed. He could not understand how a Black person could be a Christian, let alone speak as though Christianity had something good to say. The principal recounted facts Thurman painfully knew: Africans were taken from their land as slaves by Christians; there was a slave ship named "Jesus"; the institution of slavery was legitimated by Christians; self-professing Christians *still* segregate, lynch, and burn Black people. "I do not wish to seem rude to you. But, sir," the principal said to Thurman, "I think you are a traitor to all the darker peoples of the earth. I am wondering what you, an intelligent man, can say in defense of your position."[9]

Thurman listened. He tried to understand what was at stake in the question. Thurman's eventual answer was threefold. First, he offered a careful reading of Jesus's life that demonstrates that Jesus (and his people, the Jews) lived with their backs against the wall. Jesus grew up and conducted his ministry, that is, as a poor Jew who faced extensive social woundedness. Thurman's point is that, regardless of where the Christian religion stands, the historical Jesus stands in solidarity with the person whose back is against the wall.

The second part of Thurman's answer concerns Jesus's specific response to the social woundedness he experienced. According to Thurman, Jesus "focused on the urgency of a radical change in the inner attitude of the people.

He recognized fully that out of the heart are the issues of life and that no external force, however great and overwhelming, can at long last destroy a people if it does not first win the victory of the spirit against them." This intimate power makes Thurman controversial. Some figures worried that he cared more for the personal than the political—to the detriment of the personal. He continued nonetheless to emphasize the point, suggesting that the heart of Jesus's response was not focused on the social world but rather on "the inward center" of the person: "With increasing insight and startling accuracy [Jesus] placed his finger on the 'inward center' as the crucial arena where the issues would determine the destiny of his people."[10] Jesus's urgent question, Thurman argues, therefore, is what a Jewish person's interior relationship toward Rome should be. The question could not be answered from outside a person; it had to be lived authentically within. "This," Thurman writes, "is the position of the disinherited in every age. What must be the attitude toward the rulers, the controllers of political, social, and economic life?"[11]

The third part of Thurman's answer to the question of what the religion of Jesus has to say to the person whose back is against the wall concerns the inner attitude that Thurman thought Black people should cultivate. For Thurman, Jews shared the wounded psychology of Black people in the United States. In Thurman's analysis, Black people were wounded by fear, deception, and hatred. These were the "hounds of hell" that "track the trail of the disinherited."[12] The wounded interiority must be tended, Thurman thought. Jesus preached an immanent salvation of infinite rootedness in God's image, honesty, and love. This immanent salvation of the spirit was a cure for the wounds, toothmarks left by the hounds of hell. While Thurman did not abandon the social origin of the hounds of hell—the proverbial gates from which they are bred and let loose—he insisted that the ultimate path of liberation is within.

When I stood with Henrietta on the bridge, Thurman's question about what the religion of Jesus has to say to the person whose back is against the wall pulsed through me. I experienced the question as an unsettling affective force. I searched within myself—and, by extension, the tradition of Christianity that nurtured, confused, wounded, and loved me—for an answer. For an answer that was actually a real, living presence that could breathe transformative love upon Henrietta. Having one's back constantly against the wall, physically and existentially, is a common experience on the streets. Henrietta's back, however, was no longer against a wall. Her back had been thrust from the wall to a bridge. The question that became salient to me was what the religion of Jesus has to say to the woman who is going to jump off a bridge; to the woman whose life had been ravaged by a confluence of social wounds; to the woman who has almost lost faith in the world; to the woman who has nearly lost hope that she can find a life worth living; to the woman who has been fucked and asks you for drugs and then to bless her suicide; to the woman who is terrorized by the mirror; to the woman who has created a virtual bridge for us to enter into her with love.

slow down, breathe, and wonder compassionately about yourself

Responding spiritually and otherwise to homelessness can begin again (and again) with creative slownesses. To love more lovingly we can bring ourselves gentle into the healing rivers of what's slow. We can wade and wait in this river of the slow without an answer, letting whatever is present in us be an answer that we love.

I invite you, dear reader, to slow down for three minutes—and experiment with a loving slowness. Please adapt this practice until it becomes authentically free and fruitful for you.

Breathe deep and slow. Simply notice your breath as you breathe for one minute. Imagine your breath as a Friend. Invite this Friend to carry into your heart a word of tenderness that may arise freely, that may help you love yourself in the realities of your own life. Tenderly touch your heart as you breathe this word into you.

Next, for another minute, remember the last time you were on a public street or sidewalk. Picture yourself there, however long ago: the colors you wore; the smells and sounds that came into you; the creatures and objects you may have touched, even by accident; the art you felt. Be present and slow with this memory. Continue to breathe deep. With your memory, move your attentiveness up and down your (always beautiful) body and offer your word of tenderness to your feet, to your knees, to your stomach, to your chest, to your neck, to your face.

Third and finally: for one last minute, draw or paint or dance or photograph your word of tenderness. Notice if and how it becomes real.

listen and look

I return slowly, tenderly to Thurman's question and the presence of love in history. What does the religion of Jesus have to say to people experiencing homelessness? To Henrietta, on the bridge and in front of the mirror? To the human and nonhuman creatures living homeless near you? I invite you, dear reader, to live this question with me slowly and to appreciate the answers that arise within you. Before I answer this question, I propose that we allow ourselves to be gathered together into contemplative silence. Ad nauseum, Christians have spoken. Christian words have often been violent and dehumanizing. In history we see not only the presence of love, but the hateful wounds Christianity has inflicted upon the world. Most street kids I spent time with didn't think the religion of Jesus could speak lovingly to their condition. It was as though they prayed for our silence.

As I was learning how to be present on the streets of Seattle, I met one afternoon in San Francisco with Wendy Farley, one of the most influential theologians of our time. Before we started talking, we sat together in the silence, held tenderly by the beauty of sunshine, birdsong, and towering trees. We breathed together. Speaking from the silence, Wendy told me something surprising, and that reoriented my practice theology. 'It seems to me,' Wendy said, 'that perhaps the most Christian thing a Christian can do today is simply listen compassionately to what others are going through.' I began to discover through Wendy's embodied teaching that the religion of Jesus could begin not by speaking to others but by creating spaces where authentic, life-giving listening and compassionate, creative presences might become possible. Perhaps, sometimes, love begins by humbling oneself before the words and wounds in the heart of another.

On the streets of Seattle, Samantha taught me that "just listening" is an act of real love. Listening, she told me, is not a trivial but an integral response to people experiencing homelessness. 'No one takes the time to listen,' she often said. 'It's something that makes me feel like a human.' Samantha delighted in just listening to me as well, and helped me understand the mutual, reciprocal nature of listening and love. There is a hunger on the streets not only to be loved efficaciously, but to let love freely love in return.

The day before I left Seattle, I met Samantha and her dog at Target in downtown. We spanged with our backs against the wall and tried to manifest money for her and her boyfriend to get well. In the evening, Samantha put a large paper bag—filled with dog food, bread, peanut butter, and an ugly orange sweater—in the alley. 'I am sure someone who needs this will find it,' she says.

We ride the bus to the needle exchange. 'The needle exchange is one of the only places that cares,' she says. Samantha tells me they provide clean needles, naloxone, and instructions about how to safely inject heroin. Years ago, Samantha's words would have struck me as a socially detrimental rationalization of drug use. 'I can't tell you how many lives this place has saved,' she says. 'And how amazing it feels that they don't judge you like everybody else.' As Samantha goes into the needle exchange, I see heroin addiction differently than I used to. I see a person I know, and love, struggling not to suffer—and trying to liberate others from their suffering as well.

Samantha exchanges her "dirties" for "cleans." We hop on another bus. We ride to her unsanctioned encampment. Her dog, Flower, is smiling. 'Flower,' Samantha says affectionately, 'I love you. Everyone loves you, Flower.' Samantha and I create intimacy through small talk. We look out the window and say how nice it is to feel the sun and how hard it seems to be a bus driver in Seattle. I am beguiled by the sincere kindness in her cadence. We get off the bus, thank our driver, and walk a mile to her encampment. 'Right now,' she says, embarrassed, 'this is the only place the police won't harass us.'

She unzips their tent. 'Paul's here, Steady,' she says.

Samantha has a Clorox wipe in her hands. 'Give me your hands,' she tells Steady. He places his hands in her hands. Tenderly Samantha cleans the dried blood on Steady's hands. 'Honey,' she says, 'you need to take better care of yourself.'

Samantha and Steady are dope sick. They argue about who gets to use first. 'You always go first,' Steady says. 'Well,' she responds, 'I am the one working for it.' 'Well,' he retorts, 'I am the one stuck here watching our shit.'

'I am sorry,' Samantha says, turning to me, 'that you have to hear this.'

Samantha's veins are 'busted.' Lately, her only good vein is in her neck—and she can't shoot on that part of her body, alone. Samantha told me that, if she didn't need to shoot in her neck, she and Steady wouldn't be together. 'Our relationship,' she told me, 'has become too toxic. I can't wait to be on my own again, man, and free.' Steady, though, is dreaming that they will sober up together at his brother's house, find jobs, and get a little place of their own in Capitol Hill. It is a hope that holds him in this world.

Samantha reaches into her jacket. She grabs a small baggie of heroin. Samantha pulls out a clean, a spoon, a piece of cotton, and a lighter. Samantha places the heroin on the spoon, flicks her lighter lit, and puts it under the spoon. I watch the heroin transform.

They are curious about what I've learned on the streets. We talk about freedom on the streets, how people hate religion, feeling stuck, manifestation, God, The Universe. I tell them I think spirituality on the streets is about finding a presence that will help people get through another day and believe a better future is possible. It's searching in the present, even in a dumpster, for a pulse of divine love.

'I can see that,' Samantha says.

The heroin is 'cooked.' Samantha pulls the heroin into the needle through the cotton. I tell Steady and Samantha that I am thinking a lot about love on the streets. 'Love,' Steady says, 'is when someone sticks with you no matter what.'

Steady looks for a vein on Samantha's body.

'Hold on,' Samantha says, 'let me say something.' Samantha looks at Steady and then at me. 'You need to be careful, though. Out here, everything you love goes away.'

Samantha takes off her jacket: one arm through slow and then the other. Steady reads her body carefully in agony. I notice a tattoo on Samantha's arm. In black cursive, it reads: "Every saint has a past; every sinner has a path."

Steady still can't find a vein. Her neck won't 'pop.' 'Fuck, Steady,' she says. 'I am so sick right now.' Samantha cries, places her face in her hands.

'I am sorry you have to see this,' she says. 'I am honored to be here,' I say.

'I am going to smoke it,' Samantha says. She grabs another small baggie of heroin, a piece of foil, a lighter. She crawls to the back corner of the tent, lights up, and hits.

Heroin smoke fills the space we share. 'I am sorry,' I say, terrified, 'I don't mean to be rude, but can this get me high?' 'No,' Samantha says, 'you won't get high. I promise.' 'I don't think you will,' Steady says.

It is getting late anyway. I tell Samantha and Steady that I need to go home and cram the rest of my stuff into my old BMW before I leave for Spokane in the morning. 'Can I ask you before I leave,' I say, 'what you think people should know about life on the streets? Can I ask you,' I say, 'how you think people might be more loving?'

'Basically,' Steady says, 'people need to know that we are still human.' 'Yeah,' Samantha says, 'tell people we are still human—and to stop treating us like eyesores.'

'Before you leave,' Samantha says, 'we have a little something for you.' 'It's not much,' Steady says. It's a blue envelope with, they say, a gift card for Target inside. 'We thought you could get something for your new home,' Samantha says. 'Don't be a stranger, Paul.'

how to look and listen

In "The Wound of Faith," I rendered Simone Weil as a companion for ethnographers trying to understand real difference in a local world to take contemplative, loving action. For Weil, love for the Other is about learning to look, ask an open question, and listen compassionately.[13] How simple, how complex, how beautiful, how transgressive, how revolutionary. A loving look does not look first to the Other and ask its own question. Instead, a loving look looks for the real question(s) the Other is already alive in. "This way of looking," Weil writes, "is first of all attentive. The soul empties itself of its own contents in order to receive into itself the being it is looking at."[14]

By experimenting with Weil's loving look as a practice of ethnographic inquiry, I found another hint about what the religion of Jesus might say to people who are homeless. In *We Drink from Our Own Wells*, Gustavo Gutiérrez writes that "authentic love tries to start with the concrete needs of the other and not with the 'duty' of practicing love. Love," Gutiérrez continues, "is respectful of others and therefore feels obliged to base its action on an analysis of their situation and needs."[15] In *Places of Redemption*, ethnographic theologian Mary McClintock Fulkerson proposes that theology begins from "the scene of a wound."[16] In starting from the wound, Fulkerson challenges traditional modes of theology that begin from historical belief and practice. For Fulkerson, a theology that doesn't start from the wound might be violence disguised as divine love. It is hard for my theological mind to imagine a greater tragedy. Fulkerson proposes further that, instead of forcing itself upon the world, theology should emerge from dilemmas encountered in real situations where the complex forces of social woundedness bear down on people through "interpersonal forms of obliviousness and aversiveness marked and sustained by larger social-political processes."[17] Ultimately, what is at stake for Fulkerson isn't merely the description of human woundedness. Instead, what really matters is a theological response that might engender social healing.[18]

Let us slow down and return to Rilke's insight in *Letters to a Young Poet*, where I began this book. On the streets and still, I am wondering what it means and looks like to render a more loving look; what it means and looks like to listen more lovingly to what someone experiencing homelessness is going through. When we look at someone who is homeless, what are we seeing? When we listen, what are we hearing? "I ask you," Rilke writes, "to have patience with all that is unresolved in your heart and try to love the questions themselves like closed rooms, like books written in a foreign language."[19]

I invite you to pause and close this book. Please. Do not pick it up again until you wander openly and compassionately with these questions on the streets of your own city or through a visual representation of homelessness. When you return, write freely on blank pages whatever these questions evoke in you. If possible, write until it's no longer free, in a closed room and in multiple languages. Notice what might change and become real to you.

When I look at someone who is homeless, what am I seeing? When I listen to someone who is homeless, what am I hearing?

Christianity is invariably complex. It is also beautifully and painfully diverse. A central Christian challenge, nevertheless, which transcends space and time, is seeing like the person of Jesus. Christians disagree about how Jesus saw the world, but few dispute the importance of seeing as he saw. He exemplifies the loving look. Since I am a Quakerly Christian, I turned my being openly toward the person of Jesus in learning how to render a loving look and cocreate a more loving love with people experiencing homelessness. In Jesus's look, every person had infinite worth. He looked lovingly upon friends, insiders, and outcasts. The derided compelled his look. In the Parable of the Lost Sheep, Jesus shows that a loving look looks for the missing, the forgotten, and the abandoned (Matt. 18). On his cross, he looks lovingly upon his executioners and pleads for their forgiveness (Luke 23). In Samaria, when he visits with the woman at the well, Jesus shows that a loving look looks through violent social distinctions. The loving look of Jesus scandalizes those who look lovingly upon him. Nothing repelled Jesus's loving look. In *Love in the Gospel of John: An Exegetical, Theological, and Literary Study*, Francis Moloney demonstrates that Jesus's ultimate concern was to make God known. His faith was in the manifestation of divine love in the world. Moloney argues Jesus labored to help God become known through his own actions: the tender touch of his hands, the movement of his feet, the affective pulse in his eyes.[20] Jesus made God known through his loving looks. When we see how Jesus saw, we see how the living God acts in the world today. Jesus's loving look made, makes God known. In God's seeing and experiencing the world, the contemporary teacher Richard Rohr writes, "everything belongs."[21]

What did Jesus see when he saw a person? What was he looking at when he looked at people? I propose that though parts of this question will and must remain hidden, we can see that Jesus did not see isolated individuals, separated from the world. Since he saw what was real and how divine love needed to become present, which is what was and remains at stake in his life, he saw individuals in complex, emergent relationships. The loving look of Jesus did not look away. Jesus saw the worlds people were in and the impact that condition had upon them; how it pushed their backs against the wall; how it penetrated, wounded their souls. Jesus looked at a condemned woman and saw her accusers. His loving look sent her accusers away (John 8:9). The loving look of

Jesus saw religious and economic exploitation transpiring in the Temple. He saw there how the social world was wounding the people he loved through a misguided love for money and unloving economics. He saw that the human person is a radically vulnerable, interdependent creature.

Some contemporary philosophers and scientists see like Jesus. Consider Christian Smith at Notre Dame and Judith Butler at UC Berkeley. Christian Smith writes that human personhood is an emergent phenomenon constituted by complex interactions with different entities.[22] For Judith Butler, the human person is a threshold, not a point of separateness.[23] The individual self, which is like a complex world in itself, depends on a network of social relationships, sensate creatures, nonhuman environments, and social infrastructures. The Buddhist teacher Thich Nhat Hanh makes this point as well—and extends it into nonhuman life. In *How to See*, Nhat Hanh writes about "interconnection" or "interbeing" as he practiced Qi Gong in front of a tree: "The tree offers me beauty, shade, and oxygen. I offer the tree my breath, my appreciation, and my joy. The tree and I are interconnected. When we look at a human being, we can look in exactly the same way, without exaggerating what is there or imagining what is not there."[24]

Despite the porous nature of human personhood, many people in the world are inclined to imagine the human person as a point of separateness: that we are islands floating apart from each other. It is for this reason that projects like Smith's, Butler's, and Nhat Hanh's emphasize human interdependency against what might be called "individualism." Individualism is an imperfect name for a powerful force that shapes how we see, hear, and experience the world. From individualism we learn—consciously and unconsciously—that flourishing is an individual accomplishment. Individualism is not a natural way of seeing the world even though it is often encouraged in brilliant thinkers like Rousseau, Kierkegaard, and Sartre. These thinkers want us to feel alone in the world. They suggest that we find ourselves when we disconnect and lose the crowd, which is often unlovingly denigrated. Certainly, psychoanalysis has encouraged a nosedive into the private places of one's own mind. Carl Jung once wrote that he could hardly believe the social world existed at all.[25] The economic power of neoliberalism is another champion of individualism. For the MIT philosopher Noam Chomsky, neoliberalism is also a force that shapes how we see, hear, and experience the world. Fundamentally, neoliberalism prioritizes profit over people.[26] It transforms people into consumers of infinite pleasure and perpetual dislike of the present reality; it allows "free markets" to govern human affairs and control the global order. Neoliberalism tells us to tell the poor to pick themselves up by their bootstraps even though they are barefoot.

Spirituality is floating in an ocean of individualism and neoliberalism.[27] The intensity with which people make a spiritual quest within themselves for a life worth living is not new, but it is without question that the 1960s ushered in a new interest in spirituality and, at the same time, questing for ultimate reality within. Former Harvard professors Timothy Leary and Ram Dass told a generation to "turn on, tune in, and drop out." The point was to find your true self in yourself with the illuminating (but profoundly risky) power of psychedelics. Today we live in a world where, as the Jesuit theologian Philip Sheldrake put it, "the word 'spirituality' immediately implies interiority."[28] Individualism and neoliberalism have also formed faith-based responses to people who are homeless. In her groundbreaking book on homelessness, for example, Laura Stivers demonstrates that most Christian communities respond inadequately to the problem of homelessness precisely because they are seduced by individualism and neoliberalism.[29] What we see here is that we are still learning how to see and that there are complex social forces at play in the world that intentionally obstruct a loving look for profit and power.

I am proposing that a loving look, and a spirituality of loving social power for the violently uprooted, requires that we look at what we are looking at more openly, deeply. A more loving look requires an adequate look. An adequate look sees what a person is and what internal and external forces constitute their power to act. If we do not see Henrietta's mother on the bridge, we are not really looking at her. The loving look looks to the world the person is situated in and the world that has made a home within them. If we do not hear in Henrietta's voice the global despair over the lack of affordable housing and healthcare, we are not really listening to her. If we do not see the relentless violences on the streets that cut deep into the soul and a person's interior capacities, we will not really see people who are homeless and what they are going through. If we do not hear the subtle cruelties and meannesses that Henrietta will hear outside herself and then repeat like a broken record inside herself, and how we may be complicit in them, we are not listening to her when she asks us to create love with her. Our love will then be impoverished and our collective capacity to flourish will be radically undermined. It will be evident that our seeing has not yet ripened as it did for Jesus. People will continue to say, as they often did to me in Seattle, that they hear a lot about how loving God is, but they do not feel this love for themselves.

Individualism and neoliberalism hinder the loving look. Through their lenses the social wounds penetrating people soul deep move out of view. They also become places for housed people to project their discontent, resentment, and need for a culturally sanguine scapegoat. Now we are disgusted with the poor. Now we think they deserve to be swept into cages and massive encampments.

Now we don't care when a political leader says they are violent insurrectionists who destroy beauty and prosperity. We see individual failure, not social failure. It's their own damn fault. We find a personal wound that requires a personal solution, not a social wound requiring a social solution. We are free from responsibility. For a loving look at people experiencing homelessness to be adequate, and to become itself a more loving spiritual practice, we must see that they are in a world that is sustained by the complex forces of social wounding.[30] The precise, evolving, and contested names of "the powers that be" matter less than our seeing the intimate and social nature of human personhood.[31]

A loving look must do more than see that people are in worlds that wound and obstruct their power, however. A loving look for a more loving love must create creative, wild, intersectional ways of being in this world so the enlivening power of the loving look can be unleashed, and experienced, more fully.[32]

For this, I think, and as Martin Luther King Jr. taught with his life, we need another wounding look: a wounding look that wounds nonviolently and lovingly.

a more loving love invites a more social spirituality

A more loving love invites a more social spirituality. A more social spirituality can make the loving look more real. It can wound us with love for a more loving love. History remains love's intimate companion in the present; it is aglow with wisdom. Indeed, Christian theologians have been devoting their lives to illuminating how social worlds obstruct the loving look for some time, even if they do not use the language I do. Consider Walter Rauschenbusch and the Social Gospel Movement from the early 1900s; liberation theologians such as Gustavo Gutiérrez and Oscar Romero; feminist theologians like Rosemary Radford Reuther and Dorothee Soelle; civil rights figures like Walter Wink, Cesar Chavez, and Martin Luther King Jr.; contemporary public theologians like bell hooks and Natalie Wigg-Stevenson, Cole Arthur Riley, and Bo Karen Lee. These theologians have been developing what I call *a social spirituality*. A social spirituality proposes that it is essential but incomplete to try to transform only the "inward center" of a person. It challenges Thurman's spirituality and says that Christian spirituality has had a lot to say about spiritual practices that enliven the inward center but not enough to say about spiritual practices that transform social systems that grievously wound it. Our "interior castles," as Teresa of Avila beautifully calls the human soul, are being relentlessly assaulted by social woundedness. Personal prayers cannot alone carry the person to the center of the castle where divine love can be experienced. A social spirituality proposes that we need a more revolutionary *social* Christian spirituality to help engender social healing. We need more spiritual practices that put our fingers on *the social soul*. By *social soul*, I refer to the public places where social power is generated and social woundedness is freed to ravage intimately. A social spirituality is informed by Walter Wink's proposition that we are mistaken when we do not recognize that institutions have spiritualities and that the Christian is called to nonviolently transform "fallen" and demonic" institutions that undermine a person's capacity to flourish.[33] A social spirituality heeds the invitation of Philip Sheldrake to liberate spirituality from a discourse on interiority, frame spirituality as a way of "living publicly," and treat urban living as "a spiritual practice [that] includes confrontation with everything that diminishes the human spirit."[34]

In her final book, *The Need for Roots*, written in a decline and hope for France, Simone Weil saw into the human person and found the social realities that orient people in the world and undermine their capacity to be. "To be rooted," Weil wrote, "is perhaps the most important and least recognized need of the human soul."[35] Uprootedness is an apt way to frame homelessness. The person whose back is against the wall is uprooted. They are uprooted from a humanizing physical dwelling. The person who is on the bridge considering suicide is uprooted. They are uprooted from a relational dwelling and an existential ground to experience a life worth living. The person terrorized in front of the mirror is uprooted; they are grieving the excruciating absence of love, an indispensable dimension of human flourishing.[36] Without us, Henrietta cannot see and become herself. And neither can you see and become yourself without Henrietta and her love for you.

In his last State of the Union Address, Franklin Delano Roosevelt observed that the United States needs an Economic Bill of Rights. He pleaded for one to ensure domestic peace, let alone international peace. For Roosevelt, the promise of the United States in the modern world was contingent on what an Economic Bill of Rights could manifest: fair-paying jobs, adequate health care, and affordable housing. For Roosevelt, safety from foreign power was not adequate to the country's promise of life, liberty, and the pursuit of happiness. Freedom of speech and religion were integral and profound freedoms for the health of an always fragile democracy, but they were not enough. Roosevelt mapped the path toward growth into peace, democracy, and freedom in unapologetically economic terms.

I propose that we learn to experience the streets as a site of ordinary and extraordinary spiritual practice where we expose and transform precarious social conditions, crumbling infrastructures, and uprootedness to create an Economic Bill of Rights. I propose that we are too dazzled by the divine light of the inward center and that we've missed the blazing sun of the social soul. For a more loving love, we need to improve and develop spiritual practices that wound *this social soul* to help heal inward centers, nonviolently.

Shortly before he was assassinated, Martin Luther King Jr. was engaged in a social protest to make real Roosevelt's economic dream. He called the effort "The Poor People's Campaign." Realizing after the victory of civil rights legislation that racial justice could not be achieved without economic justice (and demilitarization), King was gathering poor people to the National Mall in Washington, D.C. Strikingly, he wanted to create a new city there called "Resurrection City." King wanted poor people to occupy D.C. and, through nonviolent direct action, disrupt the major institutions of the United States until economic justice was a reality for all. King wanted the nation to be wounded with love—as it had been during the civil rights movement—by exposing the wounded and uprooted human faces of poverty. The look upon the wounds of poverty, he thought, would stir people's consciousness, awaken them for the struggle for social healing, and wound them with liberatory love.

For King, religion and spirituality are inadequate unless they labor lovingly for social justice. In *The Measure of a Man*, King writes: "It may be true that man cannot live by bread alone, but the mere fact that Jesus added the 'alone' means that man cannot live without bread. Religion must never overlook this, and any religion that professes to be concerned about the souls of men [sic] and is not concerned about the economic conditions that damn the soul, the social conditions that corrupt men, and the city governments that cripple them, is a dry, dead, do-nothing religion in need of new blood."[37]

I propose, friends, that we leave our homes, if we have them. I propose that we do not return home until we (all of us) have homes. I propose that we sit down on the streets with our unhoused neighbors: learn their names, their stories, and what it might take to create authentic friendship. I propose that we companion people who are homeless and poor into loving social power by nonviolently disrupting the violences of the United States economy. One solution to the problem of homelessness is temporary, collective homelessness that, I dream, can sprout and bloom into basic economic guarantees throughout the world in a spirit of friendship. In this companionship, we might discover a homecoming that is existential and material. We might discover anew a surprising, transforming presence of divine love in the world: and a far more radical and loving Christ-presence than free meals, recycled clothing, and warm coffee. The Poor People's Campaign, which has been revitalized by William Barber II, among many others, is one model for this experimental companionship home with the homeless for a more loving love.[38]

being alone with the wound of hatred

When I left Steady and Samantha's tent, I was ready to leave Seattle. The task at hand was to write about what I had experienced on the streets. Being in the field is a postcard experience, Clifford Geertz wrote. An anthropologist is made when they return from the field and render a world with others.[39] It's also true that I was ready to leave Seattle because the social woundedness on the streets had penetrated *me* soul deep. I could hardly hear another story of rejection, see another street kid get stuck, feel another heartbreak, and learn about someone else's untimely death. Stepping off the streets seemed like a step toward some kind of sanity.

In her masterful ethnographic study of charismatic evangelicals, Tanya Marie Luhrmann, on the final page of *When God Talks Back*, describes how her ethnographic fieldwork changed her. Though she did not become a Christian, Luhrmann's work, which involved practicing charismatic evangelical spirituality, rendered for her a transformative presence of unconditional love.[40] I went in search of a similar presence on the streets. I was led into, however, or found, perhaps, an unlivable otherwise. At the end of my fieldwork, I could perhaps tell you how to look lovingly at the world, but I did not feel a loving look on my own skin. I could stand on the streets and say loving words, and perhaps people would tell me that they felt heard and, even, by grace, something like love, but I didn't much feel love speaking in my heart.

Part of me hated the world and found the world more hateful. Justice, as most people practiced it, seemed like thinly veiled demands for vengeance. Christian spirituality, as most progressives encouraged it, seemed poisoned by contempt for conservatives—and bowed prostrate at altars of trendy, egocentric knowingness rather than humbled, quiet loving. The hatreds the world has been living through are evident in children's cartoons and video games. Hatred is play on the playground. It is a normalized practice and experience on social media, where cyberbullying is a contributing factor in the mental health crisis and suicide epidemic among adolescents. It is on the front page of the news all the time and it is an unconscious, monetized campaign pitch. Hatred has woven itself subtly into the fabric of everyday conversation. It is like a native language we speak and repeat to ourselves. The fluency of hatred is and has been bearing down upon us and we cannot bear it. It is breaking us apart and weaponizing our species. To liberate our love, it seems clear to me, we need to understand the pervasive nature and wound of hatred. We must, I think, help each other understand how to get free.

In 2018, I went to a Quaker meeting in Camas, Washington. The silence among Friends cultivated a healing space that allowed the wound of hatred within and around me to be seen and tended. I kept going to these meetings, kept meeting myself, and found myself not alone with a wound of hatred. I remember a woman emerging from a long silence by describing how the human species is acting like chickens that peck violently at another's wound. Why, she wondered, are we doing this to each other? I remember another woman saying that she cannot stop hating Donald Trump and that she doesn't know how to break free from a practice that is poisoning her own soul.

I think I thought that getting rid of all my belongings and moving to Hawaii without a place to live would free me from the wound of hatred. Alas, I soon found myself homeless and an unwitting part of a colonial project uprooting Indigenous Hawaiians from their homeland. Friends, like Ben from Operation Nightwatch, held me tenderly in this flesh as I found my own way home and onto this page.

friendship, the heart, and revolution

For Dorothy Day, the founder of the Catholic Worker Movement, "the greatest challenge of the day is: how to bring about a revolution of the heart, a revolution that has to start with each one of us." A friend and Sufi teacher said, at the onset of Russia's invasion of Ukraine, and to a class we were coteaching at Seattle University, that "the real war happening today is between our rib cages." "Good Trouble" John Lewis makes a similar proposition in his memoir, *Across That Bridge: A Vision for Change and the Future of America*. Lewis writes: "The most important lesson I have learned in the fifty years I have spent working toward the building of a better world is that the true work of social transformation starts within. It begins inside your own heart and mind."[41] A compelling global initiative and body of research suggests that Dorothy Day, my Sufi friend, and John Lewis are right: to realize global sustainability goals like ending poverty, reducing inequalities, and taking urgent climate action, we need to cultivate "inner development goals."[42]

With each other we can find home within ourselves in a world that relentlessly wounds us soul deep. Friendship, I have come to discover, is a vital means of cultivating inner development and a neglected social power for a more loving love. It can help tend the ubiquitous wound of hatred and revolutionize our hearts. Friendship is a lost spiritual art being revitalized by interfaith leaders like SeiFu Anil Sing-Molares at Spiritual Directors International and US Surgeon General Vivek Murthy. Friendship, as the beloved Irish poet and philosopher John O'Donohue wrote, is a place where love can dawn.[43] For the twelfth-century monk Aelred of Rievaulx, it is how we guard each other's souls.[44] Friendship is also a practice of homecoming and an open question to live with the world.

When I moved to Capitol Hill in Seattle, I met a former street kid named Love. He was standing on Broadway with a shopping cart he manifested from "Source." He called strangers who passed by him "family." On the front of his cart, he wrote on cardboard in black ink: "Live to Love, not to Hate." When he saw me, he said that he got chills. Source told him that I was a reason he came to Seattle. A week later, when we talked at a Mexican food restaurant, he told me what love is. "Humankind has lost the concept of love and understanding," he said, "for to understand is to step out of your own truths and into another person's perception. Love," he told me, "is making sure someone can progress spiritually."

Notes

Introduction

1. For a discussion of street kids' common belief in "The Universe," see chapter 3, especially the concluding section headed "Faith in the Goodness of The Universe."
   Rebecca S. Chopp's general definition of *practice* is a useful frame to situate Hitch's spanging as a spiritual practice in. For Chopp, a practice is a "socially shared [form] of behavior . . . a pattern of meaning and action that is both culturally constructed and individually instantiated. The notion of practice draws us to inquire into the shared activities of groups of persons that provide meaning and orientation to the world, and that guide action." Rebecca S. Chopp, *Saving Work: Feminist Practices of Theological Education* (Louisville: Westminster John Knox, 1995), 15.

2. Patricia O'Connell Killen and Mark Silk, eds., *Religion and Public Life in the Pacific Northwest: The None Zone* (Walnut Creek, CA: AltaMira, 2004).

3. So began Ann Swidler's seminal sociological study of love: with collegial scoffing and indifference. Ann Swidler, *Talk of Love: How Culture Matters* (Chicago: University of Chicago Press, 2001), 1–2.

4. bell hooks, *All about Love* (New York: HarperCollins, 2001), 71, 209. In *To Flourish or Destruct: A Personalist Theory of Human Goods, Motivations, Failure, and Evil* (Chicago: University of Chicago Press, 2015), the University of Notre Dame sociologist Christian Smith argues that social scientists have exiled love from serious inquiry to the detriment of scholarship. "We are derelict in our scholarly responsibilities if we fail to appreciate and study love in human life," Smith writes (277–78). In *All about Love*, bell hooks laments love's painful absence and incites a spiritual awakening that unapologetically places love at the center of power by way of new "schools of love." For hooks, love can help liberate the world from oppression and cultivate personal and social healing.

5. "A long, loving look at the real" is from Walter Burghardt, "Contemplation: A Long, Loving Look at the Real," *Church* (Winter 1989).

6. Manuel Mejido Costoya, ed., *Land of Stark Contrasts: Faith-Based Responses to Homelessness in the United States* (New York: Fordham University Press, 2021).

7. Rainer Maria Rilke, trans. Anita Barrows and Joanna Macy, *Letters to a Young Poet: A New Translation and Commentary* (Boulder, CO: Shambhala, 2021), 33.

8. Bruce O'Neill, *The Space of Boredom: Homelessness in a Slowing Global Order* (Durham, NC: Duke University Press, 2017).

9. Though several fine books informed my practice of writing fieldnotes, which I find a beautiful art, none was more influential than Robert M. Emerson, Rachel I. Fretz, and Linda L. Shaw's *Writing Ethnographic Fieldnotes*, 2nd ed. (Chicago: University of Chicago Press, 2011).

10. Philippe Bourgois and Jeffrey Schonberg, *Righteous Dopefiend* (Berkeley: University of California Press, 2009).

11. Here and elsewhere (particularly in the second chapter), with respect to "the spiritual conditions of being" and the otherwise, I draw on Jarrett Zigon's profound ethnographic work in *A War on People: Drug User Politics and a New Ethics of Community* (Berkeley: University of California Press, 2018).

12. J. Derrick Lemons, ed., *Theologically Engaged Anthropology* (Oxford: Oxford University Press, 2018).

13. As I describe, Zigon is again illuminating here in *A War on People*.

14. Kathleen Stewart, *Ordinary Affects* (Durham, NC: Duke University Press, 2007).

15. See Ben Anderson, "Affective Atmospheres" in *Emotion, Space, and Society* 2, no. 2 (2009): 77.

16. Charles Taylor, *A Secular Age* (Cambridge, MA: Belknap, 2007); Matthew Engelke, *A Problem of Presence: Beyond Scripture in an African Church* (Berkeley: University of California Press, 2007).

17. John Lewis, *Across That Bridge: A Vision for Change and the Future of America* (New York: Hatchett Books, 2021).

18. For example, see Aelred of Rievaulx, *Spiritual Friendship, Distilled*, trans. Daniel Deforest London (Berkeley, CA: Apocryphile, 2024); John O'Donohue, *Anam Cara: A Book of Celtic Wisdom* (New York: Harper Perennial, 2022).

Chapter 1: The Wound of Faith

1. Howard Thurman, *A Strange Freedom: The Best of Howard Thurman on Religious Experience and Public Life*, ed. Walter Earl Fluker and Catherine Tumber (Boston: Beacon, 1998), viii.

2. Tanya Marie Luhrmann, *When God Talks Back: Understanding the American Evangelical Relationship with God* (New York: Alfred A. Knopf, 2012), xx.

3. Angela Garcia, *The Pastoral Clinic: Addiction and Dispossession along the Rio Grande* (Berkeley: University of California Press, 2010), 11.

4. Pierre Bourdieu et al., *The Weight of the World: Social Suffering in Contemporary Society*, trans. Priscilla Parkhurst Ferguson (Stanford, CA: Stanford University Press, 1999), 622.

5. Nancy Scheper-Hughes, *Death without Weeping: The Violence of Everyday Life in Brazil* (Berkeley: University of California Press, 1993), 24.

6. Eileen Campbell-Reed and Christian Scharen, "Ethnography on Holy Ground: How Qualitative Interviewing Is Practical Theological Work," *International Journal of Practical Theology* 17, no. 2 (2013): 232–59.

7. Joel Robbins, "Anthropology and Theology: An Awkward Relationship?" *Anthropological Quarterly* 79, no. 2 (2006): 285–94.

8. Robbins. See also Jim Spickard, "The Porcupine Tango: What Ethnography Can and Cannot Do for Theologians," *Ecclesial Practices* 3, no. 2 (2016): 173–81.

9. Robbins, "Anthropology and Theology."

10. Mary Douglas, *Purity and Danger* (New York: Routledge, 2002). I am grateful to Nancy Scheper-Hughes, who shared this insight with me in her office in Kroeber Hall.

11. Talal Asad, *Genealogies of Religion: Discipline and Reasons of Power in Christianity and Islam* (Baltimore: Johns Hopkins University Press, 1993).

12. Susan Harding, *The Book of Jerry Falwell: Fundamentalist Language and Politics* (Princeton, NJ: Princeton University Press, 2000).

13. John Milbank, *Theology and Social Science: Beyond Secular Reason*, 2nd ed. (Oxford: Blackwell, 2006).

14. For example, see Philip Fountain and Sin Wen Lau, "Anthropological Theologies: Engagements and Encounters," *Australian Journal of Anthropology* 24, no. 3 (2013): 227–34; Joel Robbins, "Afterword: Let's Keep It Awkward: Anthropology, Theology, and Otherness," *Australian Journal of Anthropology* 24, no. 3 (2013): 329–37; Eloise Meneses, Lindy Backues, David Bronkema, Eric Flett, and Benjamin L. Hartley, "Engaging the Religiously Committed Other: Anthropologists and Theologians in Dialogue," *Current Anthropology* 55, no. 1 (2014): 82–104; Eloise Meneses and David Bronkema, eds., *On Knowing Humanity: Insights from Theology for Anthropology* (New York: Routledge, 2017); Rane Willerslev and Christian Suhr, "Is There a Place for Faith in Anthropology? Religion, Reason, and the Ethnographer's Divine Revelation," *HAU: Journal of Ethnographic Theory* 8, no. 1–2 (2018): 65–78; Tanya Luhrmann, "The Real Ontological Challenge," *HAU: Journal of Ethnographic Theory* 8, no. 1–2 (2018): 79–82; James Bielo, "Anthropology, Theology, Critique," *Critical Research on Religion* 6, no. 1 (2018): 28–34.

15. Don Seeman, "Divinity Inhabits the Social: Ethnography in a Phenomenological Key," in *Theologically Engaged Anthropology*, ed. J. Derrick Lemons (Oxford: Oxford University Press, 2018), 349, 345.

16. Meneses and Bronkema, *On Knowing Humanity*.

17. Meneses and Bronkema.

18. Christian Scharen and Aana Marie Vigen, *Ethnography as Christian Theology and Ethics* (London: Bloomsbury, 2011), 67, 73.

19. Christian Scharen, *Fieldwork in Theology: Exploring the Social Context of God's Work in the World* (Grand Rapids, MI: Baker Academic, 2015), 1.

20. Meneses and Bronkema, *On Knowing Humanity*, 86.

21. Scharen and Vigen, *Ethnography*, 16.

22. Elizabeth Liebert, *The Soul of Discernment: A Spiritual Practice for Communities and Institutions* (Louisville: Westminster John Knox, 2015), 19.

23. Elizabeth Liebert, "Academic Life and Scholarship as Spiritual Practice," *Berkeley Journal of Religion and Theology* vol. 3, no. 1 (2017): 12–28.

24. Robert Wuthnow, "Spirituality and Spiritual Practice," in *The Blackwell Companion to Sociology of Religion*, ed. Richard K. Fenn (Oxford: Blackwell, 2003), 309.

25. Wuthnow, 314.

26. Søren Kierkegaard, *Training in Christianity and the Edifying Discourse Which 'Accompanied' It*, trans. Walter Lowrie (Oxford: Oxford University Press, 1941), 139.

27. Elizabeth A. Johnson, *Quest for the Living God: Mapping Frontiers in the Theology of God* (London: Bloomsbury, 2007), 13.

28. Denys Turner, "Apophaticism, Idolatry and the Claims of Reason," in *Silence and the Word: Negative Theology and Incarnation*, ed. Oliver Davies and Denys Turner (Cambridge: Cambridge University Press, 2002), 17–20.

29. Stephan Quarles, "*Foucault and the Problem of the Cross: An Apophatic Theological Reading of 'History of Madness*,'" unpublished manuscript.

30. On the dialectical relationship between the apophatic and the kataphatic, see Denys Turner, *The Darkness of God: Negativity in Christian Mysticism* (Cambridge: Cambridge University Press, 1995).

31. Pseudo-Dionysius, *The Complete Works*, trans. Colm Luibheid (Mahwah, NJ: Paulist, 1987), 49.

32. Bernard McGinn, *The Foundations of Mysticism: Origins to the Fifth Century* (New York: Crossroad, 1995), 9–61.

33. Anonymous, *The Cloud of Unknowing*, ed. James Walsh, SJ (Mahwah, NJ: Paulist, 1981), 139.

34. "John leaves to each reader and each age the task of making the suitable applications. What is essential is that the suffering and privations bring about a growing response of faith, hope, and love; without this transforming theological life the night would fail to purify and produce fruit." *The Collected Works of Saint John of the Cross*, trans. Kieran Kavanaugh and Otilio Rodriguez (Washington, DC: Institute of Carmelite Studies, 1991), 357.

35. David B. Perrin, "The *New Self* of John of the Cross," *Vinayasādhana* 5, no. 1 (January 2014): 41.

36. Perrin, 41.

37. Wendy Farley, *Gathering Those Driven Away: A Theology of Incarnation* (Louisville: Westminster John Knox, 2011), 68.

38. Farley, 77.

39. Clifford Geertz, *Works and Lives: The Anthropologist as Author* (Stanford, CA: Stanford University Press, 1988).
40. See James Clifford, "Anthropology and/as Travel," *Etnofoor* 9, no. 2 (1999): 5–15.
41. Clifford Geertz, *The Interpretation of Cultures* (New York: Basic Books, 1973), 7.
42. Veena Das, *Affliction* (Oakland: University of California Press, 2015), 15.
43. Geertz, *Works and Lives*, 144.
44. Michael Agar, *Speaking of Ethnography* (Thousand Oaks, CA: Sage, 1985), 19.
45. Geertz, *Interpretation of Cultures*, 16.
46. Geertz, 16.
47. Paul Rabinow, *Reflections on Fieldwork in Morocco*, 2nd ed. (Berkeley: University of California Press, 2007), xxiv.
48. Scheper-Hughes, *Death without Weeping*, 26.
49. Ruth Behar, *The Vulnerable Observer: Anthropology That Breaks Your Heart* (Boston: Beacon, 1996), 177.
50. I am inspired here by Pope Francis, who has encouraged priests to have the smell of sheep on them.
51. Simone Weil, *Gravity and Grace*, trans. Arthur Wills (New York: Van Rees, 1952), 115.
52. Coll Thrush, *Native Seattle: Histories from the Crossing-Over Place*, 2nd ed. (Seattle: University of Washington Press, 2017), 10.
53. Katie Herzog, "Astrologers Agree: The Eclipse Is Bad News for Trump. Astronomers Agree: Astrology Is Bullshit," *Seattle Weekly*, August 16, 2017.
54. Herzog.
55. Robert M. Emerson, Rachel I. Fretz, and Linda L. Shaw, *Writing Ethnographic Fieldnotes*, 2nd ed. (Chicago: University of Chicago Press, 2011).
56. For example, see Lawrence Wright, "Sympathy for the Devil," *Rolling Stone*, September 5, 1991.
57. Sherryl Kleinman and Martha A. Copp, *Emotions and Fieldwork* (London: Sage, 1993).
58. Elizabeth Liebert, *The Way of Discernment: Spiritual Practices for Decision Making* (Louisville: Westminster John Knox, 2008), 2414 (Kindle).
59. Simone Weil, *Waiting for God*, trans. Emma Craufurd (New York: Harper Perennial, 2009), 57.
60. Weil, 62.
61. Weil, 65.
62. Weil, 64.

Chapter 2: The Wound of Rejection

1. Kim Hopper, *Reckoning with Homelessness* (Ithaca, NY: Cornell University Press, 2003), 76.
2. Peter L. Berger and Thomas Luckmann, *The Social Construction of Reality: A Treatise in the Sociology of Knowledge* (New York: Anchor Books, 1967).

3. Berger and Luckmann, 15.
4. Berger and Luckmann, 1, 18.
5. Berger and Luckmann, 47.
6. Berger and Luckmann, 129.
7. Berger and Luckmann, 52.
8. Berger and Luckmann, 60.
9. Berger and Luckmann, 61.
10. Berger and Luckmann, 61.
11. Berger and Luckmann, 130.
12. Berger and Luckmann are intentionally unclear on when primary socialization begins and ends. In their view, it "ends" when one has developed a "generalized other": the sense that one can predict a common response from people in the social world.
13. Berger and Luckmann, 131.
14. Martin Heidegger, trans. John Macquarrie and Edward Robinson, *Being and Time* (New York: Harper Perennial, 2008), 223.
15. Berger and Luckmann, *Social Construction of Reality*, 131.
16. Berger and Luckmann, 136.
17. Peter L. Berger, *The Sacred Canopy: Elements of a Sociological Theory of Religion* (New York: Random House, 1990). In *The Sacred Canopy*, which is Berger's first robust exposition of religion as a human product, and which is nevertheless "warm-hearted" to theologians, Berger expounds on the notion that secularization (or "pluralism") has rendered religion less plausible and certain for the man on the street.
Peter L. Berger, Brigitte Berger, and Hansfried Kellner, *The Homeless Mind: Modernization and Consciousness* (New York: Vintage Books, 1974).
18. Berger, Berger, and Kellner, 185.
19. The streets are "home" not only for the street kids I spent time with. It is common for street kids from around the world to refer to the streets as home. For a fascinating ethnography of this phenomenon in Venezuela, see Patricia C. Márquez, *The Street Is My Home: Youth and Violence in Caracas* (Stanford, CA: Stanford University Press, 1999).
20. Hopper, *Reckoning with Homelessness*, 76.
21. For example, see Teresa Gowan, *Hobos, Hustlers, and Backsliders: Homeless in San Francisco* (Minneapolis: University of Minnesota Press, 2010), 434 (Kindle).
22. Kenneth L. Kusmer, *Down and Out, on the Road: The Homeless in American History* (Oxford: Oxford University Press, 2003), 30.
23. Todd Depastino, *Citizen Hobo: How a Century of Homelessness Shaped America* (Chicago: University of Chicago Press, 2005), xxi.
24. See, for example, Jack London, *The Road* (New York: Peregrine, 1906).
25. Peter Rossi, "The Old Homeless and the New Homeless in Historical Perspective," *American Psychologist* 45, no. 8 (1990): 954–59.
26. See Tanya Luhrmann, "Down and Out in Chicago," *Raritan* (Winter 2010): 140–66.

27. "Racial Disparities in Homelessness in the United States," Data and Graphics, National Alliance to End Homelessness, accessed March 1, 2020, https://endhomelessness.org/resource/racial-disparities-homelessness-united-states/; see Anna Patrick, "HUD Reports Record-High Homeless Count in 2023 for U.S., WA," *Seattle Times*, December 19, 2023.

28. Brian Goldstone, "The New American Homeless," *New Republic*, August 21, 2019.

29. "Seattle/King County Point-in-Time Count of Persons Experiencing Homelessness: 2018," All Home, accessed March 1, 2020.

30. Melinda Giovengo, "The Puget Sound Region Needs 24/7 Services for Homeless Youth," *Seattle Times*, January 4, 2018.

31. See, for example, https://facinghomelessness.org/. Facing Homelessness encourages people to humanize and "just say hello" to one's homeless "neighbors."

32. See, for example, Lisa Edge, "Despite the Data, the 'Freeattle' Myth Persists," *Real Change*, December 27, 2017.

33. Robert Bellah et al., *Habits of the Heart: Individualism and Commitment in American Life* (New York: HarperCollins, 1985).

34. Robert D. Putnam, *Bowling Alone: The Collapse and Revival of American Community* (New York: Simon and Schuster, 2001).

35. Lee Rainie and Barry Wellman, *Networked: The New Social Operating System* (Cambridge, MA: MIT Press, 2012).

36. Vivek H. Murthy, *Together: The Healing Power of Human Connection in a Sometimes Lonely World* (New York: Harper, 2020).

37. Jarrett Zigon, *A War on People: Drug User Politics and a New Ethics of Community* (Berkeley: University of California Press, 2018), 16.

38. Zigon, 20.

39. Zigon, 104.

40. Zigon, 107. Zigon gets the term "disclosive freedom" from Leslie Paul Thiele's reading of Heidegger in *Timely Meditations: Martin Heidegger and Postmodern Politics* (Princeton, NJ: Princeton University Press, 1995), 72.

41. Zigon, *War on People*, 120.

42. Friedrich Nietzsche, *Thus Spoke Zarathustra: A Book for Everyone and No One*, trans. R. J. Hollingdale (New York: Penguin Classics, 1961).

43. Joel Robbins, "Beyond the Suffering Subject: Toward an Anthropology of the Good," *Journal of the Royal Anthropological Institute* 19 (2013): 447–62.

44. James P. Spradley, *You Owe Yourself a Drunk: An Ethnography of Urban Nomads* (Long Grove, IL: Waveland, 2000), 1.

45. Elliot Liebow, *Tell Them Who I Am: The Lives of Homeless Women* (New York: Penguin Books, 1995), 25.

46. Irene Glasser and Rae Bridgman, *Braving the Street: The Anthropology of Homelessness* (New York: Berghahn Books, 1999), 58.

47. David A. Snow and Leon Anderson, *Down on Their Luck: A Study of Homeless Street People* (Berkeley: University of California Press, 1993), 215.

48. Snow and Anderson, 221–22.

49. Nels Anderson, *The Hobo: The Sociology of the Homeless Man* (Chicago: University of Chicago Press, 1923), 262.

50. Liebow, *Tell Them Who I Am*, 170.

51. Nathan Hatch, *The Democratization of American Christianity* (New Haven, CT: Yale University Press, 1991).

52. Pew Research Center, "Religious Landscape Study," accessed August 15, 2019, https://www.pewforum.org/religious-landscape-study/.

53. Pew Research Center, "American's Changing Religious Landscape: Christians Decline Sharply as Share of Population; Unaffiliated and Other Faiths Continue to Grow," May 12, 2015, 4, https://www.pewresearch.org/religion/2015/05/12/americas-changing-religious-landscape/.

54. Nietzsche, *Thus Spoke Zarathustra*, 1961. Perhaps I have coined the term "God-weight."

55. Mark Chaves, "Secularization as Declining Religious Authority," *Social Forces* 72, no. 3 (1994): 749–74; Christian Smith, ed., *The Secular Revolution: Power, Interests, and Conflict in the Secularization of American Public Life* (Berkeley: University of California Press, 2003).

56. Robert Putnam and David Campbell, *American Grace: How Religion Divides and Unites Us* (New York: Simon and Schuster, 2010).

57. Michael Hout and Claude Fischer, "Why More Americans Have No Religious Preference: Politics and Generations," *American Sociological Review* 67, no. 2 (2002): 165–90; Michael Hout and Claude Fischer, "Explaining Why More Americans Have No Religious Preference: Political Backlash and Generational Succession, 1987–2012," *Sociological Science* 1 (2014): 423–47.

58. Bellah et al., *Habits of the Heart*, 235.

59. Linda A. Mercadante, *Belief without Borders: Inside the Minds of the Spiritual but Not Religious* (Oxford: Oxford University Press, 2014).

60. Kaya Oakes, *The Nones Are Alright: A New Generation of Believers, Seekers, and Those In Between* (Maryknoll, NY: Orbis Books, 2015).

61. Jeffrey Kripal, "The Future of 'Spiritual but Not Religious,'" https://www.youtube.com/watch?v=og2SSczJ_XI.

62. Elizabeth Drescher, *Choosing Our Religion: The Spiritual Lives of America's Nones* (Oxford: Oxford University Press, 2016), 755, (Kindle).

63. Nancy Ammerman, "Spiritual but Not Religious? Beyond Binary Choices in the Study of Religion," *Journal for the Scientific Study of Religion* 52, no. 2 (2013): 258–78.

64. Robert N. Bellah, *Religion in Human Evolution: From the Paleolithic to the Axial Age* (Cambridge, MA: Belknap, 2011).

65. David Buerge, *Chief Seattle and the Town That Took His Name: The Change of Worlds for the Native People and the Settlers in Puget Sound* (Seattle: Sasquatch Books, 2017).

66. Josephine Ensign, *Skid Road: On the Frontier of Health and Homelessness in an American City* (Baltimore: Johns Hopkins University Press, 2021), 50.

67. Gary L. Atkins, *Gay Seattle: Stories of Exile and Belonging* (Seattle: University of Washington Press, 2003).
68. Doug Pray, *Hype!* (Santa Monica, CA: Lionsgate Films, 1996).

Chapter 3: The Wound of Human Being

1. "Please stop feeding the ave rats": The second epigraph to this chapter is an archived Reddit post by a Seattle resident using the name DingoDanza from approximately 2014, most recently accessed July 1, 2024, https://www.reddit.com/r/Seattle/comments/2gtzso/please_stop_feeding_the_ave_rats/.
   Beena Raghavendran, "Colorful Crosswalks Celebrate Gay Pride in Seattle," *Seattle Times*, June 23, 2015.
2. Sara Ahmed, *The Cultural Politics of Emotion* (New York: Routledge, 2004), 1.
3. Ahmed, 11.
4. Ahmed, 4, 16.
5. Ahmed, 202.
6. One could (and should) write an entire book on street names. They are clever and fascinating and, sometimes, very offensive. In many cases, unless asked to do otherwise, I do not use someone's real street name. That makes the translation difficult. "Burrito Bitch" is a name similar to and, I think, less offensive than his actual street name.
7. Kathleen Stewart, *Ordinary Affects* (Durham, NC: Duke University Press, 2007), 1.
8. Stewart, 1.
9. Lauren Berlant, *Cruel Optimism* (Durham, NC: Duke University Press, 2011), 12.
10. Berlant, 21.
11. Brian Massumi, *Politics of Affect* (Malden, MA: Polity, 2015), 114.
12. Berlant, *Cruel Optimism*, 9.
13. Gilles Deleuze, *Spinoza: Practical Philosophy* (San Francisco: City Lights Books, 1988), 18.
14. While it is helpful to discuss the specific contours of affect theory to create conceptual clarity, it is important to note that it is not a closed theory. The editors in *The Affect Theory Reader* caution one to remember that affect theory is in development. What remains true, however, is that affect theorists share a commitment to see how the world moves by human and nonhuman forces through affective encounters that make a difference. See, for example, Melissa Gregg and Gregory J. Seigworth, eds., *The Affect Theory Reader* (Durham, NC: Duke University Press, 2011).
15. Ben Anderson, "Affective Atmospheres," *Emotion, Space, and Society* 2, no. 2 (2009): 77.
16. Donovan O. Schaefer, *The Evolution of Affect Theory: The Humanities, the Sciences, and the Study of Power* (Cambridge: Cambridge University Press, 2019), 1.

17. For example, see Lane Gillespie, "Bankrate's 2024 Annual Emergency Savings Report," Bankrate, February 22, 2024, https://www.bankrate.com/banking/savings/emergency-savings-report/.

18. For a helpful resource from a fantastic organization, see Sana Khan, "Hidden Sleep Crisis: Unhoused Americans Struggle for Their Health," Sleep Foundation, updated June 6, 2023, https://www.sleepfoundation.org/sleep-news/sleep-crisis-unhoused-americans-struggle-for-health.

19. Jean-Paul Sartre, *No Exit: A Play in One Act*, adapted by Paul Bowles (New York: Samuel French, 1958).

20. For more information, see Committee to End Homelessness, http://www.cehkc.org/.

21. Steve Berg, "Ten-Year Plans to End Homelessness," in *National Low Income Housing Coalition, 2015 Advocates' Guide to Affordable Housing and Community Development Programs*, https://nlihc.org/sites/default/files/Sec7.08_Ten-Year-Plan_2015.pdf.

22. See, for example, Mark Miloscia, "King County's Plan to End Homelessness Has Failed," *Seattle Times*, March 14, 2016.

23. Daniel Beekman and Jack Bloom, "Mayor, County Exec Declare 'State of Emergency' over Homelessness," *Seattle Times*, November 2, 2015.

24. Daniel Person, "Why Ed Murray Can't Quit the Catholic Church," *Seattle Weekly*, March 1, 2017.

25. Ed Murray, "Homelessness Address to the City," January 26, 2016.

26. Christine Hauser and Ashley Southall, "Shooting at Seattle Tent City Coincides with Mayor's Homelessness Speech," *New York Times*, January 27, 2016.

27. Hannah Krieg, "After Defending Ed Murray, Can Bruce Harrell Be a Mayor to Survivors?," *Real Change*, September 8, 2022.

28. *Seattle Is Dying*, KOMO News (March 14, 2019), https://komonews.com/news/local/komo-news-special-seattle-is-dying. *Seattle Is Dying* is the third film in a series. The first film, *There but for the Grace of God* . . . explores the crisis of homelessness in Seattle "from the inside out." The second, *Demon at the Door*, explores heroin addiction in Seattle.

29. Danny Westneat, "The Backlash Fizzles: Voters Don't Seem to Believe Seattle Is Dying after All," *Seattle Times*, August 6, 2019.

30. Westneat.

31. For an extensive study on the use of banishment as a form of social control in Seattle and beyond, see Katherine Beckett and Steve Herbert, *Banished: The New Social Control in Urban America* (Oxford: Oxford University Press, 2011). Another important and more recent work that examines the criminalization of street homelessness and the detrimental effects of social banishment is by Chris Herring, Dilara Yarbrough, and Lisa Marie Alatorre, "Pervasive Penalty: How the Criminalization of Poverty Perpetuates Homelessness," *Social Problems* 67, no. 1 (2020): 1–19.

32. *Curing Spokane*, http://curingspokane.com.

33. The Council of Economic Advisers, "The State of Homelessness in America," September 2019, https://www.whitehouse.gov/wp-content/uploads/2019/09/The-State-of-Homelessness-in-America.pdf.

34. "Trump: Homelessness Is Hurting Our Country and We Are Looking at It Seriously," *Fox News*, July 2, 2019.

35. Frank Miles, "Geraldo Rivera, Dan Bongino React to US Cities in Crisis: 'Liberalism Is a Cancer,'" *Fox News*, August 20, 2019.

36. Yael Halon, "Trump Warns Newsom: If California Homelessness Crisis Persists, Feds Will 'Get Involved,'" *Fox News*, December 25, 2019.

37. See, for example, USICH, "All In: The Federal Strategic Plan to Prevent and End Homelessness," December 2022, https://www.usich.gov/sites/default/files/document/All_In.pdf.

38. See https://truthsocial.com/@realDonaldTrump/posts/110221904819759328.

39. Robert Desjarlais, *Shelter Blues: Sanity and Selfhood among the Homeless* (Philadelphia: University of Pennsylvania Press, 1997), 5.

40. Desjarlais, 3, 4.

41. In the struggle over how to view and respond to homelessness, religion has always played a critical role. In the fourteenth century, for example, people were encouraged to view persons experiencing homelessness as objects of charity. After the Black Death, however, homelessness was perceived as a threat to the social order and defined by ecclesial authorities as the result of sin. In the United States, harsh penalties were justified and/or refuted based on religious convictions. Without doubt, religion still plays a vital role in the discourse around and response to homelessness—one can see the current Poor People's Campaign led by William Barber II, which is a revitalization of Martin Luther King Jr.'s vision and leadership that I discuss in the conclusion to this book. Still, religion has relatively dull teeth and a soft bite.

42. For a fascinating ethnographic study on the deep threat of boredom on the streets, see Bruce O'Neill, *The Space of Boredom: Homelessness in the Slowing Global Order* (Durham, NC: Duke University Press, 2017).

43. Donald Winnicott, *Playing and Reality*, 2nd ed. (New York: Routledge, 2005).

44. Donald Winnicott, *Home Is Where We Start From: Essays by a Psychoanalyst* (New York: W. W. Norton, 1986), 22.

45. Mitchell Duneier, *Sidewalk* (New York: Farrar, Straus, and Giroux, 1999), 123.

46. Berlant, *Cruel Optimism*.

47. Sigmund Freud, *Civilization and Its Discontents* (New York: W. W. Norton, 1989), 11.

48. Freud, 12.

49. Friedrich Schleiermacher, *Christian Faith: A New Translation and Critical Edition: Volume 1*, trans. Terrence N. Tice, Catherine L. Kelsey, and Edwina Lawler; ed. Catherine L. Kelsey and Terrence N. Tice (Louisville: Westminster John Knox, 2016), 26.

50. Rudolf Otto, *The Idea of the Holy* (Oxford: Oxford University Press, 1958), 6.

51. Emile Durkheim, *The Elementary Forms of Religion*, trans. Joseph Ward Swain (New York: Free Press, 1965).

52. Max Weber, *The Protestant Ethic and the Spirit of Capitalism*, trans. Talcott Parsons (New York: Routledge, 2001).

Chapter 4: The Wound of God

1. Harold Garfinkel, *Studies in Ethnomethodology* (Cambridge: Polity, 1999), 36.

2. I elaborate on the concept of "the problem of presence," which is derived from the brilliant work of anthropologists Matthew Engelke and Tanya Marie Luhrmann, later in this chapter.

3. Mark A. Noll, *America's God: From Jonathan Edwards to Abraham Lincoln* (Oxford: Oxford University Press, 2002), 19, 21.

4. Max Weber, *The Protestant Ethic and the Spirit of Capitalism*, trans. Talcott Parsons (New York: Routledge, 2001.

5. Noll, *America's God*, 431.

6. See Martin Luther King Jr., *A Testament of Hope: The Essential Writings and Speeches of Martin Luther King, Jr.*, ed. James M. Washington (New York: HarperCollins, 1991), 41.

7. See, for example, Randall Balmer, *The Making of Evangelicalism: From Revivalism to Politics and Beyond* (Waco, TX: Baylor University Press, 2010), 59; David Domke and Kevin Coe, *The God Strategy: How Religion Became a Political Weapon in America* (Oxford: Oxford University Press, 2010), 101.

8. Christian Smith, *American Evangelicalism: Embattled and Thriving* (Chicago: University of Chicago Press, 1998).

9. Philip S. Gorski, "Historicizing the Secularization Debate: Church, State, and Society in Late Medieval and Early Modern Europe, ca. 1300–1700," *American Sociological Review* 65, no. 1 (2000): 138–67.

10. Friedrich Nietzsche, *Thus Spoke Zarathustra: A Book for Everyone and No One*, trans. R. J. Hollingdale (New York: Penguin Classics, 1961), 3.

11. Paul Froese and Christopher Bader, in *America's Four Gods: What We Say about God—and What That Says about Us* (Oxford: Oxford University Press, 2010), use George Herbert Mead's concept of "The Generalized Other" to help explain why God matters. In effect, they argue that God is the supreme character in the narrative of our lives and the ultimate other in our heads that we base our decisions around. God, in other words, is how we imagine others to generally respond to us. He is the "ultimate other." See George Herbert Mead, *Mind, Self, and Society: The Definitive Edition*, ed. Charles W. Morris (Chicago: University of Chicago Press, 2015).

12. Froese and Bader, *America's Four Gods*, 4.

13. Froese and Bader, 13.

14. Froese and Bader, 24.

15. Froese and Bader, 15.

16. Froese and Bader, 15.

17. I found this report in Matthew T. Lee, Margaret M. Poloma, and G. Stephen Post, *The Heart of Religion: Spiritual Empowerment, Benevolence, and the Experience of God's Love* (Oxford: Oxford University Press, 2013), 25.

18. Ana-Maria Rizzuto, *The Birth of the Living God* (Chicago: University of Chicago Press, 1979) 5.

19. David A. Snow and Leon Anderson, *Down on Their Luck: A Study of Homeless Street People* (Berkeley: University of California Press, 1993), 204, 221–22.

20. Elliot Liebow, *Tell Them Who I Am: The Lives of Homeless Women* (New York: Penguin Books, 1995), 170.

21. Robert Desjarlais, *Shelter Blues: Sanity and Selfhood among the Homeless* (Philadelphia: University of Pennsylvania Press, 1997), 6.

22. Teresa Gowan, *Hobos, Hustlers, and Backsliders: Homeless in San Francisco* (Minneapolis: University of Minnesota Press, 2010), 87 (Kindle).

23. Gowan, 3528–3536 (Kindle).

24. When I spoke to street kids about this question, I asked what they thought about God, a higher power, or The Universe. That is because a street kid might reject the idea of God but not a transcendent presence or a higher power within. Names like "higher power" and "The Universe" could get to the transcendent presence in a way that "God" couldn't. Unless important to do otherwise, to capture a street kid's own language, I will use "God" and "God concepts" more consistently. That, I think, will assist with clarity.

25. Christian Smith, "Why Christianity Works," *Sociology of Religion* 68, no. 2 (Summer 2007): 167. In the article, Smith addresses more explicitly social needs as well.

26. By foregrounding the emotional reasons Christianity works, Smith is trying to complement the social-structural reasons it does.

27. Matthew Engelke, *A Problem of Presence: Beyond Scripture in an African Church* (Berkeley: University of California Press, 2007), 132 (Kindle).

28. Engelke, 3231 (Kindle).

29. Tanya Marie Lurhmann, *When God Talks Back: Understanding the American Evangelical Relationship with God* (New York: Alfred A. Knoff, 2012), 132.

30. See another article by Luhrmann on this point: Tanya Luhrmann, "The Faith Frame: Or, Belief Is Easy, Faith Is Hard," *Contemporary Pragmatism* 15, no. 3 (2018): 302–18.

31. Charles Taylor, *Sources of the Self* (Cambridge, MA: Harvard University Press, 1992), 52.

32. Taylor, 4.

33. Taylor, 45.

34. Frederick Nietzsche, *The Gay Science: With a Prelude in Rhymes and an Appendix of Songs*, trans. Walter Kaufmann (New York: Vintage Books, 1974).

35. Albert Camus, *The Myth of Sisyphus* (New York: Vintage Books, 1983).

36. Taylor, *Sources of the Self*, 18.

37. Taylor, 16
38. Alasdair MacIntyre, *After Virtue* (Notre Dame, IN: University of Notre Dame Press, 1984), 203–4.
39. Charles Taylor, *A Secular Age* (Cambridge, MA: Belknap, 2007), 539.
40. Taylor, 63.
41. Rizzuto, *Birth of the Living God*, 5.

Chapter 5: The Wound of Love

1. Bob Smietana, "Safe Haven," *Covenant Companion* (January 2009): 6–9.
2. Rick Reynolds, *Street Stories* (Seattle: Seattle Pacific University, 2015), 21.
3. Reynolds, 22.
4. "Will You Help Ronnie?" https://www.youtube.com/watch?v=BzHpDUoCiZA.
5. Craig Rennebohm with David Paul, *Souls in the Hands of a Tender God: Stories of the Search for Home and Healing on the Streets* (Boston: Beacon, 2008), 1.
6. Ron Ruthruff, *The Least of These: Lessons Learned from Kids on the Street* (Birmingham, AL: New Hope, 2010).
7. The motif is an allusion to Song of Songs 2:5 and Isaiah 49:2.
8. Origen, "The Prologue to the Commentary on the Song of Songs," trans. Rowan Greer, in *Origen: An Exhortation to Martyrdom, Prayer and Selected Works* (Mahwah, NJ: Paulist, 1979), 223. For one of Origen's discussions on how the power of love is a wounding presence in the Song of Songs, independently of the mind, see 218–20.
9. Julian does not *explicitly* state that she was wounded with God's love, as Origen does, but her rendering of her mystical vision of Jesus's suffering is described as spiritual wounding that culminates in an intimate experience of God's love. For example, see Julian of Norwich, *Showings*, trans. Edmund Colledge and James Walsh (Mahwah, NJ: Paulist, 1978), 128–31.
10. Teresa of Avila, *The Interior Castle* VI.2, in *The Collected Works of St. Teresa of Avila*, vol. 2, trans. Kieran Kavanaugh and Otilio Rodriguez (Washington, DC: Institute of Carmelite Studies, 1980), 367.
11. Teresa of Avila, 367.
12. Wendy Farley, *The Wounding and Healing of Desire* (Louisville: Westminster John Know, 2005.
13. See Wendy Farley, *Tragic Vision and Divine Compassion: A Contemporary Theodicy* (Louisville: Westminster John Knox, 1990).
14. See John Swinton, *Raging with Compassion* (Grand Rapids, MI: Wm. B. Eerdmans, 2007).
15. Dorothee Soelle, *Suffering*, trans. Everett R. Kalin (Philadelphia: Fortress, 1975), 17.
16. Soelle, 18.
17. Soelle, 18.
18. Soelle 26.

19. Soelle, 125.
20. Soelle, 145.
21. Dorothee Soelle, *Theology for Skeptics: Reflections on God* (Minneapolis, MN: Fortress, 1992), 66.
22. Gustavo Gutiérrez, *We Drink from Our Own Wells: The Spiritual Journey of a People* (Maryknoll, NY: Orbis Books, 2003), 37.
23. Gutiérrez, 38.
24. Gutiérrez, 112.
25. Dorothy Day, "The Mystery of the Poor," *Catholic Worker*, April 2, 1964.
26. For the most part, the street kids I spent time with did not demonstrate regular psychotic behavior, though they were susceptible to psychotic episodes from the traumatizing conditions of street life, drugs and sleeplessness. It is hard to imagine any of the street kids I spent time with *not* being diagnosed with a serious mental health condition because of the trauma involved in living on the streets. The subject was difficult to understand, however, because many street kids were ambivalent about and/or had considerable antipathy to psychiatric diagnoses. For some, such diagnoses happened frequently and were considered another tool of social oppression and control. Others fully embraced certain illnesses and the impact they had on their lives. In interviews, for example, the data I got about whether they had been diagnosed with psychological maladies were often laughed at or, it seemed to me, embraced with exaggeration. In some instances, for example, street kids would tell me they had "all of the illnesses" in a way that seemed to provide positive meaning to their lives. Others experienced questions about mental health as intrusive and inappropriate for me to ask. In the end, I am not confident that I got reliable enough information about specifically what a person's actual history with mental health is.
27. David A. Snow and Leon Anderson, *Down on Their Luck: A Study of Homeless Street People* (Berkeley: University of California Press, 1993), 229–30.
28. I thank Jim Spickard for this insight, which came by way of a conversation we had at Seattle University. See also Thomas Keating, *Open Mind, Open Heart* (New York: Bloomsbury, 2019).

Conclusion: A More Loving Love

1. Bebe Rexha, "I'm a Mess," *Expectations* (Los Angeles: Warner Bros., 2018).
2. A Google search of the quote suggests it comes from a fairy-tale coloring book, *Ivy and the Inky Butterfly: A Magic Tale to Color* by Johanna Basford (New York: Penguin Books, 2017).
3. Now, as I edit this book, I have come to understand that any adequate understanding of the Other I have rendered is grace. Knowledge of the Other is only real if it invites loving action, even if that action is done in the confines of inward prayer or meditation, which is not insincere or inconsequential love. Knowledge that does not walk the path of love is illusion. Apart from the divine

Beloved, I (personally) cannot really know the Other or hope to say something true about the Other's life. Aslan has remained in Lake Washington but present still all along on the streets as I sought to unknow whatever is required to love. They are alive always in the call and question of love.

4. See for instance Elizabeth Liebert, *The Soul of Discernment: A Spiritual Practice for Communities and Institutions* (Louisville: Westminster John Knox, 2015), 13.

5. Howard Thurman, *Jesus and the Disinherited* (Boston: Beacon, 1976), 11.

6. Thurman, 13.

7. Thurman, 13.

8. Thurman, 13.

9. Thurman, 15.

10. Thurman, 21.

11. Thurman, 23.

12. Thurman, 19.

13. Simone Weil, *Waiting for God*, trans. Emma Craufurd (New York: Harper Perennial, 2009), 65.

14. Weil, 65.

15. Gustavo Gutiérrez, *We Drink from Our Own Wells: The Spiritual Journey of a People* (Maryknoll, NY: Orbis Books, 2003), 108.

16. Mary McClintock Fulkerson, *Places of Redemption: Theology for a Worldly Church* (Oxford: Oxford University Press, 2010), 13.

17. Fulkerson, 17.

18. Fulkerson, 17.

19. Rainer Maria Rilke, *Letters to a Young Poet: A New Translation and Commentary*, trans. Anita Barrows and Joanna Macy (Boulder, CO: Shambhala, 2021), 33.

20. Francis Moloney, *Love in the Gospel of John: An Exegetical, Theological, and Literary Study* (Grand Rapids, MI: Baker Academic, 2013).

21. Richard Rohr, *Everything Belongs: The Gift of Contemplative Prayer* (New York: Crossroad, 2003).

22. Christian Smith, *What Is a Person? Rethinking Humanity, Social Life, and the Moral Good from the Person Up* (Chicago: University of Chicago Press, 2010), 26.

23. Judith Butler, *The Force of Nonviolence: An Ethico-political Bind* (London: Verso, 2020), 16.

24. Thich Nhat Hanh, *How to See* (Berkeley: Parallax, 2019), 27.

25. Carl Jung, *Memories, Dreams, Reflections* (New York: Vintage Books, 1989), 16.

26. Noam Chomsky, *Profit over People* (New York: Seven Stories, 1999).

27. Christian Smith has argued, compellingly, that individualism has influenced spirituality and that individualism *is itself* a spiritual project. For example, see Christian Smith, *To Flourish or Destruct: A Personalist Theory of Human Goods, Motivations, Failure, and Evil* (Chicago: University of Chicago Press, 2015), 269–70. In a paragraph worth careful study and quoting at length, Smith writes:

Moderns are committed, however unaware, to following a particular *spiritual project*, the pursuit of *a sacred good*—namely, throwing off restraint and achieving human happiness through individual autonomy, self-definition, and self-determination. To make everything new, to leave behind the past, to be unbound by any tradition, to enjoy maximum choice, to be free from any constraint, to be able to buy whatever one can afford, to live however one desires—that is the guiding vision for what is most worthy in a sense that transcends any individual life. It is spiritual because it speaks to people's deepest personal subjectivities, their most transcendent vision of goodness, their definition of ultimate fulfillment. It is spiritual because as a deep cultural structure it occupies a position in the modern West homologous with salvation in God that was prized in the premodern Christendom that modernity broke apart. And it is spiritual because, by being sacred, it is worth protecting, defending, policing, fighting for, perhaps dying for, even killing for. Being such a sacred matter, modernity's spiritual project of unfettered individualism virtually *must* champion the currently orthodox doctrine that denies proper ends and natural goods.

28. Philip Sheldrake, "Christian Spirituality as a Way of Living Publicly: A Dialectic of the Mystical and the Prophetic," in *Minding the Spirit: The Study of Christian Spirituality*, ed. Elizabeth A. Dreyer and Mark S. Burrows (Baltimore: Johns Hopkins University Press, 2005), 282.

29. Laura Stivers, *Disrupting Homelessness: Alternative Christian Approaches* (Philadelphia: Fortress, 2011), 1485 (Kindle).

30. For a fine theological study of neoliberalism, see Adam Kotsko, *Neoliberalism's Demons: On The Political Theology of Late Capital* (Stanford, CA: Stanford University Press, 2018). Another fine study is Kathryn Tanner, *Christianity and the New Spirit of Capitalism* (New Haven, CT: Yale University Press, 2019).

31. Walter Wink, *The Powers That Be: Theology for a New Millennium* (New York: Galilee Doubleday, 1998), 39. Wink refers to the "domination system" as a complex network of powers (which he also calls "fallen" and "demonic") that can be seen in "unjust economic relations, oppressive social relations, biased race relations, patriarchal gender relations, and hierarchal power relations" that are maintained by real and symbolic violence and that undermine human flourishing.

32. Another essential concept to a loving look is "intersectionality." In short, intersectionality posits that (and analyzes how) people are disempowered by multiple sources of oppression *at the same time*. Different forms of disempowerment intersect. It is not enough to see that a person is disempowered by class, for example. One must also ask if a person is disempowered by their gender, sexual orientation, and religion. For a helpful introduction to intersectionality, see Patricia Hill Collins and Sirma Bilge, *Intersectionality: Key Concepts* (Cambridge: Polity, 2016). For an excellent discussion about how intersectionality can be applied to Christian ministry, see Nancy Ramsay, "Intersectionality: A Model for Addressing the Complexity of Oppression and Privilege," *Pastoral Psychology* 63, no. 4 (2014): 453–69.

33. Wink, *Powers That Be*, 4, 12.

34. Sheldrake, "Christian Spirituality," 296.

35. Simone Weil, *The Need for Roots: Prelude to a Declaration of Duties towards Mankind*, trans. Arthur Wills (New York: Routledge, 2001), 40.

36. "Human societies without love and bodies without blood." Smith, *To Flourish or Destruct*, 277–78. Smith argues that love has been uprooted from social science and that love's uprootedness impoverishes a social scientist's capacity to understand and explain the world.

37. Martin Luther King Jr., *The Measure of a Man* (Mansfield Center, CT: Martino, 2013), 5.

38. To learn more, visit https://www.poorpeoplescampaign.org/.

39. Clifford Geertz, *Works and Lives: The Anthropologist as Author* (Stanford, CA: Stanford University Press, 1988), 130.

40. Tanya Marie Luhrmann, *When God Talks Back: Understanding the American Evangelical Relationship with God* (New York: Alfred A. Knopf, 2012), 325.

41. John Lewis, *Across That Bridge: A Vision for Change and the Future of America* (New York: Hatchett Books, 2021), 21.

42. For example, see https://www.innerdevelopmentgoals.org/.

43. John O'Donohue, *Anam Cara: A Book of Celtic Wisdom* (New York: Harper, 2020).

44. See St. Aelred of Rievaulx, *Spiritual Friendship, Distilled*, trans. Daniel Deforest London (Berkeley, CA: Apocryphile, 2024).

Bibliography

Aelred of Rievaulx. *Spiritual Friendship, Distilled*. Translated by Daniel DeForest London. Berkeley, CA: Apocryphile, 2024.
Agar, Michael. *The Professional Stranger: An Informal Introduction to Ethnography*. New York: Academic, 1980.
———. *Speaking of Ethnography*. Thousand Oaks, CA: Sage, 1985.
Ahmed, Sara. *The Cultural Politics of Emotion*. New York: Routledge, 2004.
Ammerman, Nancy. *Everyday Religion: Observing Modern Religious Lives*. Oxford: Oxford University Press, 2007.
———. "Spiritual but Not Religious? Beyond Binary Choices in the Study of Religion." *Journal for the Scientific Study of Religion* 52, no. 2 (2013): 258–78.
Anderson, Ben. "Affective Atmospheres." *Emotion, Space, and Society* 2, no. 2 (2009): 77–81.
Anderson, Nels. *The Hobo: The Sociology of the Homeless Man*. Chicago: University of Chicago Press, 1923.
Anonymous. *The Cloud of Unknowing*. Edited and introduced by James Walsh, SJ. Mahwah, NJ: Paulist, 1981.
Archer, Margaret. *Being Human: The Problem of Agency*. Cambridge: Cambridge University Press, 2000.
Aristotle. *Aristotle's Nicomachean Ethics*. Translated by Robert Bartlett and Susan Collins. Chicago: University of Chicago Press, 2011.
Asad, Talal. *Genealogies of Religion: Discipline and Reasons of Power in Christianity and Islam*. Baltimore: Johns Hopkins University Press, 1993.
Atkins, Gary L. *Gay Seattle: Stories of Exile and Belonging*. Seattle: University of Washington Press, 2003.
Balmer, Randall. *The Making of Evangelicalism: From Revivalism to Politics and Beyond*. Waco, TX: Baylor University Press, 2010.

Barthes, Roland. *A Lover's Discourse: Fragments*. Translated by Richard Howard. New York: Hill and Wang, 1978.
Basford, Johanna. *Ivy and the Inky Butterfly: A Magic Tale to Color*. New York: Penguin Books, 2017.
Beckett, Katherine, and Steve Herbert. *Banished: The New Social Control in Urban America*. Oxford: Oxford University Press, 2011.
Beekman, Daniel, and Jack Bloom. "Mayor, County Exec Declare 'State of Emergency' over Homelessness." *Seattle Times*, November 2, 2015. https://www.seattletimes.com/seattle-news/politics/mayor-county-exec-declare-state-of-emergency-over-homelessness/.
Behar, Ruth. *The Vulnerable Observer: Anthropology That Breaks Your Heart*. Boston: Beacon, 1996.
Bellah, Robert N. *Religion in Human Evolution: From the Paleolithic to the Axial Age*. Cambridge, MA: Belknap, 2011.
Bellah, Robert N., Richard Madsen, William M. Sullivan, Ann Swidler, and Steven M. Tipton. *Habits of the Heart: Individualism and Commitment in American Life*. New York: HarperCollins, 1985.
Bender, Courtney, and Omar McRoberts. "Mapping a Field: Why and How to Study Spirituality." *SSRC Working Papers* (October 2012).
Berg, Steve. "Ten-Year Plans to End Homelessness." In *National Low Income Housing Coalition, 2015 Advocates' Guide to Affordable Housing and Community Development Programs*. https://nlihc.org/sites/default/files/Sec7.08_Ten-Year-Plan_2015.pdf.
Berger, Peter L. *The Sacred Canopy: Elements of a Sociological Theory of Religion*. New York: Random House, 1990.
Berger, Peter L., Brigitte Berger, and Hansfried Kellner. *The Homeless Mind: Modernization and Consciousness*. New York: Vintage Books, 1974.
Berger, Peter L., and Thomas Luckmann. *The Social Construction of Reality: A Treatise in the Sociology of Knowledge*. New York: Anchor Books, 1967.
Berlant, Lauren. *Cruel Optimism*. Durham, NC: Duke University Press, 2011.
Berling, Judith. *Understanding Other Religious Worlds: A Guide for Interreligious Education*. Maryknoll, NY: Orbis Books, 2004.
Bialecki, Jon. "Anthropology, Theology, and the Problem of Incommensurability." In *Theologically Engaged Anthropology*, edited by J. Derrick Lemons, 156–78. Oxford: Oxford University Press, 2018.
Biehl, João. *Vita: Life in a Zone of Social Abandonment*. Photography by Torben Eskerod. Berkeley: University of California Press, 2005.
Bielo, James. "Anthropology, Theology, Critique." *Critical Research on Religion* 6, no. 1 (2018): 28–34.
Bonhoeffer, Dietrich. *Letters and Papers from Prison*. New York: Macmillan, 1967.
Bourdieu, Pierre. *Outline of a Theory of Practice*. Translated by Richard Nice. Cambridge: Cambridge University Press, 2002.

Bourdieu, Pierre, et al. *The Weight of the World: Social Suffering in Contemporary Society.* Translated by Priscilla Parkhurst Ferguson. Stanford, CA: Stanford University Press, 1999.
Bourgeault, Cynthia. *The Heart of Centering Prayer: Nondual Christianity in Theory and Practice.* Boulder, CO: Shambhala, 2016.
Bourgois, Philippe, and Jeffrey Schonberg. *Righteous Dopefiend.* Berkeley: University of California Press, 2009.
Branch, Taylor. *At Canaan's Edge: America in the King Years, 1965–68.* New York: Simon and Schuster Paperbacks, 2006.
Brown, Frederick. *The City Is More Than Human: An Animal History of Seattle.* Seattle: University of Washington Press, 2016.
Brown, Karen McCarthy. *Mama Lola: A Vodou Priestess in Brooklyn.* Berkeley: University of California Press, 2011.
Browning, Don. *A Fundamental Practical Theology: Descriptive and Strategic Proposals.* Minneapolis, MN: Fortress, 1991.
Bruder, Jessica. *Nomadland: Surviving America in the Twenty-First Century.* New York: W. W. Norton, 2017.
Buerge, David. *Chief Seattle and the Town That Took His Name: The Change of Worlds for the Native People and the Settlers in Puget Sound.* Seattle: Sasquatch Books, 2017.
Burawoy, Michael. *The Extended Case Method: Four Countries, Four Decades, Four Great Transformations, and One Theoretical Tradition.* Berkeley: University of California Press, 2009.
Burghardt, Walter. "Contemplation: A Long, Loving Look at the Real." *Church* (Winter 1989).
Butler, Judith. *The Force of Nonviolence: An Ethico-political Bind.* London: Verso, 2020.
———. *Notes toward A Performative Theory of Assembly.* Cambridge, MA: Harvard University Press, 2015.
Bykofsky, Stuart. "No Heart for the Homeless." *Newsweek,* December 1, 1986.
Camus, Albert. *The Myth of Sisyphus.* Translated by Justin O'Brien. New York: Vintage Books, 1983.
Cerwonka, Allaine, and Liisa Malkki. *Improvising Theory: Process and Temporality in Ethnographic Fieldwork.* Chicago: University of Chicago Press, 2007.
Charmaz, Kathy. *Constructing Grounded Theory.* London: Sage, 2014.
Chaves, Mark. "Secularization as Declining Religious Authority." *Social Forces* 72, no. 3 (1994): 749–74.
Chomsky, Noam. *Profit over People.* New York: Seven Stories, 1999.
Chopp, Rebecca S. *Saving Work: Feminist Practices of Theological Education.* Louisville: Westminster John Knox, 1995.
Clifford, James. "Anthropology and/as Travel." *Etnofoor* 9, no. 2 (1996): 5–15.
Clifford, James, and George Marcus, eds. *Writing Culture: The Poetics and Politics of Ethnography.* Berkeley: University of California Press, 1986.

Coates, John, and Sue McKenzie-Mohr. "Out of the Frying Pan, into the Fire: Trauma in the Lives of Homeless Youth prior to and during Homelessness." *Journal of Sociology and Social Welfare* 37, no. 4 (2013): 65–97.
Cobain, Kurt. "Suicide Note." https://kurtcobainssuicidenote.com/kurt_cobains_suicide_note.html.
Cohen, Lawrence. *No Aging in India: Alzheimer's, the Bad Family, and Other Modern Things.* Berkeley: University of California Press, 1999.
———. "Where It Hurts: Indian Material for an Ethics of Organ Transplantation." *Zygon* 38, no. 3 (September 2003): 663–68.
Comte, August. *System of Positive Polity.* New York: Bloomsbury Academic, 2001.
Cone, James. *Risks of Faith: The Emergence of a Black Theology of Liberation, 1968–1998.* Boston: Beacon, 1999.
Crowley, Walt. *Rites of Passage: A Memoir of the Sixties in Seattle.* Seattle: University of Washington Press, 1995.
Das, Veena. *Affliction: Health, Disease, Poverty.* Oakland: University of California Press, 2015.
David, Oliver, and Denys Turner, eds. *Silence and the Word: Negative Theology and Incarnation.* Cambridge: Cambridge University Press, 2002.
Day, Dorothy. "The Mystery of the Poor." *Catholic Worker*, April 2, 1964.
Deleuze, Gilles. *Spinoza: Practical Philosophy.* San Francisco: City Lights Books, 1988.
Deleuze, Gilles, and Félix Guattari. *Capitalisme et schizophrénie.* Paris: Les Éditions de Minuit, 1972.
Depastino, Todd. *Citizen Hobo: How a Century of Homelessness Shaped America.* Chicago: University of Chicago Press, 2005.
Desjarlais, Robert. *Body and Emotion: The Aesthetics of Illness and Healing in the Nepal Himalayas.* Philadelphia: University of Pennsylvania Press, 1992.
———. *Shelter Blues: Sanity and Selfhood among the Homeless.* Philadelphia: University of Pennsylvania Press, 1997.
———. "Struggling Along: The Possibilities for Experience among the Homeless Mentally Ill." *American Anthropologist* 96, no. 4 (1994): 886–901.
Desmund, Matthew. *Evicted: Poverty and Profit in the American City.* New York: Broadway Books, 2016.
———. *Poverty, by America.* New York: Crown, 2023.
Domke, David, and Kevin Coe. *The God Strategy: How Religion Became a Political Weapon in America.* Oxford: Oxford University Press, 2010.
Douglas, Mary. *Purity and Danger.* New York: Routledge, 2002.
Drescher, Elizabeth. *Choosing Our Religion: The Spiritual Lives of America's Nones.* Oxford: Oxford University Press, 2016.
Duneier, Mitchell. *Sidewalk.* New York: Farrar, Straus, and Giroux, 1999.
———. *Slim's Table: Race, Respectability, and Masculinity.* Chicago: University of Chicago Press, 1992.

Dunlap, David. "Mark Hawthorne, a Man of Few Words, Except, 'I Hate You.'" *New York Times*, April 11, 2017. https://www.nytimes.com/2017/04/11/insider/mark-hawthorne-a-man-of-few-words-except-i-hate-you.html.

Dunlap, Susan. *Shelter Theology: The Religious Lives of People without Homes*. Minneapolis, MN: Fortress, 2021.

Durkheim, Émile. *The Elementary Forms of the Religious Life*. Translated by Joseph Ward Swain. New York: Free Press, 1965.

Emerson, Robert M., Rachel I. Fretz, and Linda L. Shaw. *Writing Ethnographic Fieldnotes*. 2nd ed. Chicago: University of Chicago Press, 2011.

Engelke, Matthew. *A Problem of Presence: Beyond Scripture in an African Church*. Berkeley: University of California Press, 2007.

Ensign, Josephine. *Skid Road: On the Frontier of Health and Homelessness in an American City*. Baltimore: Johns Hopkins University Press, 2021.

Fanon, Frantz. *The Wretched of the Earth*. Translated by Constance Farrington. New York: Grove Weidenfeld, 1963.

Farley, Edward. *Deep Symbols: Their Postmodern Effacement and Reclamation*. Harrisburg, PA: Trinity Press International, 1996.

Farley, Wendy. *Gathering Those Driven Away: A Theology of Incarnation*. Louisville: Westminster John Knox, 2011.

———. *Tragic Vision and Divine Compassion: A Contemporary Theodicy*. Louisville: Westminster John Knox, 1990.

———. *The Wounding and Healing of Desire*. Louisville: Westminster John Knox, 2005.

Favret-Saada, Jeanne. *Deadly Words: Witchcraft in the Bocage*. Cambridge: Cambridge University Press, 2010.

Fleming, David. *Draw Me into Your Friendship: A Literal Translation and a Contemporary Reading of the Spiritual Exercises*. Saint Louis: Institute of Jesuit Sources, 1996.

Foucault, Michel. *Histoire de la sexualité: La volonté de savoir*. Paris: Gallimard, 1976.

Fountain, Philip, and Sin Wen Lau. "Anthropological Theologies: Engagements and Encounters." *Australian Journal of Anthropology* 24, no. 3 (2013): 227–34.

Frankl, Victor. *Man's Search for Meaning*. Boston: Beacon, 2002.

Freud, Sigmund. *Civilization and Its Discontents*. New York: W. W. Norton, 1989.

Froese, Paul. *On Purpose: How We Create the Meaning of Life*. Oxford: Oxford University Press, 2016.

Froese, Paul, and Christopher Bader. *America's Four Gods: What We Say about God—and What That Says about Us*. Oxford: Oxford University Press, 2010.

Fulkerson, Mary McClintock. *Places of Redemption: Theology for a Worldly Church*. Oxford: Oxford University Press, 2010.

Garbacik, Jaimee. *Ghosts of Seattle Past: An Anthology of Lost Seattle Places*. Seattle: Chin Music, 2017.

Garcia, Angela. *The Pastoral Clinic: Addiction and Dispossession along the Rio Grande*. Berkeley: University of California Press, 2010.
Garfinkel, Harold. *Studies in Ethnomethodology*. Cambridge: Polity, 1999.
Geertz, Clifford. *The Interpretation of Cultures*. New York: Basic Books, 2002.
———. *Works and Lives: The Anthropologist as Author*. Stanford, CA: Stanford University Press, 1988.
Glasser, Irene. *Homelessness in Global Perspective*. New York: G. K. Hall, 1994.
Glasser, Irene, and Rae Bridgman. *Braving the Street: The Anthropology of Homelessness*. New York: Berghahn Books, 1999.
Goffman, Alice. *On the Run: Fugitive Life in an American City*. Chicago: University of Chicago Press, 2014.
Goldstone, Brian. "The New American Homeless." *New Republic*, August 21, 2019.
Gorski, Philip S. "Historicizing the Secularization Debate: Church, State, and Society in Late Medieval and Early Modern Europe, ca. 1300–1700." *American Sociological Review* 65, no. 1 (2000): 138–67.
Gowan, Teresa. *Hobos, Hustlers, and Backsliders: Homeless in San Francisco*. Minneapolis: University of Minnesota Press, 2010.
Greenfield, Susan Celia, ed. *Sacred Shelter: Thirteen Journeys of Homelessness and Healing*. New York: Fordham University Press, 2019.
Gregg, Melissa, and Gregory J. Seigworth, eds. *The Affect Theory Reader*. Durham, NC: Duke University Press, 2011.
Gutiérrez, Gustavo. *We Drink from Our Own Wells: The Spiritual Journey of a People*. Maryknoll, NY: Orbis Books, 2003.
Hadewijch. *The Complete Works*. Translated and introduced by Mother Columba Hart, OSB. New York: Paulist, 1980.
Harding, Susan. *The Book of Jerry Falwell: Fundamentalist Language and Politics*. Princeton, NJ: Princeton University Press, 2000.
Hatch, Nathan. *The Democratization of American Christianity*. New Haven, CT: Yale University Press, 1991.
Hauser, Christine, and Ashley Southall. "Shooting at Seattle Tent City Coincides with Mayor's Homelessness Speech." *New York Times*, January 27, 2016. https://www.nytimes.com/2016/01/28/us/shooting-in-seattle-homeless-encampment-kills-at-least-2.html.
Heidegger, Martin. *Being and Time*. Translated by John Macquarrie and Edward Robinson. New York: Harper Perennial, 2008.
Herring, Chris, Dilara Yarbrough, and Lisa Marie Alatorre. "Pervasive Penalty: How the Criminalization of Poverty Perpetuates Homelessness." *Social Problems* 67, no. 1 (2020): 1–19.
Herzog, Katie. "Astrologers Agree: The Eclipse Is Bad News for Trump. Astronomers Agree: Astrology Is Bullshit." *Seattle Weekly*, August 16, 2017.
Holder, Arthur, ed. *The Blackwell Companion to Christian Spirituality*. Malden, MA: Blackwell, 2010.
hooks, bell. *All about Love*. New York: HarperCollins, 2001.

Hopper, Kim. *Reckoning with Homelessness*. Ithaca, NY: Cornell University Press, 2003.
Hout, Michael, and Claude Fischer. "Explaining Why More Americans Have No Religious Preference: Political Backlash and Generational Succession, 1987–2012." *Sociological Science* 1 (2014): 423–47.
———. "Why More Americans Have No Religious Preference: Politics and Generations." *American Sociological Review* 67, no. 2 (2002): 165–90.
Hype! Directed by Doug Pray. Santa Monica, CA: Lionsgate Films, 1996. DVD.
Ideström, Jonas, and Tone Stangeland Kaufman, eds. *What Really Matters: Scandinavian Perspectives on Ecclesiology and Ethnography*. Eugene, OR: Pickwick, 2018.
Ignatius of Loyola. *Spiritual Exercises and Selected Works*. Edited by George E. Ganss, SJ. New York: Paulist, 1991.
Irvine, Leslie. *My Dog Always Eats First: Homeless People and Their Animals*. London: Lynne Rienner, 2016.
Jackson, Michael. *Lifeworlds: Essays in Existential Anthropology*. Chicago: University of Chicago Press, 2012.
James, William. *The Varieties of Religious Experience: A Study on Human Nature*. New York: Modern Library, 1902.
John of the Cross. *The Collected Works of Saint John of the Cross*. Translated by Kieran Kavanaugh and Otilio Rodriguez. Washington, DC: Institute of Carmelite Studies, 1991.
Johnson, Elizabeth A. *Quest for the Living God: Mapping Frontiers in the Theology of God*. London: Bloomsbury, 2007.
Jones, Serene. *Trauma and Grace: Theology in a Ruptured World*. Louisville: Westminster John Knox, 2009.
Jordan, Mark. *Transforming Fire: Imagining Christian Teaching*. Grand Rapids, MI: Eerdmans, 2021.
Julian of Norwich. *Showings*. Translated and introduced by Edmund Colledge and James Walsh. Mahwah, NJ: Paulist, 1978.
Jung, Carl. *Memories, Dreams, Reflections*. New York: Vintage Books, 1989.
Keating, Thomas. *Open Mind, Open Heart*. New York: Bloomsbury, 2019.
Kierkegaard, Søren. *The Sickness unto Death: A Christian Psychological Exposition for Upbuilding and Awakening*. Translated and introduced by Howard V. Hong and Edna H. Hong. Princeton, NJ: Princeton University Press, 1983.
———. *Training in Christianity and the Edifying Discourse Which 'Accompanied' It*. Translated by Walter Lowrie. Oxford: Oxford University Press, 1941.
Killen, Patricia O'Connell, and Mark Silk, eds. *Religion and Public Life in the Pacific Northwest: The None Zone*. Walnut Creek, CA: AltaMira, 2004.
King, Martin Luther, Jr. *The Measure of a Man*. Mansfield Center, CT: Martino, 2013.
———. *A Testament of Hope: The Essential Writings and Speeches of Martin Luther King, Jr*. Edited by James M. Washington. New York: HarperCollins, 1991.

Kleinman, Arthur. *What Really Matters: Living a Moral Life amidst Uncertainty and Danger.* Oxford: Oxford University Press, 2007.
———. *Writing at the Margin: Discourse between Anthropology and Medicine.* Berkeley: University of California Press, 1995.
Kleinman, Arthur, Veena Das, and Margaret Lock, eds. *Social Suffering.* Berkeley: University of California Press, 1997.
Kleinman, Sherryl, and Martha A. Copp. *Emotions and Fieldwork.* London: Sage, 1993.
Klingle, Matthew. *Emerald City: An Environmental History of Seattle.* Seattle: University of Washington Press, 2007.
Kripal, Jeffrey. "The Future of 'Spiritual but Not Religious.'" https://www.youtube.com/watch?v=og2SSczJ_XI.
Kusmer, Kenneth L. *Down and Out, on the Road: The Homeless in American History.* Oxford: Oxford University Press, 2003.
Lamott, Ann. *Help, Thanks, Wow: The Three Essential Prayers.* New York: Penguin Group, 2012.
Larsen, Timothy. *The Slain God: Anthropologists and the Christian Faith.* Oxford: Oxford University Press, 2014.
Lee, Matthew T., Margaret M. Poloma, and Stephen G. Post. *The Heart of Religion: Spiritual Empowerment, Benevolence, and the Experience of God's Love.* Oxford: Oxford University Press, 2013.
Lemons, J. Derrick, ed. *Theologically Engaged Anthropology.* Oxford: Oxford University Press, 2018.
Lescher, Bruce H., and Elizabeth Liebert, eds. *Exploring Christian Spirituality: Essays in Honor of Sandra M. Schneiders.* New York: Paulist, 2006.
Lewis, C. S. *The Chronicles of Narnia.* New York: HarperCollins, 2005.
Lewis, John. *Across That Bridge: A Vision for Change and the Future of America.* New York: Hatchett Books, 2021.
Liebert, Elizabeth. "Academic Life and Scholarship as Spiritual Practice." *Berkeley Journal of Religion and Theology* 3, no. 1 (2017): 12–28.
———. *The Soul of Discernment: A Spiritual Practice for Communities and Institutions.* Louisville: Westminster John Knox, 2015.
———. *The Way of Discernment: Spiritual Practices for Decision Making.* Louisville: Westminster John Knox, 2008.
Liebow, Elliot. *Tell Them Who I Am: The Lives of Homeless Women.* New York: Penguin Books, 1995.
London, Jack. *The Road.* New York: Peregrine, 1906.
Luhrmann, Tanya Marie. "Down and Out in Chicago." *Raritan* 29, no. 3 (Winter 2010): 140–66.
———. "The Faith Frame: Or, Belief Is Easy, Faith Is Hard." *Contemporary Pragmatism* 15 (2018): 302–18.
———. *Of Two Minds: An Anthropologist Looks at American Psychiatry.* New York: Vintage Books, 2000.

———. "The Real Ontological Challenge." *HAU: Journal of Ethnographic Theory* 8, no. 1–2 (2018): 79–82.

———. *When God Talks Back: Understanding the American Evangelical Relationship with God.* New York: Alfred A. Knopf, 2012.

Maanen, John Van. *Tales of the Field: On Writing Ethnography.* Chicago: University of Chicago Press, 1988.

MacIntyre, Alasdair. *After Virtue.* Notre Dame, IN: University of Notre Dame Press, 1981.

Marion, Jean-Luc. *The Erotic Phenomenon.* Translated by Stephen E. Lewis. Chicago: University of Chicago Press, 2008.

Márquez, Patricia C. *The Street Is My Home: Youth and Violence in Caracas.* Stanford, CA: Stanford University Press, 1999.

Massumi, Brian. *Politics of Affect.* Malden, MA: Polity, 2015.

McGinn, Bernard. *The Foundations of Mysticism: Origins to the Fifth Century.* New York: Crossroad, 1995.

McGuire, Meredith B. *Lived Religion: Faith and Practice in Everyday Life.* Oxford: Oxford University Press, 2008.

Mead, George Herbert. *Mind, Self, and Society: The Definitive Edition.* Edited by Charles W. Morris. Chicago: University of Chicago Press, 2015.

Mejido Costoya, Manuel, ed. *Land of Stark Contrasts: Faith-Based Responses to Homelessness in the United States.* New York: Fordham University Press, 2021.

Meneses, Eloise, Lindy Backues, David Bronkema, Eric Flett, and Benjamin L. Hartley. "Engaging the Religiously Committed Other: Anthropologists and Theologians in Dialogue." *Current Anthropology* 55, no. 1 (2014): 82–104.

Meneses, Eloise, and David Bronkema, eds. *On Knowing Humanity: Insights from Theology for Anthropology.* New York: Routledge, 2017.

Mercadante, Linda A. *Belief without Borders: Insider the Minds of the Spiritual but Not Religious.* Oxford: Oxford University Press, 2014.

Merton, Thomas. *No Man Is an Island.* San Diego: Harvest, 1983.

Milbank, John. *Theology and Social Science: Beyond Secular Reason.* 2nd ed. Oxford: Blackwell, 2006.

Miles, Frank. "Geraldo Rivera, Dan Bongino React to US Cities in Crisis: 'Liberalism Is a Cancer.'" *Fox News*, August 20, 2019.

Miloscia, Mark. "King County's Plan to End Homelessness Has Failed." *Seattle Times*, March 14, 2016. https://www.seattletimes.com/opinion/king-countys-plan-to-end-homelessness-has-failed/.

Moloney, Francis. *Love in the Gospel of John: An Exegetical, Theological, and Literary Study.* Grand Rapids, MI: Baker Academic, 2013.

Morgan, Murray. *Skid Road: An Informal Portrait of Seattle.* Seattle: University of Washington Press, 1982.

Mounier, Emmanuel. *Personalism.* Notre Dame, IN: University of Notre Dame Press, 2010.

Murray, Ed. "Homelessness Address to the City." January 26, 2016. http://murray.seattle.gov/wp-content/uploads/2016/01/Homelessness-address-to-the-city.pdf.
Murthy, Vivek H. *Together: The Healing Power of Human Connection in a Sometimes Lonely World*. New York: Harper, 2020.
Nhat Hanh, Thich. *How to See*. Berkeley, CA: Parallax, 2019.
Niebuhr, Reinhold. *Moral Man and Immoral Society: A Study in Ethics and Politics*. New York: Charles Scribner's Sons, 1960.
Nietzsche, Friedrich. *The Gay Science: With a Prelude in Rhymes and an Appendix of Songs*. Translated with commentary by Walter Kaufmann. New York: Vintage Books, 1974.
———. *Thus Spoke Zarathustra: A Book for Everyone and No One*. Translated by R. J. Hollingdale. New York: Penguin Classics, 1961.
Noll, Mark A. *America's God: From Jonathan Edwards to Abraham Lincoln*. Oxford: Oxford University Press, 2002.
Oakes, Kaya. *The Nones Are Alright: A New Generation of Believers, Seekers, and Those In Between*. Maryknoll, NY: Orbis Books, 2015.
O'Donohue, John. *Anam Cara: A Book of Celtic Wisdom*. New York: Harper Perennial, 2022.
O'Neill, Bruce. *The Space of Boredom: Homelessness in the Slowing Global Order*. Durham, NC: Duke University Press, 2017.
Origen. *An Exhortation to Martyrdom, Prayer, and Selected Works*. Translated by Rowan Greer. Mahwah, NJ: Paulist, 1979.
Orsi, Robert A. *Between Heaven and Earth: The Religious Worlds People Make and the Scholars Who Study Them*. Princeton, NJ: Princeton University Press, 2005.
———. *History and Presence*. Cambridge, MA: Belknap, 2016.
Otto, Rudolf. *The Idea of the Holy*. Oxford: Oxford University Press, 1958.
Perrin, David B. "The *New Self* of John of the Cross." *Vinayasādhana* 5, no. 1 (January 2014): 31–42.
Person, Daniel. "Why Ed Murray Can't Quit the Catholic Church." *Seattle Weekly*, March 1, 2017. https://www.seattleweekly.com/news/why-ed-murray-cant-quit-the-catholic-church/.
Pew Research Center. "America's Changing Religious Landscape: Christians Decline Sharply as Share of Population; Unaffiliated and Other Faiths Continue to Grow." May 12, 2015. https://www.pewresearch.org/religion/2015/05/12/americas-changing-religious-landscape/.
———. "Religious Landscape Study." https://www.pewforum.org/religious-landscape-study/. Accessed June 25, 2024.
Plato. *Plato on Love*. Edited by C. D. C. Reeve. Indianapolis, IN: Hackett, 2006.
Poloma, Margaret, and Ralph W. Hood Jr. *Blood and Fire: Godly Love in a Pentecostal Emerging Church*. New York: New York University Press, 2008.
Porete, Marguerite. *The Mirror of Simple Souls*. Translated and introduced by Ellen Babinsky. New York: Paulist, 1993.

Pseudo-Dionysius. *The Complete Works.* Translated by Colm Luibheid. Mahwah, NJ: Paulist, 1987.
Putnam, Robert D. *Bowling Alone: The Collapse and Revival of American Community.* New York: Simon and Schuster, 2001.
Putnam, Robert D., and David E. Campbell. *American Grace: How Religion Divides and Unites Us.* New York: Simon and Schuster, 2010.
Rabinow, Paul. *Reflections on Fieldwork in Morocco.* 2nd ed. Berkeley: University of California Press, 2007.
Raghavendran, Beena. "Colorful Crosswalks Celebrate Gay Pride in Seattle." *Seattle Times,* June 23, 2015.
Rambo, Shelly. *Spirit and Trauma: A Theology of Remaining.* Louisville: Westminster John Knox, 2010.
Rauschenbusch, Walter. *Christianity and the Social Crisis.* New York: Macmillan, 1920.
Rennebohm, Craig, with David Paul. *Souls in the Hands of a Tender God: Stories of the Search for Home and Healing on the Streets.* Boston: Beacon, 2008.
Rexha, Bebe. *Expectations.* Los Angeles: Warner Bros., 2018. CD.
Reynolds, Rick. *Street Stories.* Seattle: CreateSpace, 2015.
Rilke, Rainer Maria. *Letters to a Young Poet: A New Translation and Commentary.* Translated by Anita Barrows and Joanna Macy. Boulder, CO: Shambhala, 2021.
Rizzuto, Ana-Maria. *The Birth of the Living God: A Psychoanalytic Study.* Chicago: University of Chicago Press, 1979.
Robbins, Joel. "Afterward: Let's Keep It Awkward: Anthropology, Theology, and Otherness." *Australian Journal of Anthropology* 24, no. 3 (2013): 329–37.
———. "Anthropology and Theology: An Awkward Relationship?" *Anthropological Quarterly* 79, no. 2 (Spring 2006): 285–94.
———. "Beyond the Suffering Subject: Toward an Anthropology of the Good." *Journal of the Royal Anthropological Institute* 19 (2013): 447–62.
Rohr, Richard. *Everything Belongs: The Gift of Contemplative Prayer.* New York: Crossroads, 2003.
Roof, Wade Clark. *A Generation of Seekers: The Spiritual Journeys of the Baby Boom Generation.* New York: HarperSanFrancisco, 1993.
———. *Spiritual Marketplace: Baby Boomers and the Remaking of American Religion.* Princeton, NJ: Princeton University Press, 1999.
Rossi, Peter. "The Old Homeless and the New Homeless in Historical Perspective." *American Psychologist* 45, no. 8 (1990): 954–59.
Ruthruff, Ron. *The Least of These: Lessons Learned from Kids on the Street.* Birmingham, AL: New Hope, 2010.
Sartre, Jean-Paul. *No Exit: A Play in One Act.* New York: Samuel French, 1958.
Schaefer, Donovan O. *The Evolution of Affect Theory: The Humanities, the Sciences, and the Study of Power.* Cambridge: Cambridge University Press, 2019.
Scharen, Christian. *Fieldwork in Theology: Exploring the Social Context of God's Work in the World.* Grand Rapids, MI: Baker Academic, 2015.

Scharen, Christian, and Aana Marie Vigen, eds. *Ethnography as Christian Theology and Ethics*. London: Bloomsbury, 2011.
Scheper-Hughes, Nancy. *Death without Weeping: The Violence of Everyday Life in Brazil*. Berkeley: University of California Press, 1993.
———. "The Primacy of the Ethical: Propositions for a Militant Anthropology." *Current Anthropology* 36, no. 3 (1995): 409–20.
Schleiermacher, Friedrich. *Christian Faith: A New Translation and Critical Edition*. Vol. 1. Translated by Terrence N. Tice, Catherine L. Kelsey, and Edwina Lawler. Edited by Catherine L. Kelsey and Terrence N. Tice. Louisville: Westminster John Knox, 2016.
Schneiders, Sandra. "Religion vs. Spirituality: A Contemporary Conundrum." *Spiritus* 3 (2003): 165–85.
———. "The Study of Christian Spirituality: Contours and Dynamics of a Discipline." In *Minding the Spirit: The Study of Christian Spirituality*, edited by Elizabeth A. Dreyer and Mark S. Burrows, 5–24. Baltimore: Johns Hopkins University Press, 2005.
Seeman, Don. "Divinity Inhabits the Social: Ethnography in a Phenomenological Key." In *Theologically Engaged Anthropology*, edited by J. Derrick Lemons. Oxford: Oxford University Press, 2018.
Sheldrake, Philip. "Christian Spirituality as a Way of Living Publicly: A Dialectic of the Mystical and the Prophetic." In *Minding the Spirit: The Study of Christian Spirituality*, edited by Elizabeth A. Dreyer and Mark S. Burrows, 282–302. Baltimore: Johns Hopkins University Press, 2005.
Smietana, Bob. "Safe Haven." *Covenant Companion*, January 2009.
Smith, Christian. *American Evangelicalism: Embattled and Thriving*. Chicago: University of Chicago Press, 1998.
———. *Religion: What It Is, How It Works, and Why It Matters*. Princeton, NJ: Princeton University Press, 2017.
———, ed. *The Secular Revolution: Power, Interests, and Conflict in the Secularization of American Public Life*. Berkeley: University of California Press, 2003.
———. *To Flourish or Destruct: A Personalist Theory of Human Goods, Motivations, Failure, and Evil*. Chicago: University of Chicago Press, 2015.
———. *What Is a Person? Rethinking Humanity, Social Life, and the Moral Good from the Person Up*. Chicago: University of Chicago Press, 2010.
———. "Why Christianity Works." *Sociology of Religion* 68, no. 2 (Summer 2007): 165–78.
Snow, David A., and Leon Anderson. *Down on Their Luck: A Study of Homeless Street People*. Berkeley: University of California Press, 1993.
Soelle, Dorothee. *Suffering*. Translated by Everett R. Kalin. Philadelphia: Fortress, 1975.
———. *Theology for Skeptics: Reflections on God*. Minneapolis, MN: Fortress, 1992.
Song, C. S. *Jesus, the Crucified People*. Minneapolis, MN: Fortress, 1996.

Spickard, James. "The Porcupine Tango: What Ethnography Can and Cannot Do for Theologians." *Ecclesial Practices* 3, no. 2 (2016): 173–81.
Spradley, James P. *You Owe Yourself a Drunk: An Ethnography of Urban Nomads.* Long Grove, IL: Waveland, 2000.
Stevenson, Lisa. *Life beside Itself: Imagining Care in the Canadian Arctic.* Berkeley: University of California Press, 2014.
Stewart, Kathleen. *Ordinary Affects.* Durham, NC: Duke University Press, 2007.
Stivers, Laura. *Disrupting Homelessness: Alternative Christian Approaches.* Philadelphia: Fortress, 2011.
St. John, Graham, ed. *Victor Turner and Contemporary Cultural Performance.* New York: Berghahn Books, 2008.
Swidler, Ann. *Talk of Love: How Culture Matters.* Chicago: University of Chicago Press, 2001.
Swinton, John. *Raging with Compassion.* Grand Rapids, MI: Wm. B. Eerdmans, 2007.
Tanner, Kathryn. *Theories of Culture: A New Agenda for Theology.* Minneapolis, MN: Fortress, 1997.
Taves, Ann. "Detachment and Engagement in the Study of 'Lived Experience.'" *Spiritus* 3, no. 2 (2003): 186–208.
Taylor, Charles. *A Secular Age.* Cambridge, MA: Belknap, 2007.
———. *Sources of the Self.* Cambridge, MA: Harvard University Press, 1992.
Teresa of Avila, Saint. *The Collected Works of St. Teresa of Avila, Volume Two.* Translated by Kieran Kavanaugh and Otilio Rodriguez. Washington, DC: Institute of Carmelite Studies, 1980.
Thiele, Leslie Paul. *Timely Meditations: Martin Heidegger and Postmodern Politics.* Princeton, NJ: Princeton University Press, 1995.
Thrush, Coll. *Native Seattle: Histories from the Crossing-Over Place.* 2nd ed. Seattle: University of Washington Press, 2017.
Thurman, Howard. *Jesus and the Disinherited.* Boston: Beacon, 1976.
———. *A Strange Freedom: The Best of Howard Thurman on Religious Experience and Public Life.* Edited by Walter Earl Fluker and Catherine Tumber. Boston: Beacon, 1998.
Tillich, Paul. *The Courage to Be.* New Haven, CT: Yale University Press, 1967.
———. *Dynamics of Faith.* New York: Harper and Row, 2001.
Turner, Denys. "Apophaticism, Idolatry and the Claims of Reason." In *Silence and the Word: Negative Theology and Incarnation*, edited by Oliver Davies and Denys Turner. Cambridge: Cambridge University Press, 2002.
———. *The Darkness of God: Negativity in Christian Mysticism.* Cambridge: Cambridge University Press, 1995.
Turner, Victor. "Liminality, Kabbalah, and the Media." *Religion* 15 (1985): 205–17.
———. "Liminal to Liminoid, in Play, Flow, and Ritual: An Essay in Comparative Symbology." *Rice Institute Pamphlet: Rice University Studies* 60, no. 3 (1974): 53–92.

---. *The Ritual Process: Structure and Anti-structure*. New York: Routledge, 1969.
Van Ness, Peter H., ed. *Spirituality and the Secular Quest*. New York: Crossroad, 1996.
Voeten, Teun. *Tunnel People*. Amsterdam: PM, 2010.
Wacquant, Loïc. "Scrutinizing the Street: Poverty, Morality, and the Pitfalls of Urban Ethnography." *American Journal of Sociology* 107, no. 6 (2002): 1468–1532.
Weber, Max. *The Protestant Ethic and the Spirit of Capitalism*. Translated by Talcott Parsons. New York: Routledge, 2001.
Weil, Simone. *Gravity and Grace*. Translated by Arthur Wills and introduced by Gustave Thibon. New York: Van Rees, 1952.
---. *The Need for Roots: Prelude to a Declaration of Duties towards Mankind*. Translated by Arthur Wills. Foreword by T. S. Eliot. New York: Routledge, 2001.
---. *Waiting for God*. Translated by Emma Craufurd. Introduction by Leslie A. Fiedler. New York: Harper Perennial, 2009.
Westneat, Danny. "The Backlash Fizzles: Voters Don't Seem to Believe Seattle Is Dying after All." *Seattle Times*, August 6, 2019.
---. "Bad Omen: Even the Catholics Are Growing Frustrated with Seattle's Efforts on Homelessness." *Seattle Times*, January 19, 2019.
Whyte, William Foote. *Street Corner Society: The Social Structure of an Italian Slum*. Chicago: University of Chicago Press, 1993.
Wigg-Stevenson, Natalie. *Ethnographic Theology: An Inquiry into the Production of Theological Knowledge*. New York: Palgrave, 2014.
---. *Transgressive Devotion: Theology as Performance Art*. London: SCM, 2021.
---. "What's Really Going On: Ethnographic Theology and the Production of Theological Knowledge." *Cultural Studies, Critical Methodologies* 18, no. 6 (2017): 423–29.
Wijsen, Frans, Peter Henriot, and Rodrigo Mejía, eds. *The Pastoral Circle Revisited: A Critical Quest for Truth and Transformation*. Maryknoll, NY: Orbis Books, 2005.
Wilkinson, Iain, and Arthur Kleinman. *A Passion for Society: How We Think about Human Suffering*. Berkeley: University of California Press, 2016.
Willerslev, Rane, and Christian Suhr. "Is There a Place for Faith in Anthropology? Religion, Reason, and the Ethnographer's Divine Revelation." *HAU: Journal of Ethnographic Theory* 8, no. 1–2 (2018): 65–78.
Williams, Jacqueline. *The Hill with a Future: Seattle's Capitol Hill, 1900–1946*. Seattle, WA: CPK Ink, 2001.
Williams, Rowan. *The Wound of Knowledge: Christian Spirituality from the New Testament to St. John of the Cross*. London: Darton, Longman, and Todd, 2014.
Wink, Walter. *Just Jesus: My Struggle to Become Human*. With Steven Berry. New York: Image, 2014.
---. *The Powers That Be: Theology for a New Millennium*. New York: Galilee Doubleday, 1998.
Winnicott, Donald. *Home Is Where We Start From: Essays by a Psychoanalyst*. New York: W. W. Norton, 1986.

———. *Playing and Reality*. 2nd ed. New York: Routledge, 2005.
Wolfteich, Claire, ed. *Invitation to Practical Theology: Catholic Voices and Visions*. New York: Paulist, 2014.
Wright, James D. *Address Unknown: The Homeless in America*. New Brunswick, NJ: Aldine Transaction, 2009.
Wright, Lawrence. "Sympathy for the Devil." *Rolling Stone*, September 5, 1991.
Wuthnow, Robert. "Spirituality and Spiritual Practice." In *The Blackwell Companion to Sociology of Religion*, edited by Richard K. Fenn. Oxford: Blackwell, 2003.
Yoder, John Howard. *The Politics of Jesus*. Grand Rapids, MI: William B. Eerdmans, 1995.
Zigon, Jarrett. *A War on People: Drug User Politics and a New Ethics of Community*. Berkeley: University of California Press, 2018.

Paul Houston Blankenship-Lai is a spiritual companion and Assistant Professor of Spirituality at the Earlham School of Religion, Richmond, Indiana. They have contributed to volumes on spiritual and religious responses to homelessness, including *Land of Stark Contrasts: Faith-Based Responses to Homelessness* (Fordham, 2021) and *Street Homelessness and Catholic Theological Ethics* (Orbis, 2019).

www.ingramcontent.com/pod-product-compliance
Lightning Source LLC
Chambersburg PA
CBHW020410080526
44584CB00014B/1262